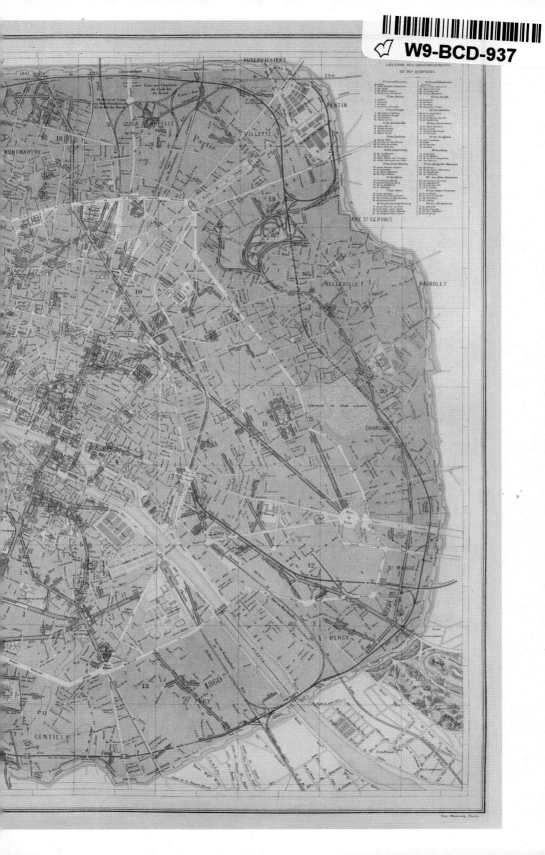

PARIS

REBORN

PARIS
REBORN

NAPOLÉON III,

BARON HAUSSMANN,

and the

QUEST TO BUILD A MODERN CITY

STEPHANE KIRKLAND

ST. MARTIN'S PRESS

NEW YORK

PARIS REBORN. Copyright © 2013 by Stephane Kirkland. All rights reserved.
Printed in the United States of America. For information, address St. Martin's Press,
175 Fifth Avenue, New York, N.Y. 10010.

www.stmartins.com

Endpaper: Plan of Paris in 1871, showing the projects of the Second Empire
(Courtesy Bibliothèque Nationale de France)

Library of Congress Cataloging-in-Publication Data Available Upon Request

ISBN 978-0-312-62689-1 (hardcover)
ISBN 978-1-250-62166-3 (e-book)

St. Martin's Press books may be purchased for educational, business, or promotional use. For
information on bulk purchases, please contact Macmillan Corporate and Premium Sales
Department at 1-800-221-7945 extension 5442 or write specialmarkets@macmillan.com.

First Edition: April 2013

10 9 8 7 6 5 4 3 2 1

CONTENTS

PARIS

REBORN

PROLOGUE

From the outset Louis-Napoléon Bonaparte had a great ambition for Paris. He wanted to transform it into the most modern and functional city in the world, a city where wide, convenient boulevards suitable for modern transportation would replace narrow streets, where elegant ladies could walk without treading in filth and decay, where new neighborhoods would rise to house the swelling population; he wanted a city that would represent the principles of order and modernity of his presidency. A pragmatist and an idealist, Louis-Napoléon was committed to personally overseeing the realization of this vision.

The "prince-president," as he was still called at the time—the future Napoléon III—did not yet know that his prefect of the Seine, Jean-Jacques Berger, would not be the man to realize this vision. Nor did he have any idea of the difficulties and tribulations that he would encounter. But, incredibly, the vision of Louis-Napoléon became a reality. Thanks to his impetus, Paris became the archetype of a modern, functional city, still perceived today as the epitome of urban beauty.

In most accounts, especially those available in English, the story fo-
cuses on Baron Georges-Eugène Haussmann. In reality, it is impossible
to grasp the story of the Second Empire transformation of Paris without understanding the fundamental role of Napoléon III, the man who
inspired and initiated it. More deeply, the transformation of Paris would
not have been possible without the convergence of a whole array of social,
cultural, and economic factors and the contributions of many individuals. To begin and end the story with Baron Haussmann is to fall into a
historiographical trap, and to miss what makes this story so compelling.

From our perspective, the transformation of Paris can hardly be
seen as unequivocally positive. It was a heavy-handed enterprise, which
achieved its ends at tremendous human and cultural cost and wiped
from the map an old, much-loved Paris that we will never know. The
work of a despotic regime, it was all too close in approach to the ego-
maniacal urban transformations of twentieth-century dictatorships
that, in some cases, it inspired. Still, the Second Empire rebuilding of
Paris was responsible for creating one of the world's great cities, a destination to which millions flock every year. There can be no question as
to Paris's beauty and allure, nor to its functional suitability as a major
city of the industrial era.

At a time when the quality and sustainability of our urban environment seems to be rising rapidly among our priorities, Paris makes a
timeless case study. It is one of history's most extravagant examples of
urban reinvention, with a surprisingly relevant set of lessons, both in-
structive and cautionary. While simple, easy-to-categorize narratives
are superficially satisfying, it is the grain of the story, the impossibility
of fully reconciling all its elements, that makes it not only fascinating
but also illuminating.

One

IN THE SHADOW OF VERSAILLES

The Seine was filled with boats carrying wine, timber, stones, and flour from the provinces and sugar, silk, spices, and other exotic goods from the colonies. On the numerous landings up and down the river, workers moored the crafts and unloaded the cargo. Around the place de Grève, the streets were crowded and hectic with pushcarts, horse-drawn carriages, cattle, and pedestrians. In the nearby market district of Les Halles, merchants removed vegetables, meat, fish, and cheese from carts and displayed them on the ground amid shouts and arguments. Across the river, on the Left Bank, the clergy and seminary students moved about in their cassocks while booksellers stood before their shops and messenger boys ran errands. Throughout the city, tailors, cobblers, blacksmiths, and basket-makers plied their trade. The year was 1749. Paris, the largest city in Continental Europe, was abuzz with activity.

Paris was a rich and impressive city. It was home to the Palais de la Cité, the Palais du Louvre, and the Palais des Tuileries, legendary centers of French power. There were churches of remarkable beauty, filled with sculptures, stained glass, and other artwork. There was the towering

Italianate Hôtel de Ville (City Hall); the veterans' residence at the Invalides, with its massive glittering dome; and the Collège des Quatre-
Nations, with its distinguished facade facing the Seine.

A visitor from a tidy Dutch town or from Britain's North American
colonies may, nevertheless, have been surprised to discover that Paris
was not, by any stretch, a clean and well-ordered city. The air was foul,
the drinking water was unsafe, and the traffic was chaotic and dangerous. The city lacked key amenities, such as a proper market, a sufficient
number of bridges, structured embankments, and a reliable supply of
drinking water. Paris was a hectic and vibrant city, but it did not resemble the capital of a country that fancied itself the most refined and
sophisticated in the world.

The jewel in the crown of the Kingdom of France was a much
smaller town, one that lay some ten miles to the southwest. Its name,
unknown a century before, was now legendary: Versailles.

Built as a seat for King Louis XIV and his court, the town of Versailles
was symmetrically arranged around its great heart, the palace. For
close to a hundred years, France's most renowned artists and artisans
had been at work making this piece of uninhabited marsh the most glorious place in Europe. Visitors from the world over marveled at its
grandeur and sought to imitate it at home.

Versailles had been created precisely so that it could be a place of
order at a safe distance from the volatile and violent Paris streets. Its
creation may have been in large part due to vivid personal memories
from Louis XIV's youth: At age ten, the young king had twice had to
flee his capital city; at fourteen, he had watched from the heights outside Paris as the troops loyal to him braved the fire of the cannons of
the Bastille to allow him to reenter the city after thirteen months of
absence. Louis XIV would not again allow the Paris populace, so easily
manipulated by disgruntled princes and dukes, to threaten the French
monarchy. In 1682, he moved the court away from the influences of
Paris to Versailles, where he could exercise complete power.

Louis XIV's reign nevertheless brought some important architectural contributions to Paris, including the Invalides, the Collège des Quatre-Nations, and the Hôpital de la Salpêtrière. His decision, in 1676, to demolish the city walls and turn them into broad thoroughfares was the genesis of the Grands Boulevards, which were to become Paris's most popular public spaces.

Louis XIV's great-grandson and successor, on the other hand, did almost nothing for Paris. King Louis XV, who reigned from 1715 to 1774, cared little about the numerous shortcomings of the urban environment, about the inconveniences, the dangers, and the risks of disease. Holed away in his gilded enclave, he focused his entire attention on the affairs of the court, the diplomacy required to maintain a kingdom with holdings that stretched from Louisiana to India, and, not least, on satisfying his leonine sexual appetite for very young girls.

The political environment in mid-eighteenth century Paris was toxic. The city magistrates had challenged the royal authority by refusing to implement a new tax wanted by the king. Vulgar and vicious satirical songs were circulating about the king and his mistress, Madame de Pompadour. The minister of the navy, the count de Maurepas, was sacked and banished from Paris for having penned, or at least imprudently repeated, such a song. And the philosopher Denis Diderot languished in the dungeon of the Château de Vincennes for the crime of having suggested that the workings of the human body could be studied by means of reason rather than dogma.

In a rickety house in a little street that would later be destroyed to build the avenue de l'Opéra lived a man of voracious intelligence with an unfailing attraction to subjects of controversy. His real name was François-Marie Arouet, but he was already much better known by his pen name, Voltaire.

A Parisian by birth, Voltaire passionately believed in civic duty and was infuriated by complacency. He loved his city as he loved the ideals of order and justice, and he could not tolerate the squalor that everyone else took for granted. In 1749, he summarized his thoughts in an essay entitled "On the Beautification of Paris."

"We need public markets," Voltaire wrote, "fountains that actually give water, regular intersections, performance halls; we need to widen the narrow and filthy streets, uncover monuments that we can not see, and build new ones to be seen."[1]

He took his fellow Parisians to task for doing nothing but grumble about the situation. During his exile across the Channel earlier in the century, he had seen how the English bourgeoisie made improvements to their cities, and he saw no reason why the citizens of Paris should not do the same. He had written in an earlier essay that "it is a disgrace that Parisians do not tax themselves to improve their city, to bring water to the houses, to build public theaters worthy of what is being presented in them, squares, fountains. Among us, the love of the public good is a chimera."[2]

Voltaire argued that the cost of making major improvements was a worthwhile investment. Paris was an industrious city and generated considerable wealth. Public works would immediately provide employment to many and would stimulate the economy for years to come. Improving Paris was certainly a better investment than underwriting the pomp of Versailles or the king's wars of prestige.

For funding, Voltaire described a pragmatic approach combining local taxes, debt raised through the municipality, state subsidies as available, and private initiative. With these resources, he asserted, "it would be easy to demonstrate that we can, in less than ten years, make Paris the marvel of the world."[3]

Voltaire compared his home city to London: "[I]n the time we've spent talking about [a royal square for Paris], the English have already built a square in London and a bridge on the Thames." He concluded the essay with another comparison to France's rival across the Channel:

When London was consumed by flames [in 1666], Europe said: London will only be rebuilt in twenty years, and even then we will see its disaster

*in the repairs of its ruins. London was rebuilt in two years, and with mag-
nificence. What! Will it only be in the last extremity that we will do
something great? If half of Paris were burned, we would rebuild it superb
and practical; and today we do not want to give it, at a thousand times less
cost, the practicalities and magnificence that it needs? But such an enterprise would make the nation's glory, bring immortal honor to the city of
Paris, encourage the arts, attract foreigners from the ends of Europe, enrich
the State, accustom to work a thousand lazy indigents who currently found
their miserable life on begging . . . ; the good of all would come of it, and
more than one sort of good. Here is, without contradiction, the effect of
the undertaking that is being proposed, that all the citizens desire, and
that all the citizens neglect. Let heaven ensure that there be a man zealous enough to take up this project, with a soul firm enough to follow it
through, with a spirit enlightened enough to draw it up, and accredited
enough to succeed!*[4]

At the time this essay was published, Voltaire's star was on the wane
at the French court. Louis XV had never thought highly of the writer,
and now he was out of favor with the king's powerful mistress, Madame
de Pompadour. Voltaire thought it wise to leave for Berlin, where he had
an offer to enter the service of Frederick II, king of Prussia. As Louis XV
approved the exit visa, he commented, "That will make one madman
less in the Kingdom."[5]

Twenty-five years later, in May of 1774, a strange expedition made its
way through the dead of night from Versailles to Saint-Denis. The body
of the deceased king, the now thoroughly detested Louis XV, was being
taken to the royal burial ground. Such was the fear of the angry Parisian crowd that the procession took a long detour around the city under
cover of darkness.

The new king was Louis XV's twenty-year-old grandson, who took

the name Louis XVI. In an increasingly tense context, Louis XVI and
his government tried to reestablish control over France. As part of this
policy, they finally acted to modernize the city of Paris.

Construction began on two new neighborhoods: l'Odéon, where
Charles de Wailly and Marie-Joseph Peyre would soon build the beautiful Théâtre de l'Odéon, and the Chaussée d'Antin, a former swamp
where, by the mid-1780s, some of the finest residences in the city were
to be found and where Paris's first sidewalks were built. Around the
same time, the duke of Chartres rebuilt the Palais-Royal, with a gallery
of shops around a central garden. The Palais-Royal instantly became a
pivotal place in Parisian life.

In 1778, four years after the death of Louis XV, the eighty-three-year-
old Voltaire was finally allowed to return to Paris. The state of the city
was still abject. Another writer, Louis-Sébastien Mercier, published his
own portrait of the city:

> If I am asked: how does one stay in this haunt of all vices and evils piled one
> upon the other, in the middle of air poisoned by a thousand putrid vapors;
> among the butchers, sewers, streams of urine, piles of excrement, shops of
> dyers, tanners, leather workers; in the middle of continuous smoke from this
> unbelievable amount of wood and the vapors from all this coal; in the
> middle of the arsenic, sulfur and bitumen particles spewed by the the work-
> shops where copper and metals are worked; if I am asked how we live in this
> abyss where the heavy and fetid air is so thick that one can see it and smell
> it for six miles in all directions; air that can not circulate and that only
> swirls around in this labyrinth of houses . . . I would answer that habit has
> made Parisians familiar with the humid fog, the wicked vapors and the
> rank mud.[6]

One contemporary remarked that the riches of Paris were all in the
interiors. The city was prosperous, houses were going up all around,

but none of the wealth went into the public space. People of means had increasingly elaborate tastes in fashion—silks, frills, powdered wigs, perfumes, and golden shoes—which made a striking contrast with the streams of sewage, the rotting refuse, and the gut-wrenching stench. Anyone who could afford it had himself or herself carried by chaise; only those who had no other choice walked the streets, and for that they wore hearty clogs.

In 1786, with political pressure mounting, King Louis XVI published a decree establishing a budget of thirty million francs for the beautifica-tion of Paris. That the king was moved to take such a step in a time of deep financial crisis was strong evidence that he and his government were aware of the need to improve the city and, even more vividly, of the political risks of continuing to tax the people of Paris without offer-ing them anything concrete in exchange. But we will never know what would have come of this change in approach, because the crisis deep-ened and, only three years later, the French Revolution began. Three and a half years later, Louis XVI's head was sliced off by the blade of the guillotine.

Paris on the eve of the French Revolution was wholly unsuited for a vibrant city with a growing population. The core of the city on the Right Bank was a compact mass of houses separated only by narrow streets and alleys. To travel across it from east to west, one had to know how to navigate this labyrinth. Going north to south, there were two streets, the rue Saint-Denis and the rue Saint-Martin, but both were narrow and crowded and went only as far as the Seine. To cross the Seine re-quired picking one's way through the densely built working-class neigh-borhood of the Ile de la Cité. The city had some wide roads, like the Grands Boulevards and the Champs-Elysées, but they were located outside the city center, making them greatly appreciated as promenades but of little use as arteries.

If the logic of Voltaire had been followed, if the French monarchy

had not simply failed to properly administer the largest city in the kingdom, Paris would have evolved very differently. Throughout the eighteenth century, architects like Pierre-Alexis Delamair, Pierre Patte, and
Charles de Wailly made carefully thought-out proposals for Paris in the
spirit of the urban tradition that created Versailles, Bordeaux's place de
la Bourse, and Paris's place de la Concorde. If these plans had been enacted, Paris would have become a unique large-city example of classical
French urban composition, with orderly perspectives and squares structuring the entire city. Instead, the legacy of the monarchy consisted of
only isolated examples of high-quality urban composition, with the bulk
of the city left to grow haphazardly.

The failure to address the needs of the growing city had an important effect on the future development of Paris. It helped establish a robust sentiment that what was needed was not incremental change, but
wholesale rebuilding. By not undertaking more in the way of improvements as they became necessary, the monarchy—and specifically the
government of Louis XV—played a critical role in setting the scene for
a much more sudden and brutal change in the landscape of Paris years
later.

But another revolution would begin first, one that would completely
change the nature of Paris's urban renewal. The venerable city of Paris
was about to enter the industrial age.

Two

A WORLD OF CHANGE

On a hot August day in 1837, Queen Marie-Amélie—wife of King Louis-Philippe—two of her daughters, assorted ministers, and other dignitaries gathered at the newly built embarcadère de Tivoli, at the northern limits of Paris. Amid much excitement, they approached the train waiting at the platform and lifted themselves aboard. In a great ruckus of steam and machinery, the engine strained and the wheels slowly began to turn. The train pulled away from the platform and out of Paris, soon speeding through the countryside on the thirteen-mile, twenty-six-minute journey to Saint-Germain-en-Laye. It was the maiden voyage of France's first passenger railway line, the most visible sign that the Industrial Revolution had come to Paris.

Those on board were fascinated by the experience:

Each of the travelers in the car in which we were sitting expressed his impressions in his own way. One was surprised that, despite such speed, it was as easy to breathe as if we were walking slowly on the ground; another was in ecstasy at the idea that he sensed no movement and felt as though

he were sitting in his bedroom; yet another noted that it was impossible to
have the time to distinguish, from three feet, on the sand, an insect of the
size of a bee, or to recognize the face of a friend; and finally another noted
with glee the surprised attitude of the country people upon the passing of
this column of smoke and this long succession of cars without horses, slid-
ing along with a slight buzz, and disappearing in the distance almost
immediately. Others, more grave, declared that the good that would come
of this invention was incalculable.[1]

More than anyone else, Emile Pereire was the man responsible for
the completion of the Paris–Saint-Germain-en-Laye line. His success
was a remarkable story.

Pereire had been born in Bordeaux to a Jewish family of Portuguese
origin. His father had eked out a meager existence as a struggling mari-
time insurance broker until 1806, when he died, leaving two small boys
and his wife, who was pregnant with their third child. The second son
died in early childhood, and the rest of the family suffered in deep poverty, their subsistence ensured only by the charity of Bordeaux's Jewish
community.

In 1822, the twenty-two-year-old Emile made his way to Paris and,
through a relative, found work as a journalist in the financial newspapers
that were beginning to flourish at the time. His younger brother, Isaac,
joined him the following year. The two men were smart and hungry;
they worked hard and learned quickly. By the end of the decade, Emile
had a coveted position as a broker on the Paris Stock Exchange, with an
office at the establishment of the most powerful banker in France, James
de Rothschild. The brothers frequented circles dedicated to the thinking of Henri de Saint-Simon, where they were exposed to grand ideas
concerning economics and visionary idealism. Infused with this exalted
spirit and filled with energy and ambition, they wrote article after article on subjects like savings banks and the modernization of the French
financial system.

The Pereire brothers' imagination was soon captured by the greatest project of the age, the railway. The world was moving into a new era of mass high-speed, long-distance transportation, a revolution sure to completely change the world as it had always existed, and Emile and Isaac Pereire were determined to lead the charge. They studied every technical and financial aspect of railway networks, from grades and profiles to rolling stock. They became vociferous and highly qualified exponents of development of the rail in France.

The brothers' efforts were rewarded on July 9, 1835, when a law granted them the concession for a future line between Paris and Saint-Germain-en-Laye. There were numerous daunting obstacles, from raising the funds to create the company to overcoming the multiple legal, technical, and practical challenges of building a new railway line. Emile Pereire, however, revealed himself to be an excellent administrator and negotiator. The Saint-Germain line was built and opened in only two years. It was an immediate sensation.

The line, together with the freight lines that had been built in other parts of the country, led to a national debate about the railway. Some anticipated unimaginable economic benefits from tying together previously distant markets; they foresaw huge military advantages from being able to move troops rapidly across the country. Others questioned the enormous cost of the many lines and wondered if the whole thing would be a passing fad. The Chamber of Deputies discussed the matter, and in 1842 a law was passed, establishing the basis for a national rail network. The first major intercity lines, from Paris to the city of Rouen, in Normandy, and to Orléans, south of Paris, were inaugurated on two successive days in May of the following year.

The question of where to situate the train stations in Paris was contentious. Emile Pereire was in favor of a single station for all the lines, as centrally located as possible, and ideally a through station. But his view was assaulted from all sides. The companies that gradually won the concessions for the major new lines out of Paris each wanted their own station. The Parisian hoteliers and restaurateurs lobbied for separate stations so that travelers passing through Paris, say from Calais to Lyon, would be forced to stay overnight and patronize their establishments. The government, police, and inhabitants preferred the new stations to be outside the city center. And the engineers claimed that it was simpler technically to avoid the urban core. Pereire managed to combine his station, today's gare Saint-Lazare, with that of the Normandy line, but after that each company—the North line, the East line, the Lyon line, the Orléans line, and the West line—built its own station. Thus was born the layout we know today, with six stations arranged in a circle around what was at the time the fringe of the city.

By this time, Paris had already changed quite a bit compared to the city it had been in the 1780s. This was in very large part due to the work of Napoléon I, who had ruled France at the beginning of the century, from 1799 to 1814, and then again briefly in 1815.

Napoléon I had ambitions for Paris. He was the first ruler in a long time to see Paris as central to his political objectives and as a projection of the glory of his reign. He wanted to turn the city of half a million souls at the time into a city of two million, a worthy capital of his empire.

Napoléon took frequent walks through the city with the painter Jacques-Louis David, who was able to describe in detail the ideas for Paris developed in the previous decades. Another figure in the cultural life of the Empire, Vivant Denon, explained to Napoléon that after years of inability to execute the ambitious schemes of the architects, the opportunity now presented itself to achieve greatness in the city of Paris. Denon said to Bonaparte: "[O]n this, as on all other things, you will imprint a definitive seal on your century."[2]

After Napoléon I became emperor in 1804, he began this undertaking in earnest. One construction site after another popped up across the city. Embankments were built on both sides of the river, replacing the old muddy banks. Five new bridges were built. The Palais du Louvre was expanded, adding the place du Carrousel, with its small arch. The église de la Madeleine was rebuilt. A new facade was erected for the Palais Bourbon, the home of the National Assembly. The Palais du Luxembourg was transformed to house the Senate. The Grand Châtelet, a fortified tower that used to guard the north end of the pont-au-Change, was knocked down. Most notable of all, construction was started on a gigantic triumphal arch at the western entrance to the city.

Napoléon also tackled much more mundane issues. He acted to address the issue of Paris's supply of drinking water, resurrecting a project that had languished on paper for years—the plan for a 130-kilometer canal from the Ourcq River to Paris. Today, water passes from the canal de l'Ourcq to the canal Saint-Martin on its way to the Seine. He built markets and other public facilities and created or widened some sixty streets. He had a large new slaughterhouse built on the edge of the city, with one important consequence: As of September 15, 1828, it became prohibited to drive cattle through the center of town.

The most comprehensive urban project to carry the stamp of Napoléon's reign was the rue de Rivoli and the adjoining neighborhood. For this prestigious project on prime land, a stone's throw from his palace, Napoléon appointed his favorite architects, Charles Percier and Pierre Fontaine. They set strict architectural rules, including a scheme of arcades that gives the neighborhood its unity and character. The result counted among the most distinguished urban achievements in Europe.

Napoléon I had more ideas for Paris. Assuredly the grandest was a palace on the Chaillot Hill—across the Seine from where the Eiffel Tower now stands. It would eclipse in size and beauty every palace in Europe, with grounds that would extend all the way to the Bois de Boulogne. The decree for the project was published in 1811, and the foundations laid, but it was never built.

Despite the volume and scope of these projects, the endeavors of Napoléon's reign were only a start. So little had been done before him that Napoléon spent much of his time and resources tending to basic needs that had been neglected. As a result, when Waterloo came and Napoléon definitively relinquished power, what had been written was only a prelude to the transformation of the city.

In the two decades following Napoléon I's abdication, the authorities accomplished little. The city grew rapidly, but it continued to lack many of the basics required to successfully negotiate the transition into the dawning industrial age. After the revolution of 1830, which brought King Louis-Philippe to power, a new generation of men more attuned to these issues began to arrive.

One of the protagonists of the July Revolution was an aristocrat from Burgundy named Count Claude-Philibert Barthelot de Rambuteau. In 1833, Rambuteau was appointed prefect of the Seine, with administrative responsibility for Paris and the surrounding territory. He would keep that position for a full fifteen years, until 1848.

Rambuteau was a well-groomed and measured man and a popular prefect. Of impeccable lineage, he led an active social life and had a robust network of friends from the most illustrious families of France. Despite this aristocratic breeding, he was, politically, a man of his time. He had embraced the Empire in his youth and, thanks to his worldly ways, eventually gained the position of the private secretary to Napoléon I. He had served as a prefect in the final years of the Empire, but, when the Bourbon monarchy returned in 1815, Rambuteau retreated to his estate in Burgundy. For more than a decade, he lived the life of a country gentleman. Then, elected as a deputy* in 1827, he became an important actor in the events that led to the revolution of 1830.

---

* A deputy was an elected representative to the Legislative Assembly. The name was changed to representative of the people in 1848, and then reverted to deputy in 1851. The assembly itself was called Chamber of Deputies from 1830 to 1848 and National Assembly from 1848 to 1851.

From the beginning of his tenure as prefect of the Seine, Rambuteau set out to improve and modernize Paris. Despite the fact that the government he was working for was not prepared to underwrite ambitious undertakings, he continued the seemingly endless task of making Paris more modern, functional, and hygienic.

In the 1830s and 1840s, essayists fretted about a phenomenon they called the "displacement" of Paris. The difficulty of getting around in Paris had grown so bad and the old neighborhoods were so dirty and dangerous that the elite had begun avoiding the historical core altogether. New centers of influence had risen in the newer and more affluent neighborhoods to the west and northwest. It was feared that Paris might in effect become two cities, with the old center simply left to wallow in its squalor while the march of progress continued in the new neighborhoods.

Civic groups and individuals responded to this threat by presenting multiple ideas for new arteries crossing through the historical center, in order to tie together the different parts of the city. Schemes were put forward for north-south crossings along the rue Saint-Denis, the rue Saint-Martin, or in between; for east-west crossings extending the rue de Rivoli or parallel to it; and for east-west crossings on the Left Bank. None of these were built at the time, but Prefect Rambuteau did create one entirely new street in the city center. It crossed Les Halles, the market neighborhood, which was one of the messiest in Paris. The new street, which was then the widest and most modern street in the historical city center, today carries his name: rue Rambuteau.

Rambuteau entirely rebuilt the Grands Boulevards from the place de la Madeleine to the place de la Bastille and built new streets outside the historical core. He added sidewalks, which greatly improved the urban experience for pedestrians. And he implemented another novelty:

From 1852 to 1870, it was literally called Legislative Body, but in this book the designation Legislative Assembly will be used.

a public lighting system of gas lamps, which completely changed the appearance of the city by night.

One of Rambuteau's greatest projects was the new place de la Concorde. Originally designed by Ange-Jacques Gabriel in 1755 to honor Louis XV, the square had been used during the French Revolution for executions, including those of King Louis XVI and Queen Marie-Antoinette. King Louis-Philippe, in an attempt to paper over the divisive political symbolism of this location, decided to erect the obelisk given to France by Mehmet Ali, the viceroy of Egypt. The place de la Concorde was redesigned between 1836 and 1846 by Jacques-Ignace Hittorff, who added the sculpted fountains. Rambuteau, again with Hittorff as architect, also began transforming the Champs-Elysées into an urban avenue in 1838.

When, in the early 1840s, it became clear that stations would be built for the new railway network, Rambuteau fully grasped their urban significance. As the location for each new station was decided, he began to restructure the surrounding neighborhoods, building new roads to serve the thousands of passengers for whom the stations would now be the entryway into the city. In 1847, when the decision was made to build the gare de l'Est, he initiated the boulevard de Strasbourg, which would lead south to the Grands Boulevards and the city center. Even though only fragments of this new street network were in place by the end of Rambuteau's time as prefect, he had nevertheless set what would prove to be critical building blocks for the city's future.

Another important innovation spearheaded by Rambuteau was the introduction of greenery. Until his tenure as prefect, there were almost no trees on the streets of Paris. Some parks were accessible to the public, but all were privately owned. Rambuteau, who had done a great deal of forestry work on his estate, had a deep love of trees. He planted them generously along the streets of Paris. He also introduced public gardens. The first of these, created in 1844, is located along the east and south

sides of Notre-Dame, on the land formerly occupied by the palace of
the bishopric of Paris, which had been burned down in 1831.

Despite his limited historical recognition, Rambuteau was seen by
contemporaries as a diligent and active prefect, a man responsible for
significant improvements:

> *Since the revolution of 1830, the embellishment of the capital has re-*
> *ceived a new impulse. The garden and palace of the Tuileries have been*
> *much altered; the quays have been some of them widened, and those on*
> *the north planted; and four new bridges have been built. The Madeleine has*
> *been finished; the Place de la Concorde has been completely re-arranged*
> *and terminated, and the Obelisk of Luxor has been erected at its centre;*
> *the Triumphal Arch at the head of the Champs-Élysées has been completed,*
> *as well as the magnificent palaces of the Quai d'Orsay and of the Fine Arts.*
> *All the public edifices of Paris that stood in need of repair have received*
> *it, and many restorations of the monuments of the middle ages are in prog-*
> *ress. Besides this, vast works have been undertaken for the drainage of the*
> *streets; gas is about to be used generally throughout the town; and the*
> *health and comfort of the inhabitants seem to be consulted by the improved*
> *quality of private edifices everywhere arising. Works of great importance*
> *are in progress, and more may be expected every year; the Government*
> *leads the way in this march of national improvement, and what is under-*
> *taken by public order is now not only* begun, but finished.[3]

With these improvements, the entry into Paris—at least for visitors
approaching the city from the west, as would those coming from across
the Channel or the Atlantic—was simply majestic. Emerging from the
pastoral landscape surrounding the villages of Argenteuil and Colombes,
travelers would reach the Neuilly plain. There they would see the regal,
newly finished Arc de Triomphe rise in the distance, marking the

entrance to Paris. After reaching and passing the monument and its ac-
companying checkpoint, they would begin the descent of the Champs-
Elysées, which offered a splendid perspective on the newly refurbished
place de la Concorde, with the greenery of the Jardins des Tuileries
beyond and, at the far end, the Palais des Tuileries, residence of the king.
Once one reached the square, the pont de la Concorde on the right led
across the Seine to the Palais Bourbon, home of the Chamber of Deputies, and to the fashionable faubourg Saint-Germain. Or one could continue along the Jardins des Tuileries, which lay straight ahead, down
the elegantly arcaded rue de Rivoli to the place Vendôme. If one turned
left into the rue Royale, toward the église de la Madeleine, fashioned
after a Roman temple, one would quickly reach the Grands Boulevards.
It was a breathtaking entrance sequence, unlike that of any other city in
the world.

The Grands Boulevards—the former fortifications of Paris, turned
into boulevards under Louis XIV—were the real center of the city's
life. They were the place where Paris surpassed itself in its Parisianness,
where elegance, frivolity, and revelry defined a life aesthetic. They
were a constant theater of humanity, where one would run into friends
and enemies, entertain wives and mistresses, and discuss business dealings and dreams of changing the world.

*In many parts of these delightful promenades, double rows of chairs are
placed, and persons of the highest respectability come from different quarters and sit for hours in them, amused with observing the happy moving
scene around them; the seats on the Boulevard Italien are often occupied
by persons of fashion, who arrive in their equipages, then take chairs for an
hour or two, whilst their carriages wait for them; the charge for each chair
is one sou, but every one takes two, one for the purpose of resting the feet,
and generally takes ices which are served from Tortoni's, long celebrated
for the supply of that cooling refreshment. It is by night that the Boulevards are seen to the greatest advantage, the innumerable lights blazing*

from the different theatres, the lamps placed before the coffee-houses, the brilliant shops, the trees, the equipages, the sound of music and singing, the houses, which resemble palaces, the gilded cafés all united has the air of a fairy scene to any one brought suddenly upon them.[4]

Parisians of the 1840s were a colorful crowd. High society was animated by a full contingent of dukes and duchesses, marquis and marquises, counts and countesses, and so on. But the bourgeoisie so well described by Balzac was also emerging, from the rich bankers and factory owners to the upwardly mobile provincials. There were the military men, the clergy, the journalists, the artists, the actors, the students, the women of moderate virtue, and a growing class of workers. Lifestyles ran the gamut, from the stultified salons of the aristocracy to the wild taverns of the Latin Quarter to the popular dance halls outside the city gates in Belleville. Never has Paris had quite the same vitality, the same sense of a society in flux, where anything was possible.

Paris was recognized as a "gay, bright, noisy, restless city—the city of the living, as beyond all others it may justly be called."[5] It was infused with an inimitable je ne sais quoi. As Heinrich Heine wrote on his arrival in 1831: "Even the terrors that one has brought along to Paris in one's own heart lose here their fearfulness. The pains become immediately softened. In this air, wounds heal faster than anywhere else. There is in this air something so generous, so worthy of life."[6]

Despite such qualities, the French capital had long since been overtaken in importance by its industrious English rival. This would seem inevitable given the greater dynamics: London was a commercial and financial hub at the head of an empire just reaching its zenith, while Paris was the capital of a nation still reeling from defeat in the Napoleonic Wars and subject to enormous political turbulence. Still, Paris, with more than one million inhabitants, remained a major center of commerce, learning, and politics. In addition, perhaps in part because of the loss of prestige in other areas, it had developed an acute sense of itself as the world's capital of art and culture. From Saint Louis on the Mississippi to Saint Petersburg on the Neva, it had established itself as the Western world's undisputed reference in cultural matters. Nikolai Gogol, who spent time in Paris in the late 1830s, described the city as "the vast showcase of everything produced by arts and crafts right to the last talent hidden away in some lost corner, the familiar dream of twenty-year-old young men, the bazaar, the great fair of Europe."[7]

Music was an unqualified passion. Gioacchino Rossini had been lured to the city in the 1820s, and Franz Liszt and Frédéric Chopin were among those who called the city home in the 1830s. But less highbrow forms of music were also wildly popular. As one contemporary commented, "In the center of the city and in the *faubourgs*,* all is but celebration and entertainment: Paris has no rest; it seems that only one type of shortage is really seriously feared: that of musicians."[8]

Literary activity seemed infectious. As an amused James Fenimore Cooper chronicled:

> *Half the voluntary visits I receive are preceded by a volume of some sort or another, as a token of my new acquaintance being a regularly initiated member of the fraternity of the quill. In two or three instances, I have been surprised at subsequently discovering that the regular profession of the writer is arms, or some other pursuit, in which one would scarcely anticipate so strong a devotion to letters. In short, such is the actual state of opinion in Europe, that one is hardly satisfied with any amount, or any quality of glory, until it is consummated by that of having written a book.*[9]

The tremendous energy devoted to art in all its forms defined important societal values. Despite production of inconsistent caliber, there

---

* The small towns immediately outside the city limits, which have since been incorporated into Paris proper.

predominated an environment of fervent respect for all things artistic, a mind-set, sustained for decades to come, that would help to establish Paris as the world's leading center for the production and commerce of art. Equally significant, the social importance accorded to art would play an essential role in shaping the buildings, avenues, and squares of the city itself.

Visitors to Paris were unanimous in the view that it was a dirty city. Nikolai Gogol, for example, wrote back to Saint Petersburg, "I don't know what to say about Paris. There is so much mud in this city that one doesn't know by which side to approach it."[10]

Even to a Londoner, the first impression of Paris was of a city dirtier and more hectic than other large cities:

> Paris at first strikes a stranger as still more bustling and noisy than London, as the streets being narrower and hack vehicles more used in proportion, the circulation gets sooner choked up, and the rattling over the stones of the carriages is still more deafening, being within so confined a space; hence also the confusion is greater. . . .
>
> [In the streets of Paris], the variety of noises which assail the ear, and the confusion of so many people bustling along upon a little bit of pavement not two feet wide, gives you plenty of occupation both to make your way, and get out of the way; when, compelled to give place to some lady, you descend from the narrow flags into the road, and whilst you are manoeuvring to escape a cart you see coming towards you, "Gare" is bawled out with stunning roar; you look round and find the pole of a coach within an inch of your shoulder, you scramble out of the way as fast as you can through mud and puddle, and are glad to clap your back against a house to make room for some lumbering vehicle, where the naves of the wheels stick out with menacing effect, happy to congratulate yourself that there is just room enough for it to pass without jamming you quite flat,

and that you are quit of the danger at the expense of being smeared with
a little mud from the wheel.[11]

Modernizers of all stripes made a great deal of the idea that Paris was but a miserable slum. For example, Victor Considerant wrote in 1845, "Paris is an immense workshop of putrefaction, where misery, pest and illness work in concert. . . ."[12] But these comments are not all to be taken at face value. They were part of an argument between the protectors of the past and the modernizers, in which it suited both sides to emphasize how different the "old Paris" was from the modern city and to create an exaggerated image of the persistence of medieval Paris into the nineteenth century. The always-entertaining Jules Janin aptly described the terms of the debate—from an unabashedly partisan perspective:

And this is the city that Mr. [Victor] Hugo and the architects that fol-
low him want to reestablish? How many tears poured on these hideous
ruins that are no more! What would they have not given for Paris to
have been rebuilt on its primal plan? Dark houses, passages without
air, the sun nowhere, thieves in every street, hungry wolves at each city
gate, anxiety everywhere. . . . Long live the gothic, black, filthy, fever-
ish city, the city of darkness, of disorder, of violence, of misery and of
blood! . . .

For example, can one understand that nothing is more boring than the
͟ɪe de Rivoli, where one can keep one's feet dry while walking, protected
͟ɴ rain in winter and from dust in summer, where the richest shops
͟ɴt all the treasures of the world? . . . [But the poets], if you push
͟ɒ their last resort, will maintain that (always for the sake of the
͟ue!) it is a great pity that we no longer hold lashings in the place
͟hat there are no more hangings at Monfaucon, and that the old
͟ɪnt-Germain-l'Auxerrois, so calm today, no longer rings from
͟he deathly toll of Saint Bartholomew.[13]

A British guidebook of 1839 provides a much less passionate description, focusing not on the layout of the city, but on Parisians' poor habits of cleanliness and maintenance:

> *Paris is inferior to most of the other capital towns in Europe as far the width, cleanliness, and general appearance of most of its streets are concerned. From the peculiar domestic habits of the greater part of the inhabitants, living not in single houses, but tenanting dwellings in common, proprietors are not anxious to make those improvements which the citizens of all other capital towns have long ago effected: the manners, too, of the Parisians still tolerate the public committal of nuisances which deprive their streets of any pretensions to cleanliness, and contribute not a little to the hindrance of any amelioration.*[14]

Paris continued to be in need of deep structural improvements. There were still no streets through the city center. There were not enough bridges, and some of those that existed were antiquated. The central market was still chaotic and unhygienic. And there was a lack of potable water. All the while, the city continued to grow, with workshops and factories springing up, laborers flocking in, and the neighborhoods outside the city boundaries rapidly expanding.

Prefect Rambuteau was entirely aware of all these shortcomings. For years, he had battled for funds to launch larger projects. In 1847, the City Council finally approved a fifty-million-franc investment program, which would include the rebuilding of the market at Les Halles; the extension of the rue de Rivoli; the building of a new hospital, a church, administrative buildings, and a new opera house to replace the previous one, which had burned down; and the construction of sewers, embankments, bridges, and streets. Since this would require borrowing funds, the approval of the Legislative Assembly was required. The debate was well argued on both sides, but in the end the city of Paris was granted permission to raise 25 million francs through debt financing to fund the program. Rambuteau knew this would be his legacy, and he was eager to get going.

But even the seemingly ambitious program put forward by the prefect was seen as insufficient. Many Parisians wanted to lead the world into the industrial age, to define a new vision of modernity, and they knew this would require much more than what the timid July Monarchy politicians could countenance. A new leader, who could capture the forces of progress and embody them in a vast urban project, was waiting in the wings, prepared to take center stage.

Three

A DREAMER IN THE
INDUSTRIAL AGE

On September 24, 1848, a well-dressed man descended from a train arriving at the embarcadère du Nord with several trunks of his belongings. At forty years of age, he had a full mustache, a rather large nose, and striking blue-gray eyes obscured by half-closed lids. He was below average in height, with legs that seemed too short for his body. He was Louis-Napoléon Bonaparte, arriving in Paris from London after an exile of thirty-three years.

Louis-Napoléon Bonaparte had a slightly complicated but prestigious lineage. His mother was Hortense de Beauharnais, which made him the grandson of Napoléon I's first wife, Joséphine de Beauharnais. His father was Napoléon I's younger brother Louis Bonaparte, who reigned briefly as king of Holland. Louis-Napoléon therefore had a double connection to Napoléon I, as his nephew and as the son of his beloved stepdaughter. After a number of deaths in the family, Louis-Napoléon was now first in the Bonaparte dynasty's order of succession.

The eyes of the newly arrived prince drank in everything they saw. The train station itself was new, and it stood in an area that had previously been well outside the urbanized part of the city. The streets were filled with people wearing the latest fashions, and omnibuses and carriages in the newest styles. As he traveled in a hired carriage to his hotel in the place Vendôme, Louis-Napoléon passed the busy Grands Boulevards, with their sidewalks, gas lighting, and bustling life.

Every avenue, every square, every building was a revelation. Since he had left Paris as a seven-year-old boy, Louis-Napoléon had gotten to know Munich, Geneva, Rome, London, and even New York, but he had only read about most places in his home city. Even the famous place des Vosges, built under Henri IV, was alien to him.

One landmark Louis-Napoléon was entirely aware of was the Arc de Triomphe, finished twelve years earlier. Towering majestically atop the Champs-Elysées, it was a magnificent monument by any standard. But to Louis-Napoléon, it had a special meaning.

Erected to commemorate the Battle of Austerlitz, the Arc de Triomphe was the most spectacular symbol of Napoléon I's unfinished project to create an imperial capital as great as the Rome of Augustus. To the eyes of Louis-Napoléon, it was not only an illustration of Paris's potential grandeur and beauty; it was an exhortation to continue the Bonaparte legacy for France.

Louis-Napoléon's view was that the monarchy that had ruled France for more than three decades had failed to lead the nation to meet the challenges of the modern era. He and his friends felt that only the Napoleonic dynasty could restore the vision and ambition that France needed.

Hortense de Beauharnais had groomed her son for power since he was a small child. She spoke to Louis-Napoléon as a future great leader, saying things like "a famous name is the first down payment that destiny gives to a man it wants to push forward."[1] She gave him advice on how to manipulate men and govern a nation. Like other men who grow up close to charismatic, protective, and ambitious mothers, Louis-

Napoléon developed an indestructible belief in himself. He also developed, from the youngest age, a taciturn, conspiratorial manner.

Louis-Napoléon had studied social issues and economics. He had seen the tremendous industrial development of England and believed that technology would lead to social and material progress. In short, he combined the Bonapartist reformist ideals of his uncle with the faith in progress of the Victorian era. He had even developed progressive political views for the time:

> Today, the reign of castes is finished—one can now only govern with the masses; it is therefore necessary to organize them so they can formulate their will, and discipline them so they can be directed and enlightened on their own interests. To govern is no longer to dominate the people through force and violence; it is to lead them to a better future, by appealing to their reason and their heart.[2]

Louis-Napoléon was an idealist. As one of his biographers would write, "He believed, as did the count de Saint-Simon and his socialist disciples, in the advent of a happy society thanks to material and moral progress, in the coming together of social classes and in the establishment of a durable peace, but he was not content with speculation, he wanted to be a man of action and he became one."[3]

In order to act, to be in a position to carry on the great work of the family, Louis-Napoléon would first need to achieve power. To all observers, in 1848 this still had every appearance of being a far-fetched proposal.

As a young man, Louis-Napoléon had brazenly, even recklessly, thrown himself into political-military adventures. First, he joined his older brother, Napoléon-Louis, in a poorly conceived revolt against the Austrian occupation of Italy, which cost Napoléon-Louis his life. In 1836, he sneaked into France at Strasbourg to try to raise the local garrison in insurrection, but he was captured and exiled to the United States. In 1840, in Boulogne-sur-Mer, he tried the same thing again. This time, it ended with three coconspirators killed and Louis-Napoléon fished out of the waters of the English Channel and sent to jail. Captive in the fortress of Ham in northern France, he was no closer to his dream of continuing the great work of his uncle.

In 1846, Louis-Napoléon made a daring escape from the fortress. He scrambled over the border into Belgium and returned to London. Wealthy since the death of his parents, he resumed his comfortable life in exile as a member of London's elite. He took part in dinners, balls, and hunts with the Victorian aristocracy. He mixed with dukes and lords, belonged to exclusive clubs, and was in contact with the likes of Disraeli and Dickens.

Louis-Napoléon lived at various addresses, all in close proximity in the neighborhood of Saint James. His daily environment consisted of supremely elegant places like Saint James Square, Carlton House Terrace, and Waterloo Gardens. He lived just steps from Saint James Park and Green Park and appreciated them greatly. He of course knew and was interested in the recent developments in London: Regent Street, Cumberland Terrace, Oxford Circus, and Regent's Park. His interest in landscape grew, and he became immersed in the design of the country properties of his English friends. In this environment of early Victorian London, an image of urban modernity, incorporating amenities and greenery, began to imprint itself on his mind.

Notwithstanding the comfort of his London life, Louis-Napoléon remained consumed by the idea of a triumphant return to France. With a small group of friends, he plotted and schemed. He published books and essays aimed at positioning himself as a credible leader. Gradually he gained notoriety.

By early 1848, the regime of King Louis-Philippe was in crisis. The

Republican opposition organized banquets that drew increasing numbers. When the government tried to break up these banquets, violence erupted. Louis-Philippe fled to England and a wave of revolutionary fervor ripped across Europe. France was declared a Republic, a provisional government was put in place, universal male suffrage was established, and parliamentary elections were held. Although no one could have known it for sure at the time, the royal lineage—whether Bourbon or Orléans—had been removed from power in France forever.

Louis-Napoléon at once grasped that the 1848 revolution presented a great opportunity for him. It removed the king who had pronounced his exile and created a power vacuum into which a man with an illustrious last name could hope to thrust himself. Unfortunately, it also established a Republic with a new constitutional order that had no place for a providential leader. Nevertheless, Louis-Napoléon's friends returned to France and began to build a network and disseminate propaganda on his behalf. Louis-Napoléon himself stayed in London through the spring and summer, until conditions were propitious for a return.

In September, Louis-Napoléon, still in London, put his name on the ballot for an off-cycle election, which he won. There ensued a heated debate about whether the heir to an emperor should be allowed to return to occupy an elected seat as representative of the people. In the end, Louis-Napoléon's exile was revoked, paving the way for his return to France.

Two days after his return to Paris, on September 26, 1848, Louis-Napoléon made his first appearance before the National Assembly. Many of the representatives had never seen him in person, but all knew who he was. He had a reputation as a hotheaded adventurer and, of course, as an admirer of the imperial system. Many were skeptical of his commitment to democracy. His appearance was a test.

Louis-Napoléon stepped up to the podium, took out a crumpled piece of paper, and hesitatingly addressed the French political class for the first time. He spoke slowly, in a monotonous voice, with a strange, indeterminate accent. The speech was vacuous: He assured the representatives of his gratitude to the Republic and committed himself to work within the democratic framework to help reestablish domestic tranquillity. In a forum accustomed to hearing paragons of eloquence such as Alphonse de Lamartine, François Guizot, and Adolphe Thiers, Louis-Napoléon's public speaking was a painful display. Even before he ended, there was a general mood of hilarity and stupefaction in the chamber. Snickers and remarks floated down from the benches. The next morning, the press skewered the newcomer.

Despite his urbanity, people found Louis-Napoléon awkward and distant. He appeared to be more comfortable listening than speaking, often leaving it unclear as to whether he agreed or not. He had little charisma and did not appear to be of particular intelligence. Alexis de Tocqueville would later say of him, "[T]he words one addressed to him were like stones one throws in a well; one hears the sound but does not know what they become."[4] An Englishman who spent time with Louis-Napoléon wrote, "[His] countenance was at all times difficult to read; his eyes, like those of others, may have been 'the windows of his soul,' but their blinds were down most of the time."[5]

On the other hand, Louis-Napoléon possessed an undeniable assurance, a way of holding himself that exuded authority. Queen Victoria would later remark that Louis-Napoléon was decidedly of northern European character, little prone to exuberance, in contrast to the other, more excitable French leaders she had known. He was indulgent and unfailingly loyal with his close friends. Women found his mysterious and refined demeanor, as well as his self-esteem and boundless ambition, alluring.

Despite his poor start on the French political scene, Louis-Napoléon was undeterred. At least he was now back in France, able to participate in political life. Furthermore, there was a presidential election to be held—the first time France would select its leader by universal male suffrage. The deck was stacked in favor of the establishment candidates, among whom the odds-on favorite was Gen. Louis-Eugène Cavaignac Nevertheless, despite the fact that everyone had written him off, Louis-Napoléon believed in his chances.

As future events would show, Louis-Napoléon had correctly identi-fied General Cavaignac's weakness and his own political opportunity. In brutally repressing the uprising of June 1848, Cavaignac had alienated much of the working class, which would be voting for the first time. Louis-Napoléon knew that the Bonaparte name, while associating him with order, had enough popularity to bring him a large part of the working class and rural vote. Although he had precious few political assets other than a recognizable name and some zealous friends, Louis-Napoléon was intent on doing everything he could to make the most of this extraordinary opportunity. His one huge weakness was that he did not have any structured political support.

In the critical weeks of the fall of 1848, Louis-Napoléon unexpect-edly succeeded in gaining the support of a major political group, the conservative faction later known as the Party of Order. The most prom-inent member of this group was Adolphe Thiers, one of the savviest French politicians of the nineteenth century, who, on this occasion, made the biggest blunder of his career.

Thiers dearly wanted to be president and, as one of France's most prominent politicians, was amply qualified. His problem was that he was much too closely identified with the regime of King Louis-Philippe, whose government he had led, to be a viable first president so soon after the 1848 revolution. But if he could get an incompetent nonentity to win the election and serve out the one term permitted by the Constitu-tion, he would be ideally positioned to win the next election, to be held in 1852.

Adolphe Thiers identified Louis-Napoléon as just the man he needed: someone electable due to name recognition, but without the capability or even, it appeared, the ambition to actually administer the nation.

That would allow Thiers and his friends to continue to run the country from behind the scenes while Thiers prepared his run for the presidency. In one of history's spectacular misjudgments, Thiers declared, "I have much studied the Prince [Louis-Napoléon] from near and far, and he is an absolute good-for-nothing."[6] Thiers decided to put his full weight behind Louis-Napoléon's bid for the presidency.

Louis-Napoléon displayed genuine political canniness. Even though he had no illusions about Thiers's views, he played along, unperturbed by the blows to his ego. This in itself was proof to Thiers that Louis-Napoléon was weak-spined and would be a pliable figurehead president.

Louis-Napoléon ran a splendid campaign, focusing on the need to bring order and stability back to the country while also putting forward his social convictions. He benefited from the work of the Bonapartist networks now covering most of the country as well as from the support of Thiers and his friends. In the days leading up to December 10, election day, Cavaignac's camp was on the defensive and the campaigns of the other candidates were in disarray. By the twelfth, enough results were in for the newspapers to call the election in favor of Louis-Napoléon. In the end, Louis-Napoléon won a remarkable 74 percent of the vote. The man everyone had, less than two months before, taken to be a bumbling amateur had just performed a political masterstroke. He was about to become the leader of France.

Paris was never ravaged by fire, razed by enemy armies, or leveled by bombs. If it was to be rebuilt to modern standards of hygiene and practicality, it would have to be by decision, and that could only be the work of a visionary leader.

Louis-Napoléon Bonaparte wanted to be that leader. He was prepared to propel Paris into the future as a modern world capital, at the same time as he realized a great many other dreams for France. But at the end of 1848, he was in a tenuous political position, elected to a single four-year term, thanks to friends who had every intention of preventing him from playing his full role as president. It was thoroughly unclear how he would gain either the power or the longevity required to make a new Paris rise up, or to achieve anything else of substance. But this reserved and inscrutable man, at once unassuming and extraordinarily ambitious, had further surprises in store.

Four

THE PRINCE-PRESIDENT
AND THE CITY

Louis-Napoléon Bonaparte was sworn in as the first president in France's history on Wednesday, December 20, 1848. Looking elegant and solemn, he stood before the National Assembly and repeated the oath of the presidency. He read a brief speech, then walked to the spot where General Cavaignac was sitting to shake his hand before leaving the National Assembly to take posession of his presidential quarters.

The next day, the new president submitted his list of appointees to ministerial and prefectoral positions. To the position of prefect of the Seine he appointed a popular politician from the neighborhood of the Bourse and the Grands Boulevards named Jean-Jacques Berger, who had helped Louis-Napoléon achieve a strong showing at the Paris polls. Along with the general administration of the city, Berger's primary responsibility would be to continue the implementation of the projects that had been started by Rambuteau and further moved forward by the temporary government over the previous year. These consisted primarily of three projects: the extension of the rue de Rivoli, the building of a new central market at Les Halles, and the creation of the boulevard de Strasbourg.

The rue de Rivoli, designed by Napoléon I's architects, Charles Percier and Pierre-François-Léonard Fontaine, was a broad, modern street,
the very image of Parisian urban sophistication. On its north side were
fine houses, with an arcade on the ground floor lined with luxurious
shops. On the south side was André Le Nôtre's classically designed Jardins des Tuileries. But the rue de Rivoli stopped after only a short distance and was therefore of little use as a thoroughfare. The plan now was
to extend it toward the center of Paris as far as the place du Louvre,
bringing its length to nearly a mile.

Les Halles, when it was first established as a market in the thirteenth
century, occupied a pastoral site on the edge of the city. Over time, it
had become the bustling heart of Parisian commerce, a veritable world
unto itself. Merchants would lay their wares about, without regard to
hygiene or order, in the midst of animals and traffic. The building of a
modern, hygienic market facility was one of the specific projects called
for by Voltaire in the mid-eighteenth century and explored by Napoléon
I, without result. In 1843, under Rambuteau, the decision had been
made to build a massive new market consisting of eight pavilions on the
existing site. An architect had been selected, and he was finalizing his
design at the time of Louis-Napoléon's election as president.

The boulevard de Strasbourg was one of the streets envisaged in
conjunction with the new train stations. It would lead from the gare de
l'Est southward toward the Grands Boulevards. Its special significance
was that it could potentially be continued straight toward the city center, forming a major artery into the heart of the city, perpendicular to
the river.

It was not a coincidence that the projects all related to the heart of
Paris. Over the previous three decades, the Grands Boulevards and the
areas beyond them, specifically the Chaussée d'Antin and Saint-Georges
neighborhoods, had been the most rapidly developing parts of the city,
the geographical base of the rising bourgeoisie. The new projects were

intended to modernize the core of the city and to better connect it to the more dynamic neighborhoods.

Louis-Napoléon's first step as president was simply to confirm the preexisting projects. His prefect of the Seine would be responsible for their prompt execution while the president focused his own attention on the broader political challenges.

The first months of 1849 were a struggle for Louis-Napoléon. In the words of his loyal friend Victor de Persigny, the new president "knew nothing of this world that he had burst into in such a dazzling and unexpected manner."[1]

A few days before the election, the National Assembly had designated the Palais de l'Elysée to be the residence of the president of the Republic. The building had an illustrious history, having served as home to Louis XV's mistress, Madame de Pompadour, and to the banker Nicolas Beaujon before becoming the residence of Napoléon I. But when Louis-Napoléon entered the palace in the gloomy early evening of the December day of his swearing in ceremony, its days of glory seemed distant. The curtains were torn and dusty, the rugs were worn, and broken windowpanes had been hastily covered with paper. It was clear that the decision to house Louis-Napoléon here, rather than in the Palais des Tuileries, which King Louis-Philippe had been occupying only months before, was meant to diminish his stature. No one had any intention of letting the new president play anything other than a nominal role— neither the National Assembly, which was not inclined to surrender the power it had enjoyed for the last ten months, spent without a head of state, nor Louis-Napoléon's allies, who saw him as their pawn.

The government, which consisted of members and friends of the Party of Order, was uncooperative. For a time, the ministers took to meeting without the president in order to present him with their preagreed conclusions. The ministers of the interior and of foreign affairs neglected to pass on important reports and missives. Louis-Napoléon had to battle even to make decisions that were his constitutional prerogative. And when things came to a head, he was more than once forced to admit his weakness publicly. For a man with ambition, it was an extremely frustrating situation.

Louis-Napoléon quickly understood that he could not win via direct confrontation, so he took another route. He remained in his quarters until late morning, doodled on his papers during official meetings, and seemed to focus only on the dinners and hunts that were organized for him. He played the role of what his opponents thought he was: a vacuous dilettante. In reality, he was putting them off their guard, again setting aside his ego in the interest of his political strategy. It worked: The government actually raised the president's stipend so that he would keep himself busy with harmless social activities. Louis-Napoléon was never more dangerous to his adversaries than when he was underestimated.

Louis-Napoléon put this period of governmental stalemate to profit by working to consolidate his popularity. He perceived that France had entered the era of mass politics and that, whatever the conflicts within the political class, a strong bond with the people would be essential to his political longevity. He kept up an intense schedule of visits across France, with inaugurations, ribbon cuttings, ceremonies to honor citizens, visits to the poor and the ill, and so on. He used the press intensively, with a carefully calibrated communications strategy that targeted messages at each segment of the electorate. He was particularly attentive to the military, reviewing troops and taking meals with the soldiers at every opportunity.

Louis-Napoléon achieved an immediate and unflagging popularity among the common people, especially in rural areas and in the army. When he traveled to Amiens, Angers, Nantes, or Rouen, as he did in the spring and summer of 1849, he was greeted by large, enthusiastic

crowds. He may have had little political backing in the Paris establishment, but from the outset Louis-Napoléon was very much a president
of the French people.

Louis-Napoléon had a genuine focus on social issues, having gone so far as
to write an essay on the subject entitled "The Extinction of Pauperism."
He was by nature compassionate, but he also perceived the importance of
social policy to maintaining order. It was clear to him that the welfare of
the working class was the key to, in his words, "calm the passions" of the
recent turbulent times.[2] He saw durable stability, which was essential to
the prosperity and the radiance of France, as his historical mission.

By the 1840s, a class of urban industrial workers was emerging. In
Paris, most workers were still employed by smaller workshops, but there
were also some larger manufacturing businesses, such as the Etablisse-
ments Cail, a manufacturer of railroad equipment that employed fifteen
hundred workers by 1848. Workers were typically employed as day laborers and paid based on output, which made the situation volatile, especially as more prospective workers came to the city. So although the
large-scale industrial working class did not yet exist, the issue of poor
urban industrial workers was plain to see.

Only weeks into Louis-Napoléon's presidency, on January 10, 1849, a
law was passed, creating the Assistance publique de Paris, a single administration overseeing hospitals, asylums, orphanages, and other public care
institutions for Paris. The new president sought other initiatives he could
take that would mark him as a champion of social-welfare policies.

In England, Louis-Napoléon had been exposed to the work of British
architect Henry Roberts on modern, hygienic housing for workers. He
had, in fact, visited a prototype developed by Roberts in London. Eager
to apply the ideas to France, Louis-Napoléon had Roberts's book *The
Dwellings of the Labouring Classes* translated into French.

These idealistic undertakings irritated the ministers, who saw them as a distraction from the serious business of governing the nation. Nevertheless, Louis-Napoléon was able to secure funding for one project. In 1849, he commissioned the architect Marie-Gabriel Veugny to build a model of modern worker housing in Paris.

The resulting complex, known as the Cité Napoléon, can still be seen today at 58, rue de Rochechouart. It offered reasonably priced dwellings, with modern lavatories on each landing, light and airy common areas, some space to grow vegetables, and even free medical care. But the unusual layout and regimented lifestyle, with gates closed at ten o'clock each night, made the building unpopular with residents. Still, the design pushed the boundaries for workers' housing. Even in Britain, architects would for decades replicate the model of the bourgeois house rather than explore innovative typologies like this one. The Cité Napoléon established a strand of activity to which Louis-Napoléon would return.

Louis-Napoléon had another area of great personal interest in which he wanted to make his mark, the art of landscape design, which he had so appreciated in Britain and and wished to bring to the French public. He decided to transform the Bois de Boulogne, a former hunting ground traversed by straight, boring paths, into a landscaped public park for Parisians. He selected a landscaper for the task and gave his instructions for the design. He was particularly insistent on the creation of a significant body of water in the Bois de Boulogne, a long lake like the Serpentine in Hyde Park. His enthusiasm for the idea that Paris would soon have a park to equal and surpass those of London was, as always, understated, but deeply felt.

Although to all appearances Louis-Napoléon held a weak political hand, he played it skillfully. He was patient and calculating, generally avoiding conflict, finding common ground with the Party of Order when he could, and playing various groups and individuals against one another. Most of all, he let the representatives, ensnared in their factionalism, disconnect themselves politically from the people. Gradually and obstinately, he asserted himself and the office of president.

By October 1849, Louis-Napoléon was strong enough to take the decisive step of dismissing the entire government and replacing it with his own men. He was beginning to grasp the reality of power, and he would use every opportunity to gain a firmer grip.

His handling of the projects for Paris followed this general approach. He appropriated the preexisting projects as his own, incorporating them into his political narrative of modernization and social welfare. In so doing, he created one of the first areas of visibility for an otherwise-beleaguered President, in which he gradually imposed greater authority.

By 1850, Louis-Napoléon was in a position to launch his first major project for Paris, the rue des Ecoles. The plans for the new street, which would form an east-west connection through the tight urban fabric of the university district, located on the Left Bank, had been drawn up by private citizens at the end of the previous year. On October 25, 1850, Louis-Napoléon reviewed and endorsed the project. As he would later say in a speech to citizens of the area, "In order to precisely understand the situation in the poor neighborhoods of the twelfth arrondissement,* I went several times to visit the narrow and insalubrious streets of your neighborhood, and I now know how just and humane your requests are."[3]

The improvement and modernization of Paris was beginning to gain prominence in Louis-Napoléon's political program. In December 1850, he gave a speech at the Hôtel de Ville, where he summarized his vision: "Paris is the heart of France, and all the useful improvements that we can adopt here contribute powerfully to the general good. . . . Let us put all our efforts to embellishing this great city, to improving the

---

* According to the configuration of the arrondissements at the time, which was changed in 1860.

condition of its citizens, to enlightening them on their true interests. Let us open new streets, clean up the populous neighborhoods that lack air and daylight, and let the sun's beneficial rays penetrate everywhere behind our walls, like the light of truth in our hearts."[4]

One of the president's most visible and decisive interventions concerned the project to expand the Palais du Louvre.

French sovereigns since the seventeenth century had dreamed of creating a Grand Louvre, a complex of palaces stretching seven hundred yards from the Louvre's historic core around the cour carrée to the Palais des Tuileries. This would give grandiose form to the locus of French political power, at the center of the capital city.

The Palais des Tuileries, which formed the west end of this complex, has since disappeared, burned in 1871 and later pulled down. But while it stood, it was one of the most prestigious palaces in France. Built at the initiative of Catherine de Medici, starting in 1564, it received contributions by many great names of French art and architecture. It was the official residence of a number of kings, including Henri IV and Louis XIV, before the latter's move to Versailles. Still today, some are calling for the reconstruction of this great forgotten monument of French history.

For close to four decades, since the most recent additions under Napoléon I, no action had been taken to build the Grand Louvre. Worse, a whole neighborhood of lowly houses had been left occupying the space between the Louvre and the Tuileries, an encroachment that was seen as a national embarrassment. The project of the Grand Louvre had been exhumed in the 1840s and, now that he was president, Louis-Napoléon was determined to see it to completion, realizing the full complex and clearing the offending hovels.

The official architect of the Louvre was Félix Duban, a renowned artist who had recently been entrusted with the restoration of the

Louvre's magnificent Gallery of Apollo. However, Louis-Napoléon, who asked to be personally briefed on the project, was not satisfied that Duban was the right man to design the complex as a whole. Instead, he asked Louis Visconti, an architect with Bonapartist credentials gained from nothing less than having designed the tomb of Napoléon I at the Invalides, to develop a proposal. Visconti did so, and his plan pleased the president. It took some time to get Visconti officially designated to oversee the expansion of the Louvre and to secure the funding. By July 1852, the obstacles were resolved and the first stone of the new Palais du Louvre was set.

Little more than a year later, on December 29, 1853, with construction of his masterpiece in full swing, Louis Visconti suffered a stroke and died. Responsibility for the project, which by now employed a small city of artisans and workers, was assumed by his colleague Hector Lefuel, an architect who would later work on the Palais des Tuileries and the Palais de Saint-Cloud and build homes for key figures of the Second Empire elite such as Achille Fould and Emilien de Niewerkerke.

The Grand Louvre seemed to some to be an idle project of prestige, but it was sent a highly symbolic message to Parisians, demonstrating that the president was serious about restoring the grandeur of Paris.

In 1851, Louis-Napoléon made another decisive intervention with lasting impact on the design of central Paris. He decided to extend the rue de Rivoli another half mile, all the way to the Hôtel de Ville. By this bold step, Louis-Napoléon created the first new artery through the heart of the city. He also settled a long-standing debate about the planning of central Paris.

There had long been a consensus among architects about the need for a new street crossing the city from east to west; there was heated debate, however, on its exact location. The traditional thinking was that the new artery should be built on the axis of the Palais du Louvre's east colonnade. It would stretch across the city to the place du Trône, today's place de la Nation, forming a majestic vista to the Palais du Louvre. The avenue would have been similar in effect to the avenue de Paris in Versailles or the Mall in London, amplifying the stature of the place du Louvre, giving the east colonnade its full urban role. It would have allowed traffic to easily cross the city through what was still an impenetrable maze of small streets and dead-end lanes. There was, however, a significant problem in that the historic church of Saint-Germain-l'Auxerrois was inconveniently positioned right in the path of the potential new avenue.

Louis-Napoléon decided to avoid polemic and not build the new avenue in the proposed location. Instead, the rue de Rivoli would be continued straight, tangential to the northern side of the place du Louvre, eventually connecting to the rue Saint-Antoine to reach the place du Trône. This was a heresy according to the precepts of classical French urban composition, but it was a pragmatic solution. The layout became the embodiment of the victory of a more functional nineteenth-century conception of urban design over the more compositional approach of the eighteenth century. The rue de Rivoli was on the way to becoming the first urban planning triumph of Louis-Napoléon Bonaparte.

Back in 1844, Prefect Rambuteau had selected an architect to design the new Les Halles market. The man he chose was a laureate of the Grand Prix de Rome who was working for the city of Paris and had built almost nothing. His name was Victor Baltard.

Baltard was the son of Louis-Pierre Baltard, one of the most famous architects of France at the time, who was just finishing a major building, the courthouse in Lyon. The younger Baltard had studied at the elite Lycée Henri IV, and then at the Ecole des Beaux-Arts, where his father was a professor. He was an intelligent and diligent young man, skilled at both freehand drawing and rendering. He had failed to win the Prix de Rome competition in 1831 and 1832, but was successful in 1833.

After spending five years of study in Rome, as entitled by the prize, he returned to Paris in 1839. Unable to win commissions, he began working for the city of Paris. There he was tasked with maintenance and restoration projects for Paris's churches and, occasionally, the design for celebrations and special events for the city.

Baltard had been developing his project for Les Halles as the revolution of 1848 unfolded. So it was that he presented his project to a new—and temporary—city administration on August 30, 1848. The project consisted of eight pavilions with a stone exterior and stone corner towers, an ambitious cast-metal structure, and a vast metal roof. Of course, the political context made things complicated. The site and program were constantly being questioned and rival architects put forward all sorts of counterproposals.

Louis-Napoléon was eager to bring Parisians a new and modern market facility. He knew that this project would touch thousands of Parisians in their daily lives. An incontestable symbol of progress toward rationalization and hygiene, it was perfectly in line with his ideals and his political program.

In 1851, the Paris City Council confirmed the project and Baltard as the architect. Later that year, Prefect Berger secured the funding, and, after a decade of work on the project, Baltard could finally start construction. Louis-Napoléon Bonaparte laid the first stone on September 15, 1851.

Among the French presidents who have wanted to make their mark on Paris, Louis-Napoléon Bonaparte was particularly fortunate to have found, upon taking office, a set of projects he could take forward. They were all now progressing, as was the project for the Grand Louvre.

The problem for Louis-Napoléon was that his four-year term as president was more than half over, and the Constitution unambiguously barred him from serving a second consecutive term. Unless something changed, elections would designate a new president of the French Republic in December 1852. Louis-Napoléon would have to hand power over to his successor, marking an end to his dreams of glory for Paris and for France.

Five

A NEW EMPIRE

Thanks to his constant campaigning, Louis-Napoléon Bonaparte was, by the beginning of 1851, by far the most popular politician in the country, especially in the small towns and villages. There was simply no opponent who could mount a credible challenge at the polls. But as it stood, he would not be allowed to run for reelection.

For a sitting president to be permitted to serve a second term, the Constitution would have to be changed, which would require a supermajority of three-fourths of the votes in the National Assembly. Throughout 1851, Louis-Napoléon's top priority was to secure that supermajority. He made the case that the Constitution as drafted was preventing the people from selecting the leader they desired. Was that not a betrayal of the democratic ideal?

Louis-Napoléon occupied the high ground, but on June 1, 1851, speaking in Dijon, he overplayed his hand:

If my government has been unable to achieve all the improvements it intended, we need to look to the maneuverings of factions that paralyze the

goodwill of even the assemblies and governments most devoted to the
public good. For the last three years, it has been notable that I have been
assisted by the Assembly whenever it was necessary to combat disorder by
measures of compression. But when I wanted to do good, to create a real
estate bank, to take measures to improve the lot of the people, I met only
inertia. . . . I take advantage of this banquet as a forum to open my
heart to my fellow citizens. A new phase of our political era is beginning.
From one end of France to the other, petitions are being signed to request
the revision of the Constitution. I await with confidence the manifesta-
tions of the country and the decisions of the Assembly, which will be in-
spired only by the public good. If France recognizes that one does not have
the right to dispose of her without her, then France has only to say it: my
courage and my energy will be there for her. . . . Whatever the duties
that the country imposes on me, it will find me determined to follow its
will; and, believe me, gentlemen, France will not perish in my hands.[1]

Many representatives interpreted this not as legitimate ambition, but as a threat to the parliamentary system. From that point on, the likelihood of getting the supermajority required to change the Constitution had vanished.

Assured of his personal popularity over the fractious and largely discredited National Assembly and now certain he would not be able to stay in power by legal means, Louis-Napoléon began quietly working with a small circle of highly trusted people on a plan for a coup d'état. The situation reminded the classically educated conspirators of Julius Caesar coming to take control of the Roman Republic, so they called the plan "Project Rubicon."

The key person behind the plan was Victor de Persigny. Son of a military man, Persigny had had a military career himself and then dabbled in journalism. He was intelligent and energetic. Most of all, he had a sense of destiny, that of bringing the Bonapartist cause to triumph. Early on, he had determined that Louis-Napoléon was the only member of the Bonaparte family with the gumption to stage a successful return to power. He had found an opportunity to meet him in 1835 and from that point onward remained his loyal and tireless accomplice: in Strasbourg in 1836, in Boulogne in 1840, in Ham in 1846, during the return to France in 1848, and now for the coup d'état.

On the evening of December 1, 1851, Louis-Napoléon hosted a reception at the Palais de l'Elysée. He chatted nonchalantly with the guests, acting as though all were normal. In reality, the wheels of a comprehensive military operation were already in motion.

During the night, the generals included in the conspiracy took their untrusted colleagues into custody and placed troops at strategic locations around the city. The police commissioners in each district pulled the most prominent members of the National Assembly and other potential leaders of a resistance movement out of bed and locked them up in Mazas Prison. A detachment of soldiers entered the National Assembly and took over the guard posts. Thousands of posters were secretly printed while the bells of the churches that could have been used to call the populace to arms were silenced.

When day broke over Paris, each street corner had a poster proclaiming that the National Assembly had been dissolved and that the president had assumed all powers. Everything was calm.

Over the next few days, barricades were built and sporadic fighting broke out. On the Grands Boulevards, nervous troops shot into the crowd and killed bystanders. In total, several hundred people were killed, but order was maintained. A plebiscite was arranged to confirm the people's support of the president and grant him a ten-year term. Most people did not regret the dissolution of the National Assembly. The plebiscite was a success.

Louis-Napoléon set about organizing a new regime. He spent the first months of 1852 putting in place a new institutional architecture, rewriting the Constitution, and preparing parliamentary elections. He appointed a government of staunch loyalists. Laws were passed reestablishing the licensing and censorship of the press and reducing the role of every institution not closely controlled by the president to near irrelevance.

The following autumn, Louis-Napoléon embarked on a tour of France to gauge public opinion. The unspoken premise was to test if the country was ready for him to proclaim himself emperor. On one of the last stops of this trip, in Bordeaux, Louis-Napoléon was greeted by the local prefect, a career civil servant named Georges-Eugène Haussmann.

The trip had been going well, but it was in Bordeaux, in the midst of a grandiose celebration magnificently orchestrated by Haussmann, that the Empire received its consecration. Louis-Napoléon gave a speech, making it clear that the Empire would be reestablished, and emphasizing again that its objectives would be more peaceful than his uncle's. He also gave an idea of his program: "I have, like [Napoléon I,] many conquests to make. We have immense fallow lands to clear, roads to build, ports to dig, rivers to make navigable, canals to finish, a railway network to complete. We have, across from Marseille, a vast kingdom [Algeria] to assimilate to France. Everywhere we have ruins to raise again, false gods to bring down, truths to make triumph."[2]

Another plebiscite was held, and on December 2, 1852—exactly a year after the coup d'état—Louis-Napoléon Bonaparte paraded under the Arc de Triomphe and down the Champs-Elysées. He would henceforth be known as Emperor Napoléon III.

In early 1853, no one yet knew what to expect from the reign of this newly installed emperor. One of the first things he did was unexpected: He got married.

Up to that point, Napoléon III had showed little inclination to marry.

He had a young English mistress, Miss Howard, as a quasi-official companion, but his romantic interests did not stop there. As his subsequent behavior would confirm, monogamy was not particularly his thing.

There were two important reasons to marry. The first was that the right spouse could help establish the new regime among the European monarchies, just as Marie-Louisa, the Habsburg princess of Austria, had done for Napoléon I. The second, even more important in the minds of most, was to produce an heir. The creation of the Empire had required the constitution of a sequence of succession, in which Jérôme Bonaparte, Napoléon I's youngest brother, was first in line. It was unanimously hoped that the emperor would quickly marry and have a child to supersede Prince Jérôme.

Over the year since the coup détat, ambassadors had been dispatched across Europe and contacts were made, but no major ruling family was willing to provide a wife to the upstart new ruler of France. Among the minor princesses whose families could be convinced, one even committed the affront of declining herself. The search was looking as if it would be difficult.

It had been in 1849, at a party given by his cousin, Princess Mathilde, that Louis-Napoléon had first noticed an attractive young Spanish lady. She was of noble extraction, as evidenced by her interminable name: María Eugenia Ignacia Augustina Palafox de Guzmán Portocarrero y Kirkpatrick de Closeburn, countess of Montijo, among a flurry of other titles, and she had grown up in Paris. She was slim and elegant, with a beautiful, typically Spanish face, but with red hair from her Scots ancestry. She was in search of a suitable match but was having some trouble, as she had pretensions that were higher still than her rank.

After the party, Louis-Napoléon remarked to his cousin about his interest in the Spanish young lady. It did not take more than that for the mechanics to kick into action. A few weeks later, on New Year's Eve, again at Princess Mathilde's, Eugenia was seated next to Louis-Napoléon.

But things did not go as planned. Of course, Louis-Napoléon, notwithstanding his relationship with Miss Howard, made overtures. And while Eugenia did not rebuff them, she made clear that she would not be a mere mistress. She was holding out for marriage.

Her resistance, of course, did nothing but stoke Louis-Napoléon's ardor. Perhaps from the sheer frustration of being able to conquer the whole country of France but not this one Spanish countess, Louis-Napoléon began to characterize his sentiment as love.

By early January 1853—that is to say, after three years of Louis-Napoléon's advances, one of which reportedly had to be repelled with the help of a riding whip—there was still no word of marriage. Aware that a search for an imperial spouse was actively under way, Eugenia saw that it was time to play her last card. She knew that if marriage did not come now, it never would.

On January 12, 1853, just weeks after the creation of the Empire, Eugenia was invited to a ball at the Palais des Tuileries. She arrived looking stunning, on the arm of the most powerful financier in France, James de Rothschild.

Napoléon III was crafty and ambitious, but he had met his match. During the course of the evening, Eugenia found a moment alone with the new emperor. She told him she was leaving Paris for good, that this was their good-bye. The response was everything Eugenia could have dreamed of. He told her she must not go, that he would ask for her hand in marriage.

Napoléon III told his entourage himself. The reaction was shock and horror. His uncle Jérôme Bonaparte bluntly told him, "[O]ne does not marry Miss Montijo."[3] No one objected to Eugenia being a mistress, but the idea that a foreigner, and not even one from a top-tier family, would be empress was seen as a catastrophe. Various members of the entourage tried to get the new emperor to back out of the reckless and unfortunate engagement. But when he had his mind made up, Napoléon III was resolute. He did not back down.

...

Less than three weeks after the ball at the Palais des Tuileries, on January 30, 1853, in the first great imperial celebration, Napoléon III and Eugenia were wed. The procession made its way through throngs of Parisians from the Palais des Tuileries to Notre-Dame. There was an elaborate Mass and wedding ceremony. Eugenia de Montijo became Eugénie, empress of France.

The marriage was popular with the French people. They were thrilled that it was a union of love instead of, as traditionally for rulers, a cynical political arrangement—it was perfect for a generation brought up with the Romantic movement. The fact that the new empress was highly Catholic reassured the conservative and clerical elements of the population. The couple handled public relations adeptly, donating the wedding gift from the nation to fund the creation of a school for underprivileged girls in the faubourg Saint-Antoine.

The new empress had many qualities. Pauline von Metternich, the wife of the Austrian ambassador, recalled her first impression:

I was subjugated by her grace, her goodness and her ravishing beauty. Her features were extremely refined, the expression of her eyes soft and intelligent, her nose, her mouth, the oval of her face, the shape of her head, her neck, her shoulders were all of rare perfection, her teeth pretty and straight, her smile delightful. . . . But what in my opinion even surpassed her beauty was her incomparable grace, for each of her movements were so gracious that one could have painted her in each of her poses.[4]

What characterized Empress Eugénie more than anything was her determination to completely fulfill her role as empress. She strictly adhered to and enforced the decorum of the court. She set the tone of fashion and taste, with the conviction that nothing was too extravagant for the Empire. Although she was not particularly good at empathy, she made the requisite visits to the poor and the sick, the orphaned children and the victims of cholera.

Despite that, Eugénie was, in the damning words of the duchess of Coburg, "neither an empress nor a princess, but just a charming and well-mannered young woman."[5] Eugénie was emblematic of the Second Empire because she, too, was a social climber; an empress not by birth, but by marriage. She led the way in an era in which those who had the appearance of the elite class—from Persigny to Morny to Walewski and the Pereires—did not have that status by virtue of lineage, but achieved it thanks to the environment of social mobility of mid-nineteenth-century France.

Despite a good start, Empress Eugénie did not win the hearts of the French. She never overcame the fact that she was a foreigner. Her staunch Spanish Catholicism translated into unwavering support of the Pope's temporal power against the emergence of the Italian Republic, which satisfied only the most rigidly conservative fringe of French public opinion. The stories from court and her elaborate taste for fashion gave her a reputation for being frivolous and profligate. The general sentiment was that she was a negative influence on the emperor's policy decisions; it was only a matter of time before she would become the national scapegoat.

Two women would rule over the Second Empire. One, of course, was the empress. The other was Princess Mathilde, the daughter of Jérôme Bonaparte, and therefore Napoléon III's cousin. Although she lacked the empress's beauty, slimness, and grace, the portly Mathilde was as sensual as the empress was cold. She had a long-lasting, passionate affair with Count Emilien de Nieuwerkerke, a tall, handsome Dutchman who, in addition to being a great seducer, was an art collector and sculptor whom Napoléon III increasingly asked to look after the artistic affairs of the Empire. Mathilde, whose décolleté was known as one of the riches of the Empire, kept brilliant intellectual company—it is hard to name a luminary of the period who was not a regular at her home in the rue de Courcelles. Gustave Flaubert, for one, had an exuberant, unrequited infatuation with her. With her sense of humor and her vivacious, often frank spirit, she could run circles around the poor empress.

From the outset, the Empire abandoned the simplicity and reserve of the Republic. The empress was to have the most magnificent outfits, the emperor the most splendid horses. An imperial court was set up with an intricate and inflexible protocol, with a ritual of audiences, meals, Masses, and balls at the Palais des Tuileries. Every autumn, the emperor and empress retreated to the Château de Compiègne, northwest of Paris, where they hosted selected guests. At Compiègne, there was hunting, theater, and dancing, especially at the grand ball in honor of the empress on November 15, the feast day of Saint-Eugene. Masquerades were all the rage, as were elaborate dances in costume performed by members of the imperial entourage. "The luxe displayed on these occasions was truly astonishing—I had almost said appalling," commented an English participant.[6]

In time, another woman would make her appearance: Virginia Oldoini, the countess of Castiglione.

The countess was a "miracle of beauty." She had captivating dark green eyes, a perfectly formed face, and long, flowing hair. Her skin was smooth, firm, and flawless. She was very tall, with long elegant arms and legs, and "the waist of a nymph." Her figure was that of a statue of Antiquity; she was "as if carved out of pink marble." "Never have we seen such beauty and never shall we see it again," wrote Pauline von Metternich.[7]

The sartorial daring of La Castiglione was legendary. Once, at the height of the success of Gustave's Flaubert's novel *Salammbô*, she attended a costume party dressed as the sultry heroine. She appeared at the ballroom of the Palais des Tuileries barefoot, her arms uncovered to the shoulder and her silk trousers slit to the hip, causing ripples of shock mixed with admiration throughout the ballroom.

La Castiglione was the cousin of the count of Cavour, the prime minister of the Kingdom of Piedmont-Sardinia. The story goes that when La Castiglione accompanied her husband to Paris in 1855, Cavour recommended that she use any means necessary to further the Italian cause with the emperor of France. She took her mission to heart.

The eighteen-year-old countess was first introduced to the forty-seven-year-old emperor at a ball at the home of Princesse Mathilde—the same place he had met Empress Eugénie—on January 9, 1856. Under their heavy lids, the eyes of Napoléon III, who was always on the lookout for a sexual conquest, did not fail to register the beauty of the Italian countess.

On July 23 of the same year, La Castiglione was present at a ball at Villeneuve-l'Étang, a property on the far end of the park of the Palais de Saint-Cloud. At one point, Napoléon III offered to take her out by rowboat to see the small island in the lake on the grounds. It took an extremely long time for the two to return. The empress grew increasingly fidgety. When the emperor and the countess reappeared, there was a wave of consternation among the guests. Not one could fail to notice that the countess's dress was heavily wrinkled; there was little doubt as to the nature of their activity during their time of absence from the party.

Empress Eugénie was furious at being upstaged by this foreign beauty, shaken at the thought that La Castiglione was younger, more beautiful, more interesting, and more fashionable than she. There ensued a veritable war of elegance between the two women. Designers and seamstresses worked in the Palais des Tuileries around the clock, maintaining an astounding production, in terms of both quantity and extravagance. Four outfits were sometimes produced for a single day: one for the morning, one for the day, one for the evening, and one for the night. Each was designed to surprise and impress.

The empress made it policy never to wear a dress more than once. As she did not want others to wear her dresses shortly after she wore them, she would wait until the end of the year and sell her dresses for charity. But sometimes Eugénie ceded to the solicitations of an actress and gave a dress away before the year-end sale. Word would get out, and people would go to the theater with great trepidation to see the dress being worn onstage. Within weeks, copies were being produced and exported. From Guadeloupe to Saint Petersburg, women were dressed "*à l'impératrice Eugénie.*"

Théophile Gautier, in his novel *Spirite,* described the fashion of the Second Empire, as visible in the salons of the Chaussée d'Antin:

> *There lounged, sitting in bubbling cascades of gauze, tulle netting, lace, satin, velvet that rose to their shoulders, women, for the most part young and beautiful, whose dress of fanciful extravagance manifested Worth's inexhaustible and expensive creativity. In their brown, blond, red and even powdered hair, of an opulence to make even the least malevolent suppose that art had enhanced their beauty, diamonds glistened, feathers ruffled, green leaves shone with droplets of water, real and chimerical flowers opened, sequined broaches rustled, pearl strings crossed, arrows, daggers, needles shone, scarab-winged gauds shimmered, golden bands circled, velvet ribbons crossed, gems trembled at the end of their spirals and generally everything that can be put on the head of a fashionable woman, without counting the raisins, currants, and the colorful berries.*[8]

There is a story that, although of doubtful veracity, is both amusing and telling. On October 4, 1856, there opened at the Théâtre du Gymnase a play entitled *Les Toilettes Tapageuses* (*The Outrageous Outfits*). In the spirit of satire, the leading actress was dressed in a ridiculously enormous crinoline dress. The next morning, claimed Maxime Du Camp, no less than twenty great ladies of high society were requesting the dress as a model for their own seamstresses, and within a week the dresses seen in Paris had doubled in size!

French haute couture became an industry during the Second Empire. The obsession with novelty and appearances had tremendous economic repercussions. On the one hand, it put France at the forefront of the luxury business, a position that it has not relinquished since. On the other, it led a whole society into significant expenditures for frivolities that some commentators saw as weakening the French economy by diverting funds from more productive uses. Some even later cited it as a contributing cause of the calamitous defeat of 1870.

There is no doubt that Parisians' passion for fashion affected the city. The luxuriant creativity could not help but be reflected in the architecture of the emerging city, from the new houses of the parc Monceau to the avenue de l'Observatoire to, its culmination, the future new Opéra de Paris. Emile Zola described the architecture of a new *hôtel* of the parc Monceau neighborhood in terms strikingly similar to those of Gautier:

> On the garden side, ... a royal set of stairs led to a narrow terrace that reigned all along the ground floor; the handrail of this terrace, in the style of the railings of the Parc Monceau, was even more laden with gold than the glass canopy and the lantern of the courtyard. . . . [The facade] was a display, a profusion, a crushing of riches. Around the windows, along the cornices, ran whorls of branches and flowers; there were balconies like baskets of greenery, upholding great nude women, hips twisted, the tips of their breasts thrust forward; and here and there were pasted whimsical escutcheons, bunches of grapes, of roses, all possible flowerings of stone and of marble. As the eye traveled up, the house continued to blossom. Around the roof ran a balustrade with, from place to place, urns carrying flames of stone. And there, between the œils-de-bœuf in the mansard roof, which opened on an unbelievable hodge-podge of fruits and leaves, bloomed the most important pieces of this surprising decoration, the pediments of the pavilions, in the middle of which reappeared the large naked women, playing with apples, taking poses, among handfuls of reeds. The roof, loaded down with ornament, surmounted with galleries of cut lead, with two lightning rods and four enormous symmetrical chimneys, sculpted like the rest, seemed to be the finale of these architectural fireworks.[9]

Even where the architecture was not so exuberant, the urban space, from the place de l'Etoile to the boulevard Saint-Michel, was approached as a stage set for the representation of oneself. Society had a passion for appearance, and the new city was to be the ideal backdrop for displays of elegance. The Second Empire went so far as to create a city to go with the lifestyle of representation and ostentation that it so valued.

In early 1852, before he became emperor, Louis-Napoléon had moved from the Palais de l'Elysée to the Palais des Tuileries. He had adorned his office in the new residence with a giant map of Paris. He knew that he would have the power and time to remake the capital, and he immersed himself into urban planning. He deepened his knowledge of the city and spent hours considering which new connections to build, which neighborhoods to develop, which avenues and squares to build. Visitors could sometimes see him at his desk, drawing lines across the map with colored pencils. The future city was gradually taking form in his mind.

Napoléon III's thoughts came together in a colored plan of Paris drawn at the beginning of 1853. It showed the planned streets in blue, red, yellow, and green, by order of priority, together with the new squares where they met. Although the original of this plan was destroyed in 1871, we have a good idea of what it contained, thanks to descriptions and the subsequent work of researchers. It was the first image of the urban possibility of the new Paris, capital of the Second Empire.

Napoléon III's thinking was a direct continuation of Rambuteau's. His initial focus was on connecting the new train stations, now the real entry points to the city, to the city center. He planned the completion and extension of the avenues leading from the stations: For the gare Saint-Lazare, he imagined the future rue Auber and avenue de l'Opéra; for the gare de l'Ouest (later named gare Montparnasse), the rue de Rennes would be extended to the Croix-Rouge intersection and potentially all the way to the Seine; for the gare de l'Est, the boulevard de Strasbourg would be extended south clear across the city; for the gare du Nord, a new avenue would lead south all the way to the place du Louvre.

Beyond these new avenues, Napoléon III's interest was focused on modernizing and providing structure to the working-class eastern section of Paris. He imagined a great square in the northeast with avenues radiating out of it; a set of new avenues around the place du Trône (today's place de la Nation); and streets structuring the faubourg Saint-Marcel in the southeast, including one major new artery, which ended up never being built but would have been parallel to the boulevard Saint-Michel on the other side of the Panthéon, passing right in front of the église Saint-Médard.

The "colored plan," as it became known, demonstrated an intuition of Napoléon III that profoundly affected the urban development of Paris. The new avenues would form connections between the major public buildings, squares, and stations, tying the city together, penetrating the neighborhoods that were until then "closed like citadels of insurrection, such as the area around the Hôtel de Ville, the Faubourg Saint-Antoine and the two sides of the Montagne Sainte-Geneviève [the hill where the Panthéon stands]."[10] Whereas Napoléon I's projects were dots on the map—a building here, a monument there—Napoléon III's approach was a comprehensive vision of how the city worked as a whole. His obsession was not monuments, but new streets that would connect, irrigate, and open up the city.

Napoléon III had already confirmed the projects under way when he came to power; then he had inflected and amplified them. Now he was mapping out the new wave of projects that would define his capital. He did not only conceive the broad ideas; he worked out exactly how his ideas would be transposed in the urban fabric. There are not many examples of the ruler of a nation sitting down with a city plan and using the basic tools and approaches that an urban planning department would use. This is one.

The paternity of the new Paris of the Second Empire is often misattributed to Baron Haussmann. But the reality is unequivocal: The man who defined the vision for Paris and gathered the political means to implement it was none other than the emperor himself.

At the same time, the content of the colored plan belies the idea that the transformation of Paris was comprehensively defined in advance of implementation. Unarguably, there was a general vision and an initial set of ideas. But while the direction was firmly set and maintained, there remained room for a great deal of flexibility in execution, with many projects added, a number changed, and some abandoned. The full nature of the undertaking emerged only as it became reality.

By the beginning of 1853, Louis-Napoléon had metamorphosed into Emperor Napoléon III, the exclusive holder of power over France. He had patiently built up a framework where there was no room for anyone who did not have absolute loyalty to him.

Napoléon III was not a man of petty party politics. He believed he had a transcendent destiny and that he should therefore remain outside and above all parties. His strategy was to give something to each faction and much to men of influence who would set aside any scruples and serve him unquestioningly. To others, he was wily and ruthless; he would refuse to get pinned down on one side of an issue, often tacking back and forth. Those whom he couldn't cajole through status and privilege or neutralize with ambiguous promises, he eliminated from the political scene altogether, through exile if necessary. It was a disconcerting dance that left the Opposition disoriented and incapacitated for years.

The Second Empire transformation of Paris was not a democratic, consensual process. It was the product of an imperial regime with a full state apparatus dedicated to implementing the will of its leader. There was no room for debate and negotiation, and no questioning of the legitimacy of the goal of imperial splendor. This autocratic stamp would be crucial to the scale and speed of its accomplishment, but it would also turn out to be the undertaking's greatest weakness.

One of the favorite topics of speculation about Napoléon III's rebuilding of Paris concerns its motivations. Was the objective urban beauty and grandeur, functionality in a new technological age, military repression, eviction of the working class from the center, or something else?

In reality, the *grands travaux de Paris* was a highly coherent, multifaceted program that included all of these. It encompassed the practical challenges facing the society that spawned it, as well as the economic and political realities. But it was also an expression of the spirit of the age, its image of the city and of society, and the ideals and sensibilities encompassed in its aesthetics.

One aspect of the program that is often overlooked today is its role as a work scheme. Despite his frequent nods toward the urban working class, Napoléon III always struggled with the urban poor politically. In the 1857 elections, for example, only five of the elected deputies were actual opponents of the regime. All five were elected from the working-class neighborhoods of Paris and Lyon. Some advisers recommended ending universal suffrage, but of course Napoléon III would not entertain that. As he told his minister of the interior of the mid-1850s, Adolphe Billault, "[I]t all comes down to finding the ways to decrease the number of malcontents in Paris and Lyon." He added, "I would have wanted long ago to ban the building of any new factories in Paris."[11] He clearly saw urban renovation as doing the next best thing: keeping the malcontents busy and employed.

This thinking was not novel. When the Left came to power after the February 1848 uprising, its first major action was to create the Ateliers nationaux, a work-welfare scheme of national workshops. In his earlier writings, the future emperor had time and time again emphasized employment schemes as a means to reduce pauperism. The rebuilding of Paris was part of a broader economic strategy, based on heavy investment in infrastructure, including ports, canals, and other facilities, both to build the basis of a modern economy and to act as an economic stimulus. When one walks the streets of Paris today, what one sees is the remnant of this political and economic strategy.

These investments were part of Napoléon III's primary political objective of maintaining order and preserving power, which he genuinely saw as being the greater interest, not only of himself but also of France. Unemployment, indigence, and idleness went hand in hand with the threat of insurrection. As Charles Merruau, a senior civil servant at the prefecture, would approvingly note when surveying Paris several years hence, "[I]t was no longer bands of insurgents going back and forth across the city, but squadrons of masons, carpenters and workers of all sorts going to their work."[12]

Another aspect of this program, one that has become less intuitive to us today, is the moral dimension. The emergence of the big city of the industrial era brought with it strong concerns about depravity among the unfixed masses. The actual layout of the streets and houses, together with the appropriate insertion of churches and other institutions to provide a spiritual framework to the citizens of the city, was seen as critical to stemming moral turpitude. The archbishop of Paris, Cardinal Morlot, articulated this point:

> [The rebuilding of Paris combats] moral misery indirectly but surely by improving the conditions and the habits of existence of the working classes. One does not comport oneself in broad and straight streets, inundated with light, with the same carelessness as in narrow, tortuous and dark streets. Bringing air, light and water to the lodging of the poor is not only to reestablish physical health; it is also to bring an encouragement to the proper upkeep of the home, to the cleanliness of the members of the family, which little by little acts on their moral state.[13]

Public health in cities was equally high in the minds of contemporaries. Paris had been traumatized by the cholera outbreak of 1832, in addition to the rise of tuberculosis and other ailments linked to the urban environment. For several decades, essayists and editorialists had made a link between the physical layout of the city and the health of the population. Michel Chevalier, one of the most prominent Saint-Simonians, had written in the 1830s:

> *Soon the mortality statistics for the different neighborhoods of Paris will be public, and we will all know what the authorities have long known . . . that there is a massive disproportion in the mortality of the workers' neighborhoods near the river compared to neighborhoods with broader streets and better-ventilated apartments. When this fact is known by all, the city or the state will undoubtedly make the sacrifices necessary to make these neighborhoods, veritable havens of epidemic, disappear.*[14]

Hygiene-driven urban renewal had, in fact, been part of the program promised by the Republicans in 1848. This policy found its legal translation in a law passed in April 1850, which, for the first time, defined insalubrious housing and put in place a procedure for its removal. By the 1850s, clearing away and opening up the dense inner-city neighborhoods was widely perceived to be a key part of a socially progressive political program.

It is often said that the broad avenues of the new Paris were created primarily to allow troop movements against the people and unencumbered cannon fire. There is no doubt that operations to ensure civil peace were a component of the urban-renewal program. It is also true that the fact that Napoléon III took power through a forceful violation of the democratic Constitution, followed by armed repression, does not give him the moral high ground. Nevertheless, the urban program for Paris was not solely or primarily conceived as an instrument of police control.*

---

*In this area, the ill-informed writings of Walter Benjamin especially have done considerable harm to the historical record.

At the same time, France had, by the middle of the nineteenth century, experienced no fewer than three revolutions, not to speak of many minor uprisings. The working-class neighborhoods of Paris, which at the time included some areas right in the city center, were political powder kegs situated within a short walk of all of the country's institutions, giving their inhabitants a disproportionate political voice in a country that was still overwhelmingly rural and non-Parisian. This was seen as a major political problem by conservatives as a whole; even some moderate Republicans were uncomfortable with the excessive power of the urban masses. From the government perspective, it certainly seemed natural to try to foil subversive operations. Haussmann, for one, was not bashful about stating his views about the danger posed to order by the Paris street:

> In reality . . . I remained and still am convinced of the wisdom of the preoccupations of all our Kings, even the most powerful, regarding the impressionable and turbulent character of the Parisian popular masses: since Philippe-Auguste, who had the Louvre fortress built to serve as his residence outside the walls enclosing his capital, to Louis XIV, who transferred the seat of government to Versailles.[15]

Napoléon III's position, typically synthetic, was to seek to improve the lot of the working class while simultaneously implementing firm measures to impose order upon the neighborhoods in which they lived—up to and including the wholesale destruction of those neighborhoods.

Grandeur and prestige were undeniably present in Napoléon III's mind as he contemplated the rebuilding of Paris. Years before becoming president, he had already stated, "I want to be a new Augustus, because Augustus made Rome into a city of marble."[16] As the beauty of the capital of the Empire had been important to Napoléon I, so, too, would it be to the leader of the Second Empire.

This aspiration was not, however, the result of a heightened artistic sensitivity. On the contrary, as Maxime Du Camp flatly wrote in his memoirs, "anything that touched to Letters or Fine Arts seemed to escape him."[17] There are anecdotes about how Napoléon III would stop for long minutes before a painting, only to make a comment about some piece of technical apparatus depicted, completely oblivious of any artistic quality the work may have had. Quite simply, his makeup was that of a military man, with a penchant for order and a taste for disciplines like science, engineering, military history, and administration. In the words of Arsène Houssaye, director of the Théâtre-Français, "[Napoléon III] was a utilitarian. What he loved most in the firmament was his own star."[18] Napoléon III did on occasion take an interest in architectural projects, but any expression of beauty that occurred was thanks to the skill of his architects, not to the guidance of the emperor.

It is often supposed that Napoléon III imported British urban concepts to Paris. In reality, except for the Bois de Boulogne, with its direct borrowings from Saint James Park and Hyde Park, there was no specific transposition of British ideas. The realizations of modern urbanism in London of course spurred the French to emulatory zeal, but their forms were quite different. The Parisian projects developed in direct relation to the thinking that was maturing in France in the 1830s and 1840s. There was without doubt a British influence, but it was more diffuse, translated through the drive toward progress and the general sense of modernity cultivated in the Victorian age.

By early 1853, construction of the rue de Rivoli was in full swing, but faced major problems. There had been no topographical survey, and it soon became apparent that the level of the new street was well below the level of the neighborhoods it was to cross. The complications seemed intractable, and would be, in any case, expensive to resolve. Behind his legendary veneer of impassibility, the emperor was beginning to get frustrated.

Prefect Berger had made basic and costly mistakes due to his inattention to the practical details of execution. But even more importantly, Berger failed to pursue the projects with the ambition that Napoléon III expected. The emperor wanted to be visionary, but Berger was everywhere toning things down, reducing the scope of the projects in order to minimize costs. As Berger saw it, the city of Paris had a limited budget, one that did not allow for significant new expenditures. He made it a point of honor to manage the city's budget as prudently as he managed his household's, adamantly maintaining that the city would pay off the debt contracted for the extension of the rue de Rivoli before committing to any further expenditures. A conservative bourgeois by nature, Berger simply did not buy in to the grandeur of the emperor's ambition.

Charles Merruau, a member of the prefecture staff, remembered an episode dating from 1851 that showed the direction things were already taking:

> One day we saw the Prefect [Berger] worried and irritated. He was coming from the Élysée, where he had been called to a council of ministers presided by the Prince [Louis-Napoléon]; he was made to understand that he was to engage the City without delay in the expenses, which were very considerable, required to take the rue de Rivoli through the populous and commercial neighborhoods of la Monnaie, les Bourbonnais, along Les Halles, across rue Saint-Denis and rue Saint-Martin to connect the Louvre and the Hôtel de Ville. The discussion included the construction of the new market building and the imminent laying of the first stone. The President of the Republic was pressing, and was insistent on a rapid execution. . . . By expressing his strong opposition to the projects that were being imposed on him, Berger had followed his initial view, assuredly very praiseworthy, of avoiding any expense that he considered excessive. . . . The President, whose days in power were strictly counted, was not free to do the public good at leisure.[19]

In fact, Napoléon III was looking not only to execute the existing projects swiftly but to go much further. It was imperative for him to have someone he could count on to implement his desires promptly and fully.

The appointment of the count de Persigny to the position of minister of the interior in January 1852 was a decisive step for the Parisian improvement projects. Persigny was a true member of the inner circle, a man of unquestionable loyalty. He certainly understood the full breadth of Napoléon III's ambitions and their political meaning. In his memoirs, Persigny presented himself as the man behind the initial implementation of the imperial vision for Paris:

> The streets of Paris were so congested, circulation had become so difficult, that upon seeing on one hand such a rapid increase in the population and on the other hand the animated spectacle of the rue de Rivoli, so successfully opened, everyone was clamoring for new openings, new connections, but without much preoccupation for the means to achieve them. As minister of the interior, it was my role to handle this matter. The Emperor, who for a long time had aspired to transform Paris, had strongly recommended this interest to me. As a consequence, six weeks after my arrival in the ministry, on the basis of my report and my presentation, the Prince-President of the Republic, by the decree of March 10th [1852] decided the opening of boulevard de Strasbourg. . . . But this project . . . was but a detail in the overall plan of which everyone understood the necessity. The matter at hand was to resolve the general plan of operations, and especially the financial plan for these operations.[20]

Under Persigny, there was indeed progress. During the course of 1852, decrees were published for the extension of the rue de Rivoli to the rue Saint-Antoine, for the rue de Rennes leading to the gare de l'Ouest, for the rue des Ecoles, and for the boulevard de Strasbourg leading to the gare de l'Est.

The minister of the interior struggled with Berger. He spent time with the prefect, elaborating and discussing the idea that, by driving future revenues, the urban projects would pay for themselves, justifying that the city should raise debt to complete them. Berger would simply not let himself be convinced. He remained obstinately opposed to further expenditures.

By 1853, after Napoléon III had been in power for more than four years, progress on the improvements to Paris was decidedly unsatisfactory. A first set of works was under way, but at every turn obstacles and frustrations sprang up. New projects had been approved, but they remained on paper. The emperor's vision was clear and his determination was strong, but unless he found someone with the will and capability to overcome roadblocks and achieve results, the new city he imagined would never emerge.

Prefect Berger had already been given quite a bit of leeway. But now, with the Second Empire firmly in place, the emperor's wish was to be diligently carried out, without hesitation or afterthought. Time was pressing—Napoléon III did not know how long he would have to build his urban legacy. It was clear that Berger needed to be replaced.

The last straw was the new market at Les Halles. The first pavilion went up in the spring of 1853. The design had undergone a number of revisions to make the metal skeleton less prominent and a great deal of stone masonry had been added. The satirists had already dubbed the building "the Les Halles fortress." Napoléon III decided to visit himself, and he did so on June 3. He found a heavy stone building that wholly failed to conform to his vision of a modern market. He instructed that construction be stopped immediately and the brand-new building be pulled down.

Napoléon III was looking for a new prefect of the Seine. Of course, he knew Georges-Eugène Haussmann, whom he had promoted to prefect of the Var shortly after being elected president and who had masterfully hosted him in Bordeaux a few months earlier. Persigny presented the emperor with a list of civil servants suitable for the position. When Napoléon III saw Haussmann's name, the choice was clear. "We need look no further," said the emperor.

And indeed, if there was ever an instance where the appointment of a civil servant brought together the appropriate aptitudes and capabilities for a specific mission, this was it. The combination of Napoléon III and Georges-Eugène Haussmann would change Paris forever.

Six

THE MAN FOR THE JOB

On June 23, 1853, Georges-Eugène Haussmann was at the underprefecture of Bazas, a small town in the Gironde, enjoying dinner with notable citizens of the district. As he sat conversing with the underprefect's wife, a member of the prefecture staff interrupted to give him a message that had come via the aerial telegraph. Haussmann read it, told the other diners that it was nothing serious, stuffed the note in his pocket, and rejoined the conversation.

That note would change Haussmann's life. It was from Victor de Persigny, the minister of the interior. It informed him that he had been appointed to the position of prefect of the Seine and that he was to come to Paris at once.

After returning to Bordeaux and putting his affairs in order over the weekend, Georges-Eugène Haussmann arrived in Paris on Tuesday, June 28. He took possession of a room at the Hôtel du Danube and went straight to see his friend from Burgundy, the former deputy Louis Frémy. Haussmann learned about the conflict between Prefect Berger and the emperor regarding the pace and scale of the public-works program for

Paris. He quickly inferred that Berger was incapable of properly understanding and implementing the task at hand.

Three years earlier, at the time in the more junior position of prefect of the Yonne, in Burgundy, Haussmann had come to meet Berger
about a new tax that would affect Burgundy's wine producers and merchants. He had come away appalled. He had felt that Berger, essentially
a local Parisian politician, did not have the stature commensurate with
his post. He had discussed this with Frémy, who was then a deputy
representing Burgundy. Haussmann told his friend that nothing could
be expected from the position of prefect of the Seine if it was occupied
by Berger "or any other political veteran who has come there seeking,
in the words of the poet, *otium cum dignitate*"* but that one could expect
everything from "a man who, by his status in government, . . . has sufficient authority to undertake great works and bring them to completion and who also has the vigor of spirit and of body necessary to
combat routine, which is so powerful in France. . . ."[1] The account was
written by Haussmann years later, nakedly for the benefit of posterity,
but it does reflect his thinking: He saw the position of prefect of the
Seine as a potentially powerful one and felt that it was wasted in the
hands of someone like Berger.

Haussmann's impressions were confirmed at his next meeting with
Victor de Persigny, the minister of the interior, and therefore Haussmann's superior. Thinking back upon a meeting of this period in his
memoir, Persigny recalled the individual he had before him: a "big,
strong, vigorous, energetic, man, who was at the same time clever and
resourceful." Persigny also remembered how extremely enthralled with
himself Prefect Haussmann was. "[H]e would have spoken for six hours,
provided it was about his favorite subject: himself,"[2] Persigny wrote.

Persigny was not disturbed by this. He recognized that Haussmann

---

*"Leisure with dignity," referring to the ancient Roman practice of occupying positions to retain
influence and status in retirement, similar to many vice chairmen in today's corporate America.

was just the person needed to fight the entrenched interests of the financial and political worlds, because, in Persigny's words, he had the same "brutal cynicism" that they did. "Where a gentleman with an elevated spirit, the most upright and noble character, would inevitably fail, this vigorous athlete, with robust backbone and coarse collar, full of audacity and skill, capable of countering each expedient with an expedient of his own, each trap with a trap of his own, would certainly succeed."[3]

Haussmann was a true Parisian, born in what is today's eighth arrondissement, educated in the city's finest schools. But in several respects, his strong personality was rooted in a background that made him an outsider to the capital's circles of power. This heritage resulted in an unusual combination: someone with a great need to belong and a fundamentally conservative outlook who at the same time was more than willing to risk compromising everything for his convictions.

His family origins were in Alsace, in the northeast of France. Barred, like all Protestants, from careers in officialdom, the Haussmanns had turned to commerce. Toward the middle of the eighteenth century, they had started a large and successful business as producers of printed fabrics in the Alsatian town of Wintzenheim.

George-Eugène Haussmann's paternal grandfather, Nicolas, had moved to Versailles to represent the family business. As a bourgeois and as a Protestant, and as a man of some idealism, he became an active participant in the French Revolution and was elected to the Legislative Assembly in 1791. He later became an enthusiastic supporter of Napoléon I and the mayor of Chaville, a town near Paris, at the time of the First Empire. Two of his sons, including Georges-Eugène Haussmann's father, had served in the imperial army.

Haussmann's maternal grandfather, Georges Dentzel, had similar geographical origins and political views but a much more fantastic trajectory. As a young man, he had enlisted in the Royal Deux-Ponts, an infantry unit at the service of the French king composed of soldiers from Alsace and Dentzel's native Palatinate. In 1780, he was sent as part of the expeditionary corps under Marshall Rochambeau to help Washington's Continental army in the American Revolution, during which he fought in the Battle of Yorktown. Then, back in France, Dentzel took part in the French Revolution. Out of grace for a time, he later managed to join Napoléon I's staff and was appointed governor of Vienna during its occupation by the French.

Haussmann credited his grandfathers for much of the influence that molded his character. From Nicolas Haussmann, he got his methodical spirit, his taste for order, and his vocation as an administrator. As his grandfather told him when he was growing up, "We do not sufficiently realize how many resources France holds and how rich and powerful France would be if she were well governed and, especially, well administered!"[4] From Georges Dentzel, he got his verve and boldness. The attachment and admiration he felt for his grandfathers, both firmly committed to Napoléon I, would directly feed his own dedication to the cause of Napoléon III.

Georges-Eugène Haussmann went to Paris's prestigious Lycée Henri IV, where he was a top pupil. Despite his family's political leanings, he was friendly with the elder son of the future king Louis-Philippe, who was his classmate. He continued his studies at what is today the Lycée Condorcet before going on to study at the Paris School of Law.

Everything changed for Haussmann in July 1830. His father, Nicolas Valentin Haussmann, had been a staunch member of the opposition throughout the restoration of the Bourbon monarchy and naturally embraced the cause of the revolution of 1830. Georges-Eugène surprised his father by joining him, even taking part in combat around the Palais-Royal. It was on this occasion, as an insurgent armed with a musket, that Georges-Eugène Haussmann for the first time entered the gilded halls of the Hôtel de Ville, which would later be his domain.

The revolution of 1830 opened entire new avenues for a young

Protestant. Haussmann boldly solicited a meeting with his former classmate, now heir to the throne, to discuss his interest in becoming a magistrate. The prince suggested he consider the prefectoral corps—then, as today, a prefect was the government representative in a French administrative district (the *département*), supported by underprefects posted in the secondary towns. Following this advice, the twenty-one-year-old Haussmann wrote to the minister of the interior, François Guizot, clumsily claiming the prince's support and making a number of arrogant and less than credible claims about his qualifications. What he was lacking in finesse, he made up for in persistence, barraging Guizot and the two men who succeeded him as minister of the interior with letters. Finally, after close to nine months of effort, he was appointed to the position of general secretary of the prefecture of the Vienne *département,* based in Poitiers.

Haussmann was smart, hardworking, and ambitious. After just one year, he was promoted to underprefect. Thereafter, however, his career stalled: He spent the next sixteen years as underprefect in a succession of provincial backwaters: Yssingeaux, in the Haute-Loire; Nérac, in the Lot-et-Garonne; Saint-Girons, in the Ariège; and Blaye, in the Gironde. He was always extremely active in improving life in his district and serving the government's political agenda, but his high opinion of himself, his brusque and autocratic manner, and his tendency to short-circuit his hierarchical superiors proved to be significant encumbrances to career progression in the civil service. Still, the job suited him well. In a godforsaken village like tiny Saint-Girons, hundreds of miles from Paris, he was the highest figure of authority, the proverbial big fish in a small pond.

By the time he was posted to Blaye, Haussman was married, with in-laws who were rich merchants in nearby Bordeaux, where he had his own growing interests. He was seriously considering leaving his stagnant career in the civil service to join his father-in-law in business.

But the revolution of 1848 and Louis-Napoléon's election as president gave Haussmann's career new promise. In January of 1849, right after Louis-Napoléon's victory, Haussmann traveled to Paris to meet the new minister of the interior, and he was earmarked as one of the politically dependable civil servants carried over from the previous regime. Days later, he was received by the new president, who was eager to meet senior civil servants he could count on. From the start, there was a certain complicity between the two men. Shortly after the meeting, Louis-Napoléon granted Haussmann his long-awaited promotion.

Haussmann's first position as prefect was in the Var, a stronghold of leftist Republicans, whom he combatted forcefully. In 1850, he moved to Auxerre, where he was prefect of the Yonne, and twice had the opportunity to receive Louis-Napoléon on the president's profile-building visits in the field. Haussmann was gaining a reputation as a highly effective representative of the government in political and police matters. He was rewarded in 1851 when Louis-Napoléon appointed him to one of the highest-profile prefectures: that of the Gironde, based in Bordeaux.

As prefect of the Gironde, it was up to Haussmann to organize the local leg of Louis-Napoléon's tour of France in the fall of 1852. This tour was of paramount political importance, as Louis-Napoléon was testing the waters in advance of declaring himself emperor. The local prefect at each stop had to elaborately stage-manage a visit that would serve as a gradual buildup to a popular plebiscite of the Empire. The visit to Bordeaux, organized by Haussmann, was perfect, with cheering crowds and fireworks, which served as the ideal backdrop for Louis-Napoléon to give a historic speech on the road to the constitution of the Empire. Haussmann had proved that he could flawlessly execute everything that was expected of him. Six months later, he was given the supreme position for a prefect: Paris.

After taking leave of Persigny, Haussmann made a few more visits and then, in the afternoon, presented himself at the door of the Hôtel de Ville.

Jean-Jacques Berger received his successor cordially, but the discussion between the two men reflected their tremendous differences. The conversation revealed to what a great extent Haussmann exemplified the emergent thinking that would allow him to become the most illustrious civil servant of the Second Empire, in contrast to a man firmly anchored in the now-obsolete preconceptions of Parisian politics during the July Monarchy.

Berger was the product of a political system that, even with election limited to qualified citizens, operated with the inevitable clientelism of elected office. He had grown to be pragmatic and accommodating; as a politician, he was concerned first and foremost with his popularity. Haussmann, on the other hand, was a pure product of France's administrative apparatus, used to working without public accountability. He held up pure and simple conceptions, to be implemented and enforced by the administrative apparatus. He personally did not subscribe to the tenets of mass democracy: He saw the voice of the masses as fluctuating and malleable, in no way reflecting the good of the nation, which could only be ensured from the top-down by the ruler of the nation.

Berger was not a strict or particularly competent administrator. As Haussmann would later say, he "reigned more than he governed."[5] Haussmann, on the contrary, as a worthy representative of the prefectural corps, was focused on the rigor and effectiveness of public administration. Once in place he would implement major changes in the operating practices of the Seine administration.

The most concrete and immediate difference between the two men related to the very need to undertake an ambitious public-works program for Paris. In Auxerre and Bordeaux, Haussmann had already shown his appetite for building, modernizing, and restructuring the territories under his responsibility. He deeply believed in the sanitization, beautification, and reconfiguration of the city as part of a holistic project of building a better society. Politically, he wholeheartedly adhered to Napoléon III's vision of progress and modernity for France.

Where Berger saw no pressing need, Haussmann saw the defining challenge of the age.

Haussmann was a vigorous proponent of the idea of "productive expenditures," the concept that investments financed by borrowing would drive the economy in the future, yielding incremental revenues that would be used to pay back the debt. This idea, popular with the Bonapartists, was profoundly counter to the dominant view of the bourgeois class since the French Revolution. In the paradigm of July Monarchy conservatives, the mortal sin of the old-style monarchy had been to run up massive public deficits to fund wars and the life of the court; the responsible course now was to keep balanced budgets and enforce disciplined use of public finances, well within the revenues raised by the government. The Bonapartists felt that this timid thinking was holding back growth and progress in France in an increasingly competitive international economic environment. One writer summarized the sea change in public financing at the beginning of the Second Empire: "Until then, borrowing appeared to all as an accidental event, provoked by rigorous necessities. Starting in 1852, it took an entirely different aspect: it became the rule, a system of government."[6]

Haussmann, for his part, saw the problem from the perspective of a territorial administrator. For him, the city was a revenue base to be managed as an asset. He was absolutely convinced that wise investments would make that asset grow. The great challenge, especially visible in Paris, was to increase tax revenues by developing the plentiful land on the periphery of the city. He was therefore, for fiscal reasons, particularly attuned to the need for new arteries connecting the city center to the periphery.

Haussmann had spent decades quashing local uprisings and ensuring the regime's candidates won the elections without misstep, so there could be no question that he adhered to the agenda of keeping the peace. He was particularly attuned to the issue in Paris, which he saw not quite as a city, but as the meeting point of a large number of people come to pursue their diverse fortunes. Even though Paris had a separate police prefect with this specific duty, Haussmann would contribute as he could, with a view that, in Paris more than elsewhere, authority should reign with a firm hand.

Haussmann, like Napoléon III, did not see a place for municipal democracy in Paris. "Paris is not a municipality; it is the Capital of the Empire, the collective property of the entire Nation, the 'city of all the French.'"[7] He gave the example of Washington, D.C., the capital city of the archetypally democratic Americans, managed as a federal territory. Paris, in fact, had no mayor, only a prefect reporting to the minister of the interior and an unelected city council. The reluctance to give Parisians local democracy would be long-lived: Other than a brief time during the Paris Commune, the city of Paris did not have an elected mayor until 1977.

Haussmann belonged to those who saw the glory of the nation as the greatest goal to which any honorable civil servant could contribute. At one of the early meetings in the Hôtel de Ville after his appointment as prefect of the Seine, when those in attendance gave the customary cheer of "*Vive l'Empereur,*" Haussmann replied, "Yes, long live the Emperor, who wants to make Paris the greatest city in the world, a capital worthy of France."[8]

The meeting between Berger and Haussmann, two men opposed in so many ways, was an exercise in talking past each other. Berger explained why an ambitious program of public works for Paris was impossible and unreasonable. Haussmann sat opposite him, ignoring these claims and focusing on an entirely different question: how he would secure the funds to drive the program for Paris forward at a whole new pace and scale.

·——·

Seven

EVISCERATING WITH GLEE

On Wednesday, June 29, 1853, at a little before ten in the morning, Georges-Eugène Haussmann's rented carriage exited Paris through the barrière de l'Etoile. In the bright sun of the warm summer morning, the vehicle sped through the Bois de Boulogne, turned right into the Longchamp plain, and then followed the bucolic landscape of the Seine. It crossed the river at the pont de Saint-Cloud and climbed the incline toward the entrance of the Palais de Saint-Cloud, where it paused only a moment before the great gates flew open, imperial guards standing in salute.

Haussmann, wearing the uniform of the imperial civil service, stepped down from the carriage. As he started up the palace steps, the sweeping landscape of Paris at his back, he could not repress a feeling of elation. He was embarking on the greatest adventure of his life, finally a mission worthy of his measure.

Haussmann had harbored dreams of greatness since his youth, but, despite his hard work and obvious talent, the success he yearned for had always eluded him. In Bordeaux, he had come close to resigning himself to a life as a provincial notable, perhaps leaving the civil service to seek his fortune in private business. Now he knew that he held a rendezvous with history. It meant more to him than anything.

Haussmann was greeted and ushered up the grand staircase to the floor where the emperor was finishing the weekly Council of Ministers meeting. As he waited, he thought of the historical significance of this palace, the very place where, on 18 and 19 Brumaire, year VIII,* Napoléon I started his decisive rise to power. This was the heart of the French power structure.

A little later that morning, there was a brief ceremony. Georges-Eugène Haussmann was among the tallest of the men arranged around Napoléon III, listening solemnly as the emperor said a few words. Each new prefect swore to the sermon read by the minister of the interior, Victor de Persigny.

"In the present circumstances I attach special importance to the position you now occupy" were the words Napoléon III said as he held Haussmann's hand. It was a typically vapid formula, but Haussmann already knew the emperor well enough to understand that he never spoke without intent. The phrase was an allusion to Napoléon III's frustration with Berger and his hope that Haussmann would be able to implement the vision for Paris.

The new prefect of the Seine had not yet received his instructions from the emperor, but he had an idea of what needed to be done. Broad streets would be cut through the city core, "eviscerating the neighborhoods of the center," in the words of Haussmann.[1] Then new avenues would be created leading toward the unbuilt areas on the periphery of the city, opening up whole new tracts for development. Paris would be rebuilt for a future of development and prosperity, an era of technology and modernity.

---

* November 9 and 10, 1799.

Haussmann was invited to stay for lunch, during which he clumsily tried to impress the empress with his pedigree—or rather, that of his wife. Afterward, Napoléon III invited Haussmann into his study to discuss the affairs of Paris. A number of streets, together with the transformation of the Bois de Boulogne, had already begun, and the first priority was to bring them to completion promptly. But the emperor did not want to stop there. He was keen to show Haussmann the colored plan he kept in his office at the Tuileries, which showed the new avenues he imagined. There were two immediate projects: the boulevard Malesherbes and the boulevard du Centre, later to be renamed the boulevard de Sébastopol, which would extend the boulevard de Strasbourg straight into the heart of the city. And when those were done, there would be more new squares and avenues to be built in every part of the city. Napoléon III showed Haussmann the ideas that had been occupying his mind for many months: streets radiating out of the place de l'Etoile, a major new square in the east of Paris, boulevards across the entire city in all directions.

Napoléon III took advantage of the meeting to inform Haussmann that he had created a Commission on the Beautification of Paris and had appointed as its head Count Henri Siméon, a senator whom Haussmann suspected may have harbored a secret desire to become prefect of the Seine himself. Perhaps the emperor did not notice the momentary look of concern that passed over the prefect's face upon hearing this news. In any case, Haussmann did not respond, and the interview was soon over.

On the return journey to Paris, Haussmann had plenty of time to consider the situation. Between the projects that were under way and those that the emperor wanted to launch, there was a great deal of work to be done. He would set about it immediately, and simply show the emperor that, with his new prefect, there was no need for any commission. Through the vigorous action of which he knew himself amply capable, he would make it clear to all that he had full and sole executive responsibility for the realization of the Emperor's vision for Paris.

In the months that followed, Haussmann would indeed achieve his objective of making the commission redundant. But in December 1853, shortly before it was disbanded, the commission published a report that made two notable points. The first was to assert that the mechanism for the new streets should be the *percée*. This term referred to the creation of entirely new roads through the middle of the city blocks, as opposed to widening existing roads on the edges of the blocks. In Haussmann's expressive language, "[I]t is easier to cut through the center of the pie than through the crust."[2] The second point was the idea of actively beginning to structure the areas outside the city limits of the time—the territory covered by today's twelfth to twentieth arrondissements. The reasoning, of course, was that this could be done much less expensively before this space was built up, creating a structure for the expanding city to grow into. These two ideas would be core principles of the upcoming transformation that Haussmann happily presented as his own. In truth, they had been conceived of, and even broadly accepted, before he arrived.

As the new prefect of the Seine, Haussmann had an immediate political challenge: to convince the predominately hostile thirty-six-member city council to commit to the emperor's *grands travaux* and to accept a much more aggressive style of financial management. Maneuvering this conservative group, and especially its president, Claude-Alphonse Delangle, a senator and future minister of the interior, was to be one of Haussmann's main occupations for the coming months. Fortunately, as concerns Delangle, Haussmann quickly understood that constant deference to the senator's age and rank would allow him to get whatever he needed from Delangle. He used this ploy shamelessly.

Louis Véron, a doctor who had turned to other endeavors—
entrepreneur, newspaper owner, director of the Paris Opera—observed
the interactions with the city council as an outside party and gave a wonderful description of Haussmann's approach:

> *I love your prefect: he amuses me. It appears as if he believes what he
> spews out to those imbeciles listening to him, mouth agape, as if all
> that were really going to happen. When one of them ventures to make
> an observation, the Prefect listens with a very well executed air of con-
> descension, approving the less harebrained comments with a nod; then,
> when the time has come for him to respond, he starts by agreeing with
> his contradictor on some secondary points and then, taking the argu-
> ment developed in the opposite direction, he turns it around, without hur-
> rying, like a glove he is removing from his aristocratic hand, and he ends
> by nailing the offending individual to the wall with a decisive phrase,
> but with such perfect urbanity that, delighted with such good grace,
> the other person thanks him and declares himself satisfied. It would be
> impossible to mock the world with more irreproachable glibness. It is very
> amusing.*[3]

Haussmann applied his skills to assuaging the susceptibilities of the
City Council members, three of whom were senators and therefore
higher in the imperial hierarchy than Haussmann himself. He also had to
contend with ministers, civil servants, and other important people somehow involved in the affairs of the city. His ability to manage all these egos
to the furtherance of his own objectives, together with his carefully cultivated proximity to the emperor, would be critical to his success in ex-
ecuting the *grands travaux*.

The core obstacle to an ambitious program of public works for Paris was
simply that not enough money was being made available. To achieve the

outcome the emperor desired, Haussmann knew that he would need to find a way to increase the quantity of investment radically.

At his meeting with Berger, Haussmann had asked for the full financial accounts of the city to be delivered to him. In the evening, as he sat at the little desk in his hotel room, poring over the numbers, Haussmann discovered that Berger's extremely conservative financial management actually put him in an excellent position now. Berger had systematically left himself extra margin: Revenues were baselessly assumed to decrease, costs included items that would never materialize, and expenses allowed for spurious items that Haussmann would hasten to eliminate. Adding it up, Haussmann calculated that, out of a total city budget of 69 million francs, he could immediately free 22 million for the *grands travaux*. Convincing the city council to go along with this would, however, be another matter.

When Haussmann assumed office as prefect of the Seine, a key city council meeting had already been organized for July 14, 1853.* On the agenda was the budget for 1853 and the proposed preliminary budget for 1854. Much to Haussmann's chagrin, the documents had already been prepared and even distributed to the city council members by Berger. So Haussmann spent his afternoons in early July combing through every table and footnote in these documents. He articulated his own perspective in a "Note to the City Council on the Financial Situation of the City."

In the note, which he read to the council members, Haussmann picked apart Berger's system of financial management. He informed the council of the 22 million francs that he had identified in the city budget. In addition, he asserted that the payments required to pay off the city's debt would henceforth allow at least a further ten million francs

---

*This was a working day in 1853. The national holiday during the Second Empire was August 15, as in the First Empire. July 14 was instituted as the national holiday in 1880.

to be invested in the *grands travaux* each year. He concluded by telling the council that the city should not only continue the "transformation of the old Paris" but accelerate its pace.

The speech was greeted with an icy silence. No one was surprised at the direction the new prefect was taking, but the councilors were stunned by his audacity. Haussmann could have done nothing to make it more clear that the chummy, consensual days of the Berger administration were a thing of the past.

To impose the new municipal strategy, Haussmann had to fight each step of the way. He waged battle at the Finance Commission, in city council sessions, through more memoranda and endless meetings and visits. Over the course of weeks, François Jules Devinck, a wealthy chocolate entrepreneur who presided over the city council's Finance Committee and also served as a deputy, gradually gave in to Haussmann's stubbornness. Devinck even ended up becoming a key supporter whenever the financial matters of Paris were discussed at the Legislative Assembly. Others, however, were not won over: Five city councilors refused to accept the new approach and resigned. This suited Haussmann perfectly well, as he could guide the hand of the emperor in the choice of more favorably minded replacements.

Haussmann was dismayed by the administrative practices that had taken hold under Berger's tenure, and he immediately set about imposing stricter rules and processes. He implemented a process for handling the daily incoming mail, complaints, and approvals. He also made changes in organizational structure of the prefecture and some staff changes, although it must be said that he kept much of the personnel, including Berger's general secretary, Charles Merruau.

By the fall of 1853, Haussmann had made great progress. He had vanquished the resistance of the city council, improved the effectiveness of the municipal administration, and identified funds. There was now a perfect alignment of the political, financial, and practical requisites.

I then felt that I was firmly in the saddle to undertake the conquest of the old Paris, with an army that was gaining confidence in its new leader. With its help, I would be able to begin ripping open the neighborhoods of the center of the city with their tangle of streets almost impossible to navigate by carriage and their crowded, sordid, and unhealthy houses; these neighborhoods that are for the most part a seat of misery and disease and a subject of shame for a great country such as France.[4]

Although the principles of the transformation of Paris had nothing to do with Haussmann, he undertook the *grands travaux* with unconcealed glee:

It was a great satisfaction for me to start out in Paris by razing [the shoddy neighborhood around the Louvre]. Since my youth, the uncared-for state of the Place du Carrousel in front of the courtyard of the Tuileries seemed to me to be a shame for France, an avowal of its government's powerlessness, of which I was resentful.[5]

Haussmann's words affirm his defining values: the assertion of the power of government authority, the aspiration for rigor and order, and single-minded zeal in pursuing these principles. The destructions that had begun were to be only the start of a full-scale transformation of the city.

Before going any further, Haussmann had a major concern: No geometrically and topographically precise plan of the city of Paris had ever been established. He therefore asked Eugène Deschamps, who was in charge of the Roads Department at the Seine prefecture, to conduct a comprehensive survey of Paris.

In the fall of 1853, Parisians were intrigued to see workers erecting wooden towers around the city. These formed a triangulated network, in relation to which reference points across Paris were measured. An altitude survey was also conducted, using the level of the water of the La Villette basin as the reference point. The surveying work lasted more than a year. When it was finished, Haussmann finally received a complete and accurate plan of Paris, which he had printed at the scale of 1:5000. A copy of the plan, which measured ten feet high by sixteen feet wide, was mounted on canvas and hung in his office. He could now precisely and comprehensively embrace the city he was to rebuild.

The most pressing project Haussmann needed to put back on track was the extension of the rue de Rivoli to the Hôtel de Ville. The street itself was built, but in some places it lay many feet below the surrounding area. This topographical discrepancy had made major work necessary on all the connecting streets, causing the destruction of numerous houses beyond what had initially been planned. It also led to acrobatic works to hold up the Tour Saint Jacques while a base was built underneath it. The pont Notre-Dame had to be entirely rebuilt, as the access to the bridge had become too steep for traffic. When all was said and done, the bill increased by 63 percent, to 31 million francs; the number of houses demolished increased from 236 to 423. Throughout the changes and course corrections, Haussmann mercilessly disparaged his predecessor while demonstrating his own prowess at overseeing the works.

Parisians were enthused as they saw the rue de Rivoli begin to emerge. It was an impressive realization that gave Parisians a taste of what was to come. It met a real need but also symbolized a new, modern Paris. At the same time, the rue de Rivoli caused the destruction of some of the oldest neighborhoods in the city, eliminating from the map many little streets with picturesque names, such as Tanners Street, Dyers Street, Basketmakers Street, Old Lantern Street, Calves Place, and so on. Haussmann, who considered them "dirty, putrid, and unsanitary," was delighted to see them disappear.

The Bois de Boulogne was envisioned as another project that would give Parisians a sense of the emperor's vision for the city. But here, too, Haussmann found the relics of technical and administrative sloppiness under Berger. To build the lake desired by the emperor, excavation work had begun at either end of the proposed site, but no one had thought to consider issues of topography. Haussmann, concerned about the fact that one end of the lake seemed much higher than the other, had some surveying work done. Indeed, the difference was such that, if the area were built as a single lake, the upper end would not hold any water. The excavations were well advanced, so options were limited; all Haussmann could do was make the best of the situation, creating two separate lakes at different heights, with a dam and a small cascade between them. This is how Paris's version of the Serpentine became not one lake but two. Napoléon III was exceedingly disappointed by this mishap.

Haussmann fully grasped that the Bois de Boulogne was Napoléon III's pet project and, astute civil servant that he was, the new prefect did everything he could to use it as an opportunity to win the Emperor's confidence. Napoléon III began to sense that his new prefect of the Seine was reliable in taking his guidance and saw firsthand Haussmann's remarkable effectiveness as an administrator. The project for the Bois de Boulogne, the first time the two men worked closely together, was an important step toward building the iron trust that Napoléon III would retain in Haussmann in the years to come.

Les Halles was yet another project Haussmann needed to put back on sound footing. The architect, Victor Baltard, had been working on the project for twelve years when he had been instructed to demolish the one pavilion he had built and stop work. Seeing this major public embarrassment, Baltard's colleagues had thrown themselves at the opportunity, publicizing their own counterprojects in hopes of winning the commission. The situation was one of total confusion.

Baltard was at a loss. He had been told by the city administration that the buildings should have a monumental character; now he was being told that he should build a railway shed. He immediately wrote to the emperor, proposing to rework the project as necessary to meet his satisfaction. As he frenetically prepared new designs, it was decided that a new architectural consultation would be held.

On July 5, a month after Napoléon III's visit to the site and only a week after Haussmann's appointment, Baltard submitted three new variants to the prefect and requested a meeting. Both men knew they were not strangers: many years earlier, they had been among the small group of Protestant students at the Lycée Henri IV that was taken weekly to the Reformed service instead of the Catholic Mass. Haussmann agreed to meet Baltard and decided to do what he could to help him.

Around that time, Napoléon III shared with Haussmann his vision for the new market building. He imagined an airy metal structure, similar to the Crystal Palace, built in London for the Great Exhibition of 1851, or the sheds of the recently built gare de l'Est: "I just want a huge umbrella," he summarized. Based on this information, Haussmann was able to coach Baltard through several iterations of his project for Les Halles until it matched the emperor's vision.

When it was time to review the architectural submissions with the emperor, Haussmann kept Baltard's design aside. Napoléon III reviewed the proposals: One was a massive stone monolith with arches all around; another was in the eighteenth-century neoclassical style of Ledoux. None of them matched what the emperor desired.

Haussmann asked for permission to present one last design, without mentioning that it was by Baltard. Napoléon III was delighted. "That's it!" he exclaimed, "That's exactly what I wanted!"[6] Haussmann claimed that he managed to decamp before the emperor thought to ask who had authored the design. It was, allegedly, only later that Napoléon III discovered that he had again selected the discredited Baltard.

Les Halles put Victor Baltard in architectural history as an early protagonist of metal architecture in France. But it was also the cause for bad feelings between Baltard and Haussmann. Haussmann, typically dismissive of the architect's craft, considered that the building was his brainchild, and he was appalled that Baltard did not give him credit. Baltard, while grateful that Haussmann had helped him regain the commission, did not consider that Haussmann had played any role in its architectural design.

The Les Halles pavilions were built between 1854 and 1874. The architecture was extraordinarily audacious, a massive structure using the new industrial language of cast iron and glass in the heart of one of Paris's oldest neighborhoods. When the last pavilions were going up, Emile Zola wrote *The Belly of Paris,* a novel that revolves around the new market and its neighborhood. Here is how Zola wrote of the poetic force of the architecture:

> . . . *at the end of each street they could see a corner of the cast-iron giant. There were sudden perspectives, unexpected architectures, the same horizon offering itself again and again under different aspects. Claude would turn around, especially on rue Montmartre, after having passed the church. In the distance, Les Halles, seen from an angle, filled them with enthusiasm: a huge arcade, a high, gaping entrance, and then the pavilions crowded in, with their two stories of roofs, their continuous blinds, their immense awning; they appeared as if superimposed profiles of houses and palaces, a metal Babylon, with a Hindu lightness, crossed by suspended terraces, aerial corridors, flying bridges thrown over the void.*[7]

Baltard's pavilions functioned as a market until 1969 and are still remembered by many Parisians. Then the wholesale market and all the noise, traffic, and filth it generated were moved to the southern suburbs. In its place were built a rapid transit hub and shopping center, an architectural monstrosity that the current city administration is in the process of replacing with a new scheme. Baltard's pavilions were demolished in 1973, except for one, which was moved to Nogent-sur-Marne, in the eastern suburbs of Paris, where it serves as a concert venue.

·————·

Eight

THE EMPIRE BUILDS

The Great Exhibition of 1851, held in London's Hyde Park, marked the start of a new age. It was the first exhibition that overcame the forces of nationalism and protectionism, inviting all nations to take part. Exhibitors from around the world came to London with their newest and greatest creations. Now, it was hoped, countries would compete on the terrain of commerce and innovation instead of on the battlefields.

Hector Berlioz, the future composer of the *Symphonie Fantastique,* was one of the Frenchmen in London for the exhibition. Although he disliked the job that had brought him there, judging musical instruments for the exhibition prizes, he was, like all the visitors, spellbound by the central symbol of the Great Exhibition, the Crystal Palace. The enormous assembly of glass and cast iron designed by Joseph Paxton was itself a thrilling example of the possibilities of the industrial age.

Louis-Napoléon did not visit the Great Exhibition of 1851, but he heard a great deal about it and became determined to host an equal, if not superior, event. The date for the Paris Universal Exposition was set for 1855.

The exposition would be a chance to show the new France to the world, in large part through its rapidly changing capital. Not much would be finished by the date of the exposition, but there could at least be one completed project to give a sense of what was to come: the new, extended rue de Rivoli. On the south side of the street, visitors would be able to see the newly built north gallery of the Palais du Louvre. On the north side, the arcaded sidewalk conceived by Percier and Fontaine, Napoléon I's architects, would continue, with fine buildings just like those of the first section of the street. For the new and enlarged place du Palais-Royal, Napoléon III envisioned a huge modern hotel to rival those that were beginning to be built abroad.

For Napoléon III and Haussmann, quickly showing finished pieces of the new city, with impressive amenities, was not only aimed at achieving international prestige. There was also the important objective of winning Parisians over and overcoming the inertia and resistance to the broader plan for Paris. The exposition would be the perfect vehicle to establish momentum for the rebuilding of the city.

There was, however, a major problem. Although the rue de Rivoli itself had been built, there were no buildings along it, and developers did not seem interested in making the investments necessary to build them. Perhaps the cost of complying with the architectural rules was too high or the French political situation still seemed too volatile for the financiers to feel comfortable underwriting such a large project. In any case, no one had bought the land. At the end of 1853, Haussmann had 170,000 square feet of undeveloped land on his hands, despite the prime location, right across the street from the Palais du Louvre. It was at this time that he enlisted the help of Emile and Isaac Pereire.

By 1848, the two Pereire brothers, raised in poverty in Bordeaux, had become leaders of the largest modernization project the country had ever known. Emile Pereire managed his original train line and had developed the Northern line from Paris to Lille, while Isaac played a leading role in the Paris-Lyon line. They were prominent, but they had not become particularly rich themselves, as they owned only small stakes in the companies. They were increasingly thinking about how to play a larger role not just as administrators but as capitalists. However, the political instability of the 1840s led them to bide their time. When the coup d'état of December 2, 1851, occurred, they knew the moment had come for them to increase their role dramatically. They jumped on the opportunity with all the vigor of a second youth.

Again, the brothers worked on a grand scheme, directly inspired by their ideas of the 1820s, when they had first arrived in Paris: the creation of a new sort of industrial bank.

Traditionally, French banks were family establishments. Over time, they had grown by funding trade, foreign exchange, and government debt. For the bankers of the French *haute banque,* foremost among which stood James de Rothschild, banks should be self-financing. Having recourse to outside sources of funding was unheard of.

The Pereire brothers were critical of this model, which they considered an inefficient way to gather and deploy capital. The idea that occupied the Pereire brothers and their friends was to capture funds from a much wider base. This had been tried in France as early as 1818, when the Caisse d'Epargne, a mutual saving organization, was created. To take the idea further, the Pereires wanted a bank that could float tradable shares. This would provide much greater quantities of capital to fund large infrastructure projects.

French capital markets had developed greatly during the July Monarchy and were now sufficiently structured to make such innovations possible. The 5 percent government bond, the "*rente à 5%*," formed a benchmark for the pricing of all securities. Publicly traded joint stock companies funded large-scale coal extraction, as well as railway and canal ventures. In French society, the currency of wealth had begun to shift from landholdings to securities. As Louis-Napoléon understood, the emergence of effective conduits to source funding from a broad base and channel it toward investment opportunities was critical to funding the capital-intensive national infrastructure projects needed to support economic growth.

Inspired by German real estate banks, the French Republic had been seeking to introduce the idea of institutions focused specifically on mortgage lending. Victor de Persigny, the minister of the interior, who at the time was still trying to force Berger, the prefect of the Seine, to invest more into the city on the basis that it would pay itself back in the future, was a major proponent of creating such institutions: "[W]here these establishments exist they have the effect of decreasing property costs, reducing interest rates, developing agricultural productivity, stimulating economic activity of all sorts, and increasing the revenues of the State."[1] In May of 1852, after two years of political debate, the Banque Foncière de Paris was created; a few months later, it was modified to cover all of France and renamed Crédit Foncier de France, which it is still called today. The institution would go on to play a critical role in the rebuilding of Paris in the 1850s and 1860s.

The Pereire brothers' idea was different. They imagined a private bank that would operate for industry in a way analogous to how the Crédit Foncier was to operate for real estate. They wanted the institution to issue interest-bearing obligations, to be secured by the assets of the industrial undertakings in which the proceeds were invested, just as the mortgages issued by the Crédit Foncier were secured by the real estate assets. The Crédit Mobilier would be allowed to issue obligations of a value up to ten times its assets—600 million francs of obligations for 60 million francs of shareholder equity. The idea was to use the magic of leverage to release funds to finance French industry.

These forms of access to capital became explosive when combined with the mechanism of the concession. Concessions were—and remain—extremely useful for governments: Instead of putting up the capital itself, the government can get the private sector to provide funding against the promise of future revenues, while retaining public ownership of the asset. For the investor, a concession represents a virtually guaranteed stream of cash flow that can, in principle, justify highly leveraged investments. In mid-nineteenth-century France, mines, railroads, canals, real estate developments, utilities, and projects for the colonies were all developed in this way—even the Suez Canal, opened in 1869, was a concession granted to a French joint-stock company.

The emerging financial instruments and the mechanism of concession turned out to be an essential foundation of the rebuilding of Paris. The large-scale expropriations and rebuilding to come would require huge amounts of capital. The *grands travaux* of the Second Empire, at the scale at which they occurred, would quite simply have been impossible without this new capitalist infrastructure.

Naturally, the new ideas were threatening to the traditional Parisian *haute banque,* which functioned according to a model largely untouched since the ancien régime and remained, until this point, the government's only port of call for its financing needs. But it was increasingly felt by industrialists that stimulating France's growth required more innovative thinking. The ideas appealed to Napoléon III because they would support the modernization of the country and allow the emperor to fund his ambitious plans, but also because they would reduce the historical dependence of the French government on the old families, whose ultimate loyalty to the Empire was not above question.

The Pereire brothers were very ambitious and ideologically completely aligned with the Empire. But to put in place their plan for a new type of bank, they still needed political patronage. They turned to a charismatic man they had known since the mid-1840s, who was now in a prime political position. His name was Charles-Auguste de Morny.

Morny was of immaculate appearance: Largely bald, he sported a well-tended mustache, had a svelte physique, and always dressed impeccably. Despite his affable manners and conversational ease, he was steely and unscrupulous. He was about to become one of the most powerful figures of the Second Empire.

A former military man and Parisian socialite, Morny had, years earlier, bought a factory that produced sugar from beetroot in the Puy-de-Dôme region in central France. He had then been elected to represent the area at the Legislative Assembly and, as an early convert to the promise of the rail, had taken part in a number of schemes to bring the railway to the region.

Charles-Auguste de Morny had a very special secret, reflected in the mysterious fact that his birth certificate gave no name for his parents. He was in fact the illegitimate son of Hortense de Beauharnais, wife of Napoléon I's brother Louis and mother of Louis-Napoléon. This made Morny the younger half brother of the emperor of France.

Despite the awkward nature of the family connection, Morny was accepted into the presidential entourage in 1851. He gradually gained Louis-Napoléon's confidence and played an important role in the coup d'état. Immediately thereafter, he was made minister of the interior. A remarkably effective backroom dealer, Morny orchestrated the selection of Louis-Napoléon's candidates for deputy in each district. He managed the arsenal of measures to rein in the press. He was the man who could always be trusted for the unsentimental work of holding things together. But in January 1852, after less than two months as minister, Morny resigned in protest over Louis-Napoléon's decision to confiscate the property of former king Louis-Philippe.

Charles-Auguste de Morny turned to his private affairs. He was an inveterate speculator, with no ideals beyond his financial interests and pleasures. He loved nothing more than to be surrounded by the smell of money and the naked shoulders of the wives and daughters of elite bankers. He was masterful at profiting from lobbying and acting as an intermediary. A member of numerous company boards, he increased his holdings with every restructuring and won considerable sums on the stock exchange through his access to information in the corridors of power. When the Pereire brothers approached him, he was happy to act as political patron of the Crédit Mobilier.

Victor de Persigny, Morny's replacement as minister of the interior, was not close to Morny, but he, too, supported the Pereires' project. Persigny's motivation was simple: It was an excellent way to diminish the influence of James de Rothschild, who had been all too close to King Louis-Philippe. Despite the opposition of a number of ministers, including the minister of finance, Achille Fould—who himself was from one of the traditional French banking families—Persigny and Morny were able to convince Louis-Napoléon to approve the plan.

The decree creating the Crédit Mobilier was published on November 18, 1852. Along with the Pereires, the founders included Adolphe d'Eichtal, who had been one of the main underwriters of their railway projects from the beginning, and a number of other Parisian bankers—Mallet, André, Pescatore, de Galliera, de Mouchy—and the Fould-Oppenheim bank; in other words, the family bank of Achille Fould, who had so vociferously opposed its creation!

The Crédit Mobilier was floated on the Paris Stock Exchange on November 23. The shares, which had been sold at five hundred francs apiece in the private offering only days before, reached eleven hundred francs on the first day of trading. On November 30, they hit fourteen hundred francs. The rise in the share price, achieved with the help of the press and abundant rumors, provided a lucrative liquidity opportunity for the first circle of owners. Although the shares went down in December and remained volatile, the Crédit Mobilier became the highest-profile stock on the French market. Asserting its status, the company acquired the Hôtel de Gramont on the place Vendôme—the building that is now the Ritz Hotel—to serve as its headquarters.

In late 1853, with the Crédit Mobilier firmly established, Prefect Haussmann approached Emile and Isaac Pereire about developing the rue de Rivoli. This was not the first time their paths had crossed—the brothers had already contacted Haussmann to solicit approval to develop land belonging to their railway line leading out of the gare Saint-Lazare. The Pereires had also begun to work on some of the emperor's other schemes. They were absolutely receptive to Haussmann's request.

Not surprisingly, the Pereires turned out to be savvy negotiators. At the price of significant financial concessions, they agreed to acquire and develop the land along the rue de Rivoli. They committed to having it ready, including the hotel, in time for the 1855 Universal Exposition. They created a limited liability company with equity funding from a consortium of Parisian bankers and debt funding provided by the Crédit Mobilier and took charge of the rue de Rivoli development project.

The centerpiece of the development was the Grand Hôtel du Louvre, built "on the plan of the colossal hotels for which the United States are so celebrated."[2] It had seven hundred rooms, a glass-covered central court, a thirty-four-foot-high dining room, and all the modern conveniences: electric bells to call for service, elevators for the luggage, hot and cold water in all the rooms, a steam laundry service, and a telegraph. The perimeter of the ground floor consisted entirely of shops, all bought up by one tenant to create one of Paris's first department stores, the Grands Magasins du Louvre, opened in July 1855. An American guidebook raved: "The situation of the Hôtel du Louvre is delightful and the amusements about the house so varied that you hardly want to go out to look for any other."[3] For the Pereire brothers, the hotel and the property holdings around it became one of the most profitable parts of their financial empire.

It was soon apparent to all that the Empire was consumed by speculation and materialism. One contemporary noted that "the French bourgeoisie, ordinarily so parsimonious, almost instantly became imprudently prodigal."[4] The new minister of the interior, Adolphe Billault, publicly called for a stop to the "exploitation of public greed and gullibility," and the minister of war published a memo to officers to tell them to stop constantly making requests for money from the emperor.

Napoléon III had seen and enjoyed a satirical play by François Ponsard called *La Bourse* (*The Stock Exchange*), which condemned the passion for speculation and financial shenanigans. The emperor heartily commended the author for putting his talent to work to expose and combat such tendencies. But everyone knew that Napoléon III was given to luxury and condoned exactly the behavior described in the play within his entourage. The Second Empire had the paradox—that both the emperor and empress cultivated—of being in principle inclined to a sort of austerity but ultimately unable to resist habits of outrageous luxury.

Morny was the most publicly known figure involved in this unscrupulous capitalism. In 1853, he gained the position of president of the Legislative Assembly, with the responsibility of making sure that the lawmakers reliably voted for whatever was the emperor's desire. This did not slow down his appetite for deal making, nor, incidentally, his appetite for his other passions: women, horses, and vaudeville theater. He became president of a British-backed company aimed at building a railway through central France, the Compagnie du chemin de fer Grand-Central de France, an obvious case of monetizing his political role. In August of that year, he provided political patronage for a scheme by the Pereires, Emile de Girardin, and other bankers to develop a new neighborhood in the former parc Beaujon, to the east of the place de l'Etoile. The outcry over Morny's actions became so damaging that Napoléon III had to give him a talking-to. Morny momentarily stepped back, but, incorrigible, he soon returned to his ways.

Morny, among his various activities, was a member of the Jockey Club, an elite club for the idle rich with an interest in horse racing. In this capacity, he was sent as an emissary to win over Haussmann to the Jockey Club's plan to build a hippodrome in the Bois de Boulogne so that races could be held there, rather than on the Champ-de-Mars, where they were being held at the time. Haussmann adopted the idea

and decided to expand the Bois de Boulogne by expropriating the
Longchamp plain, the area between the park and the Seine that was being
used to grow vegetables, together with the adjacent park of the Château
de Madrid. The agreement with Morny was that the Jockey Club would
build the Longchamp Hippodrome at its own expense, then operate it for
fifty years for a symbolic annual concession fee of twelve thousand francs.

The Longchamp Hippodrome was designed by the architect Antoine-
Nicolas Bailly and inaugurated on April 27, 1857, in the presence of the
emperor and empress. It has had a long and illustrious history that continues to this day. But Haussmann's approach, offering extremely
favorable terms to someone widely believed to be corrupt, with no
competition, transparency, or public disclosure, appeared suspect. No
specific accusations of personal gain were ever made against Haussmann, but he inevitably began to be perceived as one of the insiders
taking advantage of the imperial system.

In acquiring the Longchamp plain, the city also acquired the house
of Longchamp Abbey. It was restored at the expense of the city and at-
tributed to the prefect of the Seine, who started using it as a summer
residence upon its completion in 1856.

By 1855, with work on the Bois de Boulogne nearly completed, the new
park began to emerge as the delightful place of recreation and contem-
plation that would be so appreciated by elite Parisian society.

In addition to the park, Napoléon III's vision included a grand avenue leading from the gate of Paris at the place de l'Etoile to the entrance of the new and improved Bois de Boulogne. The city of Paris had
committed to building the road in 1852 and, the following year, decided
to name it avenue de l'Impératrice in honor of the new empress. It is
known today as avenue Foch.

The avenue de l'Impératrice was yet another undertaking taken
over by Haussmann in mid-development. To design the avenue, Na-

poléon III had already selected one of the most prominent architects of
the time, Jacques-Ignace Hittorff, a distinguished-looking gentleman
with wavy hair and rich gray sideburns.

The fact that Hittorff was French at all was a historical oddity. After
the French Revolution, war had broken out between the new French
Republic and the European monarchic powers that surrounded it. On
October 8, 1794, the French Revolutionary troops led by Gen. Jean-
Baptiste Jourdan entered Cologne, in what is now Germany, marking
the start of what would be a twenty-year occupation. The city happened
to be the home of a two-year-old boy named Jakob Ignaz Hittorff. The
French officers could not have imagined the impact their military actions would have on the architectural history of Paris.

The young Hittorff was skilled in drawing, and he soon became
destined for the profession of architect. Having grown up in a French-
controlled territory, he naturally went to pursue his studies in Paris,
where he began using the French version of his given name, Jacques-
Ignace.

His talent readily apparent, Hittorff was admitted to the studio of
Charles Percier, architect of Emperor Napoléon I. He quickly immersed
himself in the Parisian architectural world, marrying the daughter of
Jean-Baptiste Lepère, another architect of Napoléon I's entourage. So
even though the French occupation of Cologne ended in 1814 and Hittorff lost his French citizenship the following year, he was too deeply
entrenched in Parisian life to consider returning to Cologne. He would
later regain his French citizenship, through naturalization, in 1842.

As a student, Hittorff developed a passion for the architecture of
antiquity, and particularly that of ancient Greece. He spent several
years in the early 1820s in Italy and specifically in Sicily studying archaeological vestiges. Throughout his life, whenever he was not building,
Hittorff continued to pursue his scholarly interests.

With his father-in-law, Lepère, Hittorff built Paris's église Saint-
Vincent-de-Paul. After building the Théâtre de l'Ambigu-Comique,

another high-profile commission, he was put in charge of the design of the Champs-Elysées and the place de la Concorde. He was the architect responsible for the current design of the square, incorporating the Obelisk of Luxor. In this period, he also built a theater at the Rond-Point des Champs-Elysées* and the town hall of what is now Paris's fifth arrondissement, facing the Panthéon.

Hittorff was one of the rare architects to go from being an official architect of the July Monarchy to being a favorite architect of Napoléon III, aided perhaps by the fact that he had been a student of Percier. In any case, he became the beneficiary of a considerable number of commissions directly from the emperor: a pavilion for the 1855 Universal Exposition, the Bois de Boulogne and the avenue de l'Impératrice, the buildings of the place de l'Etoile, the town hall of the first arrondissement, and the Eugène Napoléon Foundation.

One might think that with common Rhinelander family origins and strong links to the service of Napoléon I, Haussmann and Hittorff may have had a natural affinity. That was most decidedly not the case. The relationship between the two men was tempestuous from the outset.

Their first run-in occurred shortly after Haussmann became prefect of the Seine, as Hittorff was finishing the église Saint-Vincent-de-Paul. Hittorff had published a scholarly book on the polychromatic architecture of ancient Greece and was implementing such ideas in the decoration of his church. Haussmann, however, did not approve. He found the multicolored ornamentations offensive, in that they hid the "simple and noble beauty of the materials used in the construction," reminding him of "the tattoos with which barbarous people hide their naked bodies." Haussmann stated bluntly, "I cannot help but find grotesque this pretentious mode of decoration."[5]

Hittorff found it outrageous that a career bureaucrat with no artistic

---

*The building was destroyed in 1855. The new Théâtre du Rond-Point, built subsequently, was designed by Gabriel Davioud.

education—sixteen years his junior, no less—was brazenly imposing his architectural judgment upon one of the country's foremost experts on architectural history. To make matters worse, Haussmann instructed another architect, Baltard, to rework the monumental staircase that Hittorff had built in front of the church. Hittorff, naturally, was furious.

Napoléon III appreciated Hittorff and his work, and had appointed him to be the architect of the Bois de Boulogne. He was therefore also responsible for the grand avenue leading to the park. Hittorff had no desire to work with Haussmann, but at the same time he could not turn down a commission personally requested by the emperor.

One day, Hittorff went to Haussmann with his design for the avenue: a broad street, which, at forty meters, was wider than the Grands Boulevards, with side paths for pedestrians and for riders, which were each to be planted with a double alignment of trees for shade. In response, he got a rant from the prefect:

> No trees! The Emperor doesn't want any! And do you really think that His Majesty will be satisfied by a 40-meter boulevard? Is that the extension of the Bois de Boulogne toward Paris that the Emperor desires? 40 meters! . . . But, sir, we need two, even three times that. Yes, I am saying triple: 120 meters! Add to your plan two lawns, each four times wider than your side paths, that is to say 32 meters. . . . Beyond your lawns, add two alleys of 8 meters each to give access to the properties along the avenue, which I will require be built with a 10 meter setback decorated by parterres and closed off by iron railing.——In this way we will have 140 meters between the buildings on either side—100 meters more than in your project!——Completed in this way, I hope it will be approved by His Majesty![6]

Hittorff was livid at having his design dictated to him as if he were a mere draftsman. Nor did the cavalier, decidedly unarchitectural approach to the width of the new avenue impress the sophisticated

Hittorff. Hittorff was too urbane to respond in kind, but he turned violet with repressed wrath and indignation.

Relations between the two never improved. Haussmann was jealous of the high regard in which Napoléon III held the architect. The erudite Hittorff could not stand Haussmann's self-importance and his insistence that he knew best in all matters, especially in the area of architecture, in which Haussmann was grossly ignorant. Hittorff subsequently did little work for the city, and the two collaborated only when required to satisfy specific requests made by the emperor—each was a new opportunity for a scuffle.

Hittorff's final work was the gare du Nord, one of the new gateways to the city and an important part of the new layout of Paris. It is a good example of Hittorff's strengths and weaknesses. While the inside is well designed and skillfully uses innovations of metallic architecture, the facade is heavy and awkwardly composed. The building was completed in 1865, in time for the travelers arriving for the 1867 Universal Exposition. During the exposition, Hittorff passed away.

Napoléon III had not abandoned the cause of housing for the working class. In 1852, his position bolstered by the coup d'état, he decided to press forward. In January and March, decrees were published, establishing a budget of ten million francs for workers' housing in the major cities. A competition was held for designs to house workers "better, but less expensively, while allowing the building owners to receive a fair return on their money."[7]

The competition was won by an architect named Charles Gourlier, but his design was never realized. Instead, the money was used for sixteen buildings on the boulevard Diderot designed by Eugène Godeboeuf and for homes for convalescent workers in Vincennes and Le Vésinet.

The fundamental problem was that the workers did not like the visions proposed by the architects. An official of the buildings administration wrote to his superior, "The solutions proposed by the various architects and engineers who have applied themselves to this type of building have only imperfectly met the needs that were to be satisfied."[8] Prosper Mérimée was blunter: "[O]ur workers do not want to go live in the houses that the Emperor has built for them. They say they do not want to be parked."[9]

Napoléon III decided to use the remainder of the original grant, three and a half million francs, for a program of subsidies for private-sector workers' housing. It is estimated that this program yielded some fifteen hundred new apartments for workers, despite the difficulties of making the projects profitable at Parisian prices for land and materials while meeting the standards required for the subsidies.

Compared to the immense needs for low-cost housing in Paris, these results were negligible. The government soon pulled out of housing nearly completely so as not to interfere with the private sector. For Parisian workers, the problems remained unsolved. Housing was constantly becoming more expensive, forcing many to move far from the center of the city and to live in small, cold, unsanitary, and unsafe homes.

Haussmann was focused primarily on the projects for the city center: Les Halles and the continuation of the rue de Rivoli to the Hôtel de Ville. As work progressed, he took advantage of every opportunity to amplify the undertaking. What Berger had thought of as only a building and a street were, to Haussmann, the rebuilding of an entire chunk of the city.

Among Haussmann's additions to the original plan for Les Halles were two broad new streets departing from the south end of Les Halles: the rue du Pont-Neuf, which leads to the Pont-Neuf, and the rue des Halles, which leads to the place du Châtelet. In this way, traffic coming from the north could use the rue Montmartre, cross Les Halles through the now-defunct rue Baltard, which bisected Les Halles north to south, and continue on to either the Pont-Neuf or the place du Châtelet. Piece by piece, the old inability to cross the center of Paris was being overcome.

The city core, with key institutions like the Hôtel de Ville and the Palais de Justice, was becoming the focal point of a network of streets radiating toward the rest of the city rather than being in the middle of an inextricable jumble.

Haussmann also vastly expanded the project for the place de l'Hotel de Ville, to which the rue de Rivoli now extended. This square, historically known as the place de Grève, had been a river landing at the heart of the city's economy in medieval times. It would now be increased to more than double its previous size, providing a broad perspective on the east facade of the Hôtel de Ville. In addition, a monumental avenue would be created from the place de l'Hôtel de Ville, in the axis of the Hôtel de Ville, to the place du Châtelet.

Haussmann took advantage of the redesign of the area to build new barracks right next to the Hôtel de Ville, the caserne Napoléon. This was a convenient location for a garrison, which would stand between the faubourg Saint-Antoine, a historic area of unrest, and the Hôtel de Ville. With the new rue de Rivoli, troops could easily be sent to the place de la Bastille and the faubourg Saint-Antoine.

New barracks were also built on the place du Château d'Eau, the future place de la République. They were equally strategically located, right at the point where working-class hordes descending from Belleville and the faubourg du Temple would arrive on the Grands Boulevards.

This new layout would unquestionably increase the availability of troops in the city center and facilitate their movements. Still, Haussmann maintained it was not the primary reason for the design:

Certainly the Emperor, in drawing the boulevard de Strasbourg and its extension to the Seine, and beyond, was not thinking of the strategic utility of this extension any more than that of many other major streets, like the rue de Rivoli, for example, whose straight layout did not lend itself to the usual tactics of local insurrections. Even if he was not primarily seeking this objectives, as the Opposition claimed, one can not deny that it is

*the very fortunate consequence of these new streets created by His Majesty
to improve and sanitize the old city.*[10]

As the zone of construction expanded, the center of Paris under-
went a massive disruption. Hundreds of houses were destroyed, whole
neighborhoods were cleared away, and the familiar urban landscape
was remodeled day by day. Although some were saddened that the old
Paris was disappearing, the general sentiment regarding the project was
favorable. Parisians were keen for the center of the city to receive the
improvements everyone knew were long overdue and to finally see a
solution to their practical problems of simply getting around.

Having established momentum, the emperor and his prefect launched
the next phase: the completion of the crossing of Paris. In 1854, a decree
was passed for the last section of the rue de Rivoli, to the place Birague,
connecting it to the rue Saint-Antoine, completing the east-west route
through Paris. The day when a carriage could race through the historical
center of the Right Bank, straight from the place de la Concorde in the
west to the place de la Bastille in the east, was within reach.

The north-south crossing was also well in hand. An artery leading
south from the gare de l'Est, the boulevard de Strasbourg, had been
completed in 1853, shortly after Haussmann became perfect of the
Seine. Napoléon III's intention was to continue the artery south, straight
across the center. Now it was time for the next phase, the boulevard du
Centre—later renamed boulevard de Sébastopol to commemorate a
victory of the Crimean War—which would lead as far as the Seine.

However, the boulevard de Sébastopol did not encounter the general
public support of the rue de Rivoli. The public did not understand why
it was necessary to create a new street when there were already two
north-south streets, the rue Saint-Denis and the rue Saint-Martin, which
could be widened or, to further reduce costs, where a new setback could
simply be imposed for future buildings.

It was here that the combined stubbornness of Napoléon III and

Haussmann made a difference. If they had been the sort to have doubts or to seek expedients, Paris as it now exists would never have been built. Perhaps the existing streets would simply have been remodeled. But that was out of the question. Haussmann, at his most inflexible, tirelessly repeated the arguments regarding the high cost of widening existing streets and the impracticality of a gradual rebuilding at a new setback. He felt that a new boulevard was the only way to achieve a broad, arrow-straight artery with all the modern conveniences and with the grand appearance he desired. A new boulevard would also, he argued, greatly increase the value of large quantities of landholdings that were either at the heart of blocks or otherwise difficult to access through the existing infrastructure. Napoléon III, with whom authority ultimately rested, did not waver from his vision. Paying no heed to the murmurs of public opinion, he saw to it that the new street was created in all its grandeur, without compromise.

Nine

CELEBRATING THE NEW CITY

Fashionable carriages pulled up one after another at the Hôtel de Ville's main entrance. Men emerged in the ceremonial dress of the imperial elite, accompanied by women wearing fanciful dresses of crinoline and exposing bare shoulders and deep décolletés. Butlers bowed and opened doors. To the music of an orchestra, the guests made their way into the Great Hall. These were the lucky few, the 140 guests invited by the new prefect of the Seine and his wife to the first gala dinner of his tenure, graced by the presence of the emperor and the empress of France.

It was August 14, 1853. The date was important because it was the eve of Napoléon I's birthday, the national holiday during the First Empire and again now in the Second Empire. By hosting an exclusive gathering on the eve of the first celebration of this holiday since it had been reinstated, Prefect Haussmann, less than two months after assuming office, was asserting his position within the Empire.

Haussmann felt that under Berger the Hôtel de Ville and the office of the prefect of the Seine had been degraded. From the moment he arrived in Paris, one of Haussmann's obsessions had been to restore the splendor of the Hôtel de Ville. The social elite of Paris had stayed away from the Hôtel de Ville fetes since the departure of Rambuteau. But on this night, they ate, drank, and danced well into the night.

This festive evening was only the first of many. In 1854, Haussmann orchestrated another grand celebration for the national holiday, with cannons, fireworks, orchestras, dancing at the Hôtel de Ville, and a giant public ball from the Palais des Tuileries to the top of the Champs-Elysées. On January 22, 1855, the Hôtel de Ville was covered in lights and decorations for an unforgettably sumptuous party for six thousand guests. For the entire time he occupied the Hôtel de Ville, Haussmann continued to host these extravagant affairs. He understood the importance of pageantry in Napoléon III's construct, and put the full symbolism of the Hôtel de Ville behind it.

The evenings were full of glitter, but during the days something altogether less glamorous was on Georges-Eugène Haussmann's mind. He was thinking about shit.

Every night, the workers of several private companies would fan across Paris. They would open the latrine reservoirs and shovel the accumulated human waste into barrels, causing a vile stench to envelop the streets. A ballet of carts then hauled the filth to storage tanks in La Villette, to the north of Paris, from where it was channeled to a dumping ground in a forest farther afield.

Paris needed a modern sewer system. Auguste Mille, the engineer responsible for the La Villette storage facility, embraced the issue. He made a trip through England and Scotland to observe the most advanced networks in operation and wrote an exhaustive account of his findings in 1854. That same year, he published a detailed proposal for a major expansion of Paris's sewer network according to the same model.

Haussmann was not won over by the English system of sending

solid waste into the sewer with the rainwater and household waste. He did, however, agree with Mille that solving this problem was the "greatest, most meritorious, if not the most spectacular and most appreciated, service that an administration conscious of its duties can provide the population of the Queen-City."[1]

On January 22, 1855, the city council approved Haussmann's plans for a major extension of the sewer system. Enormous collector pipes would be built across the city, sending the waste into the Seine far downstream from Paris, in Asnières. A network of smaller sewers would be built in every neighborhood, including areas designated for future development. The total size of the Parisian sewer network would be increased from 66 miles to 350. Within years, visitors in top hats and fine coats would come from across Europe to inspect and admire the conduits for Paris's filth. The workers of the night with their shovels, barrels, and putrid carts were about to become a thing of the past.

Paris's drinking water was another embarrassment to the city. The water came directly from the Seine and was of such poor quality that Parisians would first let it sit for a day so that the solids it contained would settle to the bottom. Drinking this pestilential water killed many foreigners, including Anna Maria Mozart, mother of Wolfgang Amadeus. It was commonly said that the only reason why the water didn't kill more Parisians was that if one made it through childhood drinking the stuff, one developed an unusual tolerance. Nor was there a distribution network. Instead, an army of water carriers—a workforce heavily composed of men from Auvergne—pushed heavy barrels of water mounted on wheels across the city and would carry the barrels up five, six, or seven stories to their customers.

To address the drinking water–supply problem, Haussmann had brought to Paris Eugène Belgrand, an engineer with whom he had worked when he was prefect of the Yonne, in Burgundy. Belgrand started by performing a complete hydrological study of the Seine basin to identify the best sources of drinking water for Paris. Haussmann and Belgrand wrote lengthy reports in 1854 and 1858, requesting authority to build an aqueduct to bring water from Champagne, sixty miles northwest of Paris. But the subject was technically complex and politically controversial. The scheme was not approved by the city council until March 18, 1859.

After years of administrative procedures and technical challenges, the new aqueduct became operational in August 1865, channeling one million cubic feet of high-quality drinking water to Paris each day. Three reservoirs were built, as well as a vast distribution network to carry the water directly into each home. Implementation of this comprehensive plan lasted until 1924.

In parallel, the city prepared to outsource the water-distribution operations. In 1860, a fifty-year contract was signed with the Compagnie Générale des Eaux, a company chartered by Napoléon III in 1853, which was already managing the Lyon water network. The company still exists today under the name Veolia and manages the water for many cities around the world, although Paris later reverted to an in-house model.

In addition to waste and water, there was the issue of the gas network. By the mid-1850s, a number of companies in Paris were already producing natural gas from coal and distributing it through small local networks. In 1856, Emile and Isaac Pereire decided to spearhead the consolidation of these companies. Although this was not in his area of responsibility, Haussmann assisted the Pereires in the negotiation. He also increased the value of the gas monopoly by expanding the city's system of street lighting, which at the time functioned by burning natural gas. The generalization of street lighting improved both the appearance and the safety of Paris's streets at night and was greatly appreciated by Parisians.

The Second Empire ushered in the age of utilities such as the waste-management, water, and natural gas systems. Networks were built and innovative mechanisms, much like the ones we have today, were put in place to manage them. Basic services that make modern urban life possible, even if they are taken for granted by Parisians today, have their origin in these initiatives.

As the date of the Universal Exposition approached, Haussmann had another issue to resolve: the chaotic situation of public transportation in Paris.

A little more than two decades earlier, in 1828, mass public transportation had been introduced to Paris in the form of the omnibus. This was a fifteen-seat vehicle, pulled by two or three horses, that one could ride along any part of the route for the fixed price of five sous. Omnibuses met a real need and were a great success. By the 1850s, they had proliferated, with a confusing array of companies with amusing and inventive names operating lines that crisscrossed the city. Each company had its own colors and design: the white Dames Blanches, the green Parisiennes, the yellow Hirondelles, and even the Scottish-inspired Ecossaises in tartan.

An exciting new twist was introduced in 1853: the *omnibus à impériale,* an omnibus in which one could ride on the open upper deck. Even though the railings were completely inadequate and there were regularly deaths and serious injuries from people falling off, the *impériale* became very popular. By the 1855 Universal Exposition, they had become a hallmark of Paris.

By that time, a dozen separate companies were transporting 36 million travelers a year on three hundred and fifty omnibuses pulled by nearly four thousand horses.[2] Prefect Haussmann decided that all these assets and activities needed to be consolidated into a single company that would have a monopoly on public transportation in Paris. There would be a set network of twenty-five lines, identified by the letters of the alphabet. Prices would be standardized: thirty centimes to ride inside and fifteen centimes to ride on top.

The acquisition and consolidation of all the existing lines was a considerable financial operation. The Pereire brothers' Crédit Mobilier provided the requisite funds, and on February 22, 1855, the Compagnie Générale des Omnibus was created. The CGO operated as Paris's bus company for years, until it was absorbed into the RATP, which operates the Parisian public-transportation system today.

If one had the means and wasn't in town long enough to hire a carriage, horses, and a driver, one could simply pay for a car by the ride at any of 158 designated locations in Paris, much like one takes a taxi today. These vehicles were known as *voitures de place,* for the specific places where they were required to stand as they awaited customers.

The approach taken with the *voitures de place* was similar to that taken for the omnibuses. The Compagnie Impériale des Voitures de Paris was created and given a monopoly. The company improved the quality of the vehicles available in the city and organized the service— for example, by training drivers and enforcing the systematic issuance of receipts. The system was unpopular with drivers, however. The discontent eventually culminated in a strike, in June 1865, after which it was decided to reverse course and allow for-hire carriage drivers to work independently.

With these undertakings to consolidate and modernize the fleet, Paris's public-transportation system was in order. A growing and rapidly changing city, full of buses and carriages in an increasing spiral of movement, was now ready to greet the world.

There was no small sense of expectation when the Exposition Universelle de Paris opened on May 15, 1855. Unfortunately, the day was cold and rainy. Only two of the buildings were finished, many exhibits were not in place, and visitors were sparse. Despite the fact that a bitter war was being fought between European nations in Crimea, Napoléon III pompously proclaimed the opening of "this temple of peace that brings together all people in concord."[3] The general feeling was one of disappointment and disinterest.

The centerpiece of the exposition was the main exhibition building, the Palais de l'Industrie, a 227-yard-long behemoth with a huge glass-covered interior courtyard. The outside was of masonry, of no particular interest, with a dollop of sculpture around the main entrance to try to overshadow the tedium of the rest. There was genuine technical prowess in the cast-iron beams, which spanned 157 feet, but it was not remotely as spectacular as Paxton's Crystal Palace. Although it was meant to be permanent, the Palais de l'Industrie was unloved and ended up being demolished in 1896 to make room for the Petit Palais and the Grand Palais of the 1900 Universal Exposition.

On May 26, the first foreign dignitary arrived. He was Don Pedro V, king of Portugal. Parisians greeted the likable seventeen-year-old king, who had a military bearing and a mustache not dissimilar to their own leader's, with enthusiasm.

In the 1850s, as today, summer was the calmest time of the year in Paris, with much of the population in the habit of retreating to cooler country residences. Eighteen fifty-five was an exception. With the buildings and attractions beginning to fill in, the exposition gained momentum. Giuseppe Verdi was in town for the premiere of his opera *Les Vêpres siciliennes,* which took place on June 13 and was a massive success. The theaters were full, with the two great actresses of the age, Adelaïde Ristori and Rachel, performing at the same time across town from each other. One Parisian marveled, "Never, at any point in its history, had the great capital been as brilliant and as animated."[4]

Without doubt, the greatest event of the summer was the visit to Paris of Queen Victoria. On August 18, Napoléon III traveled to Boulogne-sur-Mer to greet the British sovereign. He waited patiently for the royal yacht to arrive, considerably late, and helped the queen, Prince Albert, and two of their children—Vickie, fourteen, and Edward, thirteen—disembark. They all boarded a train to Paris.

The queen's train pulled in to the gare de l'Est at twenty past seven in the evening to the sound of the French National Guard playing "God Save The Queen." An open carriage decorated with white silk and pulled by four magnificent horses waited in front of the station. As evening gently descended over the capital, thousands and thousands of Parisians, many of whom had been waiting for much of the day in the sweltering heat, cheered the queen. For two countries who had fought a terrible war within living memory—with many veterans of these wars alive and in attendance—it was an extraordinary moment.

The party proceeded down the new boulevard de Strasbourg to the Madeleine, then down the rue Royale, across the place de la Concorde, and up the Champs-Elysées, all of which were decorated with festive banners. The queen, who had never before seen Paris, was fascinated by the spectacle before her. As night fell, the lanterns of the procession were lit, creating a magical effect.

Thousands of soldiers lined both sides of the street along the entire route. Every house from the gare de l'Est to the place de la Concorde had some sort of sign or emblem to welcome the queen. Statues and other tributes had been erected along the way, such as the triumphal arch on the boulevard des Italiens, crowned by immense eagles holding escutcheons with the monograms of the sovereigns of Britain and France intertwined. A British observer later recalled:

> I have seen a good many displays of bunting in my time; I have seen Turin and Florence and Rome beflagged and decorated on the occasions of popular rejoicing; I have seen historical processions in the university towns of Utrecht and Leyden; I have seen triumphant entries in Brussels; I was in London on Thanksgiving day, but I have never beheld anything to com-

pare with the wedged masses of people along the whole of the route, as far
as the Bois de Boulogne, on that Saturday afternoon.[5]

From the Arc de Triomphe, the royal family was taken down the vast new avenue de l'Impératrice and through the Bois de Boulogne, which was completely illuminated. They reached the Palais de Saint-Cloud, which Napoléon III considered to be his finest residence, and where Empress Eugénie was waiting to greet them. The private apartments of the queen had been entirely refitted to resemble those of Windsor Castle, and paintings had been brought from the Louvre to decorate them. Absolutely everything had been done to make the stay unforgettable.

On Monday, August 20, Queen Victoria visited the Fine Arts section of the exposition. After that, she and her family were taken down the Champs-Elysées, which was still decorated with Venetian masts, to the brand-new rue de Rivoli and onward to the Bastille, then back along the Grands Boulevards, again surrounded by throngs of cheering Parisians. In the afternoon, there was a reception at the Palais de l'Elysée and in the evening, back at the Palais de Saint-Cloud, the actors of the Comédie-Française performed Alexandre Dumas's play *Les Demoiselles de Saint-Cyr*. The thrilled queen wrote in her diary, "What could I say about this most wonderful city in the world?"

The visit offered the thirty-six-year-old Victoria the opportunity to immerse herself in the glamour and excitement of the French capital, the sort of trip she rarely got to make. During nine days, her feet hardly touched the ground. She was even able to escape for an incognito outing at the Grands Magasins du Louvre, opened only the month before. She found the shops and galleries enchanting.

Fashion was a bit of an issue. Whereas Empress Eugénie and the French imperial court defined the height of elegance, Queen Victoria was, to put it mildly, considerably less sophisticated. She arrived in France with a bright green parasol and a huge handbag embroidered with a poodle. Other outfits were equally questionable. Parisians had a hearty laugh at the queen's attire, but they did not let that interfere with the genuine abandon with which they celebrated her presence.

On August 23, there was a reception at the Hôtel de Ville. The decorations and flowers alone were said to have cost 350,000 francs.

For Georges-Eugène Haussmann, this was the realization of all his dreams. He, a bourgeois Protestant who had entered the Hôtel de Ville for the first time as part of a mob during the 1830 revolution, who ten years earlier had been a minor civil servant in a town of fewer than five thousand people, was now the host of this brilliant reception. Haussmann lived for status and recognition, hoping to emulate his two illustrious grandfathers. This evening was a glorious, unforgettable milestone in his life.

As he gave the queen a tour of the building, the prefect pointed out the construction site across the street. He said he could think of no greater honor than to name the avenue that was being built there after the visiting sovereign. And so, when it was completed, it became avenue Victoria. Queen Victoria was apparently sensitive to the gesture: She made special mention of Haussmann's reception to Napoléon III, which led to his subsequent appointment to the Legion of Honor.

The whirlwind did not stop. On Friday, August 24, Queen Victoria was taken to the Champ-de-Mars for a review of forty thousand soldiers. At the time, the French army was thought to be among the greatest in the world, and it was certainly among the best accoutered. The endless rows of glistening troops filling the grounds with the Ecole militaire as a backdrop were an impressive sight.

The following night, there was a ball at Château de Versailles, which was magnificently illuminated and decorated. The ball itself took place in the Galérie des Glaces, filled with three thousand wax candles. Empress Eugénie, wearing a white dress decorated with green leaves and a profusion of diamonds, was resplendent. After nightfall, there was a fireworks show, accompanied by the spectacular fountains of the Versailles gardens, while orchestras played. And then there was dancing—quadrilles and waltzes—during which the emperor danced with the young Princess Victoria.

Finally, on the twenty-seventh, with her head spinning from the experiences she had had, Queen Victoria returned with her family to Boulogne-sur-Mer, whence she sailed back to England. "This trip," she later wrote to the emperor, "will never be erased from my memory."[6]

Napoléon III was highly satisfied. The nonstop succession of events had gone off perfectly, constituting the high point of his reign to date. The visit served the immediate diplomatic objective of solidifying the alliance between Great Britain and France, but it also marked a critical moment in the history of Paris. It was the beginning of a new identity for the city, not only capturing and amplifying the excitement it already embodied but asserting that it was now a center of modernity and sophistication.

Queen Victoria and her family were not the only ones to travel to Paris in 1855. That year, Parisian hotels registered half a million stays, of which 128,000 were made by foreigners—nearly double the previous year's number. For the first time, more than four million travelers passed through Paris's train stations.

As was clear to contemporaries—but is completely forgotten today—the Universal Exposition of 1855 was the beginning of a new phenomenon: mass tourism. For some time, the railway had allowed Britons to travel conveniently to Paris, but these visitors tended to be either aristocrats or businessmen with a specific purpose or, at any rate, with introductions and some notions of French. In 1855, middle-class British tourists descended on the French capital en masse, often speaking no French at all. Parisian shopkeepers started posting signs in their shop windows that said ENGLISH SPOKEN HERE. They gamely tried to make themselves understood in English—it was only much later that they developed their famous grumpiness about serving people in any language other than French.

The beginning of mass tourism brought the mass development of cheap hotels, cheap restaurants, souvenir shops, and legions of dubious guides who seemed to have instantaneously materialized on the streets of Paris. And so it turns out that not just the glories but also the crassest aspects of the tourist's experience of Paris are a legacy of the Second Empire.

Nearly all the projects for the city so far had been for the Right Bank. Now it was time to continue on the Left Bank. The first step was to extend the new north-south axis southward, as figured in the emperor's colored plan, through the Ile de la Cité, over the pont Saint-Michel, past the Luxembourg Gardens, and straight to the barrière d'Enfer (today's place Denfert-Rochereau). This new street was initially referred to as the boulevard de Sébastopol, like its Right Bank counterpart, but this soon proved confusing, so it was renamed boulevard Saint-Michel.

Nearby on the Left Bank, the Napoléon III–initiated rue des Ecoles was under construction, but Haussmann found the street totally unsatisfactory. It was crooked, went uphill and downhill, and was poorly connected to the rest of the city. Haussmann approached the emperor with a new idea: to build, notwithstanding the imminent completion of the rue de Ecoles, a new east-west street parallel to it, as straight and broad as the boulevard de Sébastopol. This street would go through the historic neighborhoods of the Left Bank, past the abbey church of Saint-Germain-des-Prés, in order to form a connection all the way from the faubourg Saint-Germain to the place de la Bastille. At first, Napoléon III did not see the need for this new street. But the prefect dug in, and in the end the emperor consented. The idea of the future boulevard Saint-Germain was born.

The new projects for Paris's Left Bank were formally adopted on

August 11, 1855, in the middle of the Universal Exposition and the Crimean War. The decree ordained the completion of the rue des Écoles, as well as the building of the boulevard Saint-Michel from the Seine to the rue Cujas, including the place Saint-Michel. It also made official the construction of the easternmost part of the boulevard Saint-Germain, from the quai de la Tournelle to the boulevard Saint-Michel. With this step, the armature of the central Left Bank as we know it was defined.

In the early 1850s, France was still a diplomatic pariah. The victors of the Napoleonic Wars had held France at bay and, until now, prevented it from regaining its erstwhile military strength.

Initially a bit of a gamble, the Crimean War, in which France led a coalition against Russia in support of the Ottoman Empire, turned out to be a military and diplomatic success. Napoléon III demonstrated that the French military could act in concert with the other European powers, and he did not make any attempt at territorial expansion. The leaders of Europe began to accept the prospect of the return of France as a military force.

On December 29, 1855, a portion of the troops engaged in the Crimean War made a triumphant return to Paris. They paraded through the city to the place Vendôme, decorated by Victor Baltard, where thousands of guests occupied the bleachers. A giant celebration had the people of Paris dancing until late into the night.

Two months later, from February 26 to March 30, 1856, the city hosted the Congress of Paris, the largest diplomatic meeting since Vienna. During these weeks, delegations from all the European powers gathered in the brand-new building of the Ministry of Foreign Affairs on the quai d'Orsay, finished and fully decorated for the occasion. In the evenings, the diplomats threw themselves on the opera houses and the theaters, the restaurants and the brothels.

On March 16, 1856, in the middle of the Congress of Paris, everyone in the city was awakened at six o'clock in the morning by the cannons of the Invalides. The firing went on until the salvo of 101 shots was complete. The empress of France had given birth to a dynastic successor.

The birth was of the utmost political significance for a regime aimed at establishing a lineage and of tremendous personal importance to Napoléon III. That day, the plenipotentiaries of the Congress of Paris came to congratulate the emperor, the Te Deum was sung in churches across the country, theaters were opened to the public free of charge, poems were composed by the greatest poets, gifts to charities were made from the imperial treasury, and the emperor and empress declared themselves godparents of all the newborn babies in France.

The baptism of the Imperial Prince, which took place three months later, was one of the greatest days of celebration France has known. Hundreds of thousands of people lined the streets as the imperial family went to Notre-Dame, where six thousand attended the ceremony. The cathedral itself was adorned with elaborate decorations, making it look to some more like a garish opera set than a place of worship. The dinner that evening was sumptuous, with the finest dishes and wines accompanied by music composed specially for the occasion by Charles Gounod and Daniel Auber. The day culminated with fireworks as sweets rained down from the skies onto the Parisian public.

At one o'clock on the afternoon of March 30, the documents of the Treaty of Paris were ready to be signed. The dignitaries assembled in the Salon des Ambassadeurs of the new Ministry of Foreign Affairs—"probably the most elegant official apartment in all Europe," according to the *New York Times*[7]—for the signing ceremony. Cannons sounded from the Invalides and from the eighteen forts surrounding Paris. The city was again lit up, and on the following Tuesday, Napoléon III conducted a grand review of sixty thousand troops in honor of the peace. His efforts to recover France's international stature had met with success.

The frequency and grandeur of all these celebrations may seem anecdotal, but they have a real importance in relation to the history of

Paris and to the genius of Napoléon III as an urban planner. These events were not idle rejoicing; they were intended to give the transformation of Paris and the Empire itself a transcendent meaning within France and abroad. Napoléon III was acting with political purpose to imprint prestige on his regime and instill a shared vision for the capital.

Napoléon III did not understand art, but he certainly understood politics. He knew the value of symbols and the role they can play in society's adherence to a collective project. Some saw this as fawning and considered it a ploy to distract the people from revolution by appealing to the French sense of self-aggrandizement. But Parisians were in large part responsive to the call to civic pride and to the sense of a civilizing mission for France and for Paris. The emperor's vision for the city, far beyond functional concerns, as a symbol of national unity, of shared ideals of progress and beauty, resonated with the spirit of the time.

From our perspective, the expense and energy that went into all these celebrations is astonishing. Even at the time, some questioned in hushed voices this use of funds. But Napoléon III was not just administering a nation; he was giving it a new sense of itself and a vision for the future. Napoléon III was building a country that he wanted to be a beacon for humanity, and a city that he wanted to be nothing less than the capital of the world.

Ten

A LANDSCAPE
OF RUINS

The process of road building, performed without the help of modern equipment, was impressive. Rows of laborers advanced, using pickaxes to break up the dirt and stones. They shoveled the unneeded material into wheelbarrows and horse-pulled dumpers waiting by the dozen to haul it off to other parts of the city to be used as infill. Trenches fifteen feet wide and twenty deep were dug by hand, with wooden hoardings holding up the sides and wooden spanners every ten feet or so, where masons would build stone channels, walls, and vaults to make the sewer. The whole area was covered with earth and leveled to form the structure of the future street.

Preparing the street surface was another enormous job. Big slabs of granite were firmly set into the earth along the edge of the road, marking where the sidewalks would go. A gutter was built using small, square granite paving stones, with cement joints to prevent the water from seeping through. From place to place, workers built a collector, connecting down to the sewer below.

The nicest roads in Paris used a variant of the technique developed by John Loudon McAdam. The procedure was simple. Stones, broken down to the size of a walnut at the quarry, were brought to the new road by dumpers for the workers to spread out in the slightly convex shape of the road. Heavy cylinders were then pulled by horses again and again over the surface until the stones formed a solid mass. Finer matter was spread over the road and water was poured to compact it further. Again, the cylinders were used, until the surface was hard and smooth. Although the technique is long forgotten and few know that the name comes from a Scottish engineer, to this day Parisians refer to the surface of roads as *macadam*.

Although it provided for the smoothest ride, the McAdam technique required a great deal of maintenance. The surface of the road needed to be swept regularly, but softly, so as to take away the fine sand that built up as horses and carriages crushed the surface matter. When the weather was wet, the workers needed to take away the excess mud. When the weather was dry, teams of maintenance workers had to sprinkle the road with water so that it did not get too dusty. And whenever the road became damaged, it needed to be repaired immediately. Because of all this expensive maintenance, the McAdam technique could be used only for the most prestigious arteries.

The roads of more strictly functional use were built with stone pavers. These were more expensive to build and did not offer the same smooth ride, but they lasted much longer and required minimal maintenance. Qualified workers were needed to build these roads. They had to lay and compact the sand foundation, set the pavers in place at the right height using a paver's hammer, properly offset the joints so that the narrow wheels of the carriages would not get caught in a rut, set the pavers level so that the horses' hooves would not slip or twist. It was careful, repetitive work.

Napoléon III once remarked, "[I]n London, they are concerned only with giving the best possible satisfaction to the needs of traffic."[1] In Paris, there was a much broader approach to the design of streets, the continuation of an urban tradition of creating streets as places where people could promenade. It was in the Second Empire that broad sidewalks with lines of trees were systematically included in major arteries, together with carefully designed street furniture, such as benches, lanterns, and columns for posting advertisements. This attention to streets as more than places for the circulation of vehicles—even tempered by the subsequent careless interventions of engineers in the twentieth century—played an immense role in giving Paris the overall character that distinguishes it.

In total, the Second Empire built eighty-five miles of entirely new streets in Paris—with an average width of eighty feet, more than three times the average width of the preexisting streets of the city center. Four hundred and twenty linear miles of sidewalks were built. The number of gas streetlamps went from 15,000 to more than 32,000. The number of trees along the roads went from 50,000 to 96,000.

Building a new street was a long and painstaking job, but when it was finished, it was a glorious sight. As far as the eye could see, the surface was as smooth as a ballroom floor. The street was so wide that many carriages could comfortably pass. Elevated sidewalks with a new material called asphalt ensured that pedestrians could circulate, safe from the traffic, and without being inconvenienced by splashing water or mud. Everything had been thought of: elegant gas lights made the street safe and festive at night; rainwater was captured in the gutters and streamed away; the sewers below carried away the city's filth unseen. These newly finished avenues truly were a marvel of engineering and of art.

As grandiose as the achievements seemed once finished, the immediate consequence of the *grands travaux* was to turn Paris into a gigantic and unending construction site. New streets were cut right through the city blocks. The landscape of the city was dominated for years by half-dismantled buildings surrounded by the simple wooden fences that were used to enclose a construction area. Pedestrians, horses, and vehicles stealthily picked their way around ripped-apart roads and mountains of rubble. Twenty-seven thousand buildings were knocked down between 1852 and 1870.

To some, Paris resembled the ruins of an ancient city. The writer Théophile Gautier's evocation prefigures the haunting poetry of war zones:

> It is a curious spectacle to see these open houses with their colored or flowered wallpaper still showing the shapes of bedrooms, their stairs that no longer lead anywhere, their strange declivities and their violent ruins. . . . This upheaval is not without beauty; shadow and light play in picturesque effects on the rubble, on these accidents of stones and beams fallen at random.[2]

The work was labor-intensive, making construction sites lively places, full of workers with pickaxes, horses pulling dumpers, men delivering and removing materials by wheelbarrow, and the odd steam-powered lifting device spewing white clouds over the scene. All around stood mounds of rubble awaiting the tedious process of loading and removal.

The construction industry took on an unprecedented prominence in Paris. Contractors flourished. Workers arrived daily from distant regions; they walked in clusters from job to job, chatting in their funny accents and slang. Barges of stones and sand were hauled by boat down the Seine and unloaded onto the docks. Horse-drawn dumpers and handcarts weighed down with rubble and construction material clanged through the city streets.

The rapidly changing landscape posed the problem of people's orientation in their own city. Emile Zola's novel *The Belly of Paris* starts with the return of the main character, Florent Quenu, from the labor camps of Guyana, where he had been sent in 1848. When he returns to the neighborhood of Les Halles only a few years later, he is unable to recognize the streets where he grew up. The pioneer of photography, Nadar, is just one of many real-life Parisians to have felt the same sense of disorientation and upheaval with the rebuilding of their home city: "I am like a traveler arrived yesterday in a foreign city. I find myself isolated and new in this place where everything was familiar."[3]

Théophile Gautier wrote of the landscape changing before the eyes of Parisians:

Deep trenches, some of which have already become magnificent streets, crisscross the city; city blocks disappear as if by magic, new perspectives are opened, unexpected views appear, and someone who thought he knew his way gets lost in streets born yesterday. In many places the physiognomy of Paris is completely and utterly transformed.[4]

All the rebuilding led to lots of moving. Families that had lived in Paris's oldest neighborhoods for generations, who had all their friends and acquaintances there, loaded their belongings into moving carts to be taken away, often to other working-class neighborhoods, such as the faubourg Saint-Marcel or the faubourg Saint-Antoine, or else to the areas north and east of Paris that were just beginning to become truly urbanized. In total, between 1852 and 1870, 117,553 families, representing 350,000 people—more than 20 percent of the population of Paris—were forced to move because of the *grands travaux*.

The expropriation plans, some of which are preserved in the Paris archives, reveal the details of the process. The draftsman meticulously positioned the existing buildings on the plan, drew the lines of the new thoroughfares, and shaded all the affected properties pink. To the side, a table, in immaculate handwriting, gave the precise address of each property, the name of the owner, the total surface of the property, the surface to be expropriated, and any additional notes. This gave way to a well-oiled administrative choreography of notifications and judgments, appraisals and appeals. Dozens of lives were overturned with each line of the table. This, with all its painful human consequences, was the concrete reality of the old Paris giving way to the new dream of urban grandeur and modernity.

The construction inconvenienced not only the living Parisians but also the dead. Traditionally, Parisians had been buried in numerous small cemeteries all around the city, many of which were inevitably engulfed in the wave of construction. Vast quantities of human bones were recovered and sent to the old Vaugirard Cemetery. By 1859, forty thousand cubic feet of them had piled up.[5] The city administrators then decided to move all these bones to the Municipal Ossuary, better known as the Catacombs, where they joined those that had been stored there since the late eighteenth century. The bones exercised a fascination on Napoléon III. One day in 1860, he decided it would be the perfect destination for an outing with his son, then only four years old. One assumes the young Imperial Prince was suitably impressed.

Many regretted the destructions, and none were as eloquent as the exiled bard of medieval Paris, Victor Hugo, and Charles Baudelaire, a lifelong resident of the city who was only beginning to acquire fame for his poetry. Both were deeply attached to the character of the old Paris, which was in the process of disappearing forever, including the house at 13, rue Hautefeuille, where Baudelaire was born. Hugo decried the endlessly straight rue de Rivoli; Baudelaire lamented the scaffolding and new buildings and the "dear memories more heavy than rocks." But for neither of the two did Paris cease to be a source of poetic inspiration. As Baudelaire wrote, "Paris changes, but nothing in my melancholy has moved."[6]

While both poets were vehemently against the wholesale destruction of historic neighborhoods and what they saw as the artlessness of the *grands travaux,* neither was entirely against modernization. Baudelaire— an inveterate walker, both for *flânerie* and due to the lack of funds for a carriage or the omnibus fare—had complained bitterly of the muddy streets and appreciated the introduction of sidewalks and other improvements. Hugo supported making Paris a capital for humanity, later writing the most lyrical and sweeping articulation of the idea in his 1867 introduction to *Paris-Guide*. Still, both men despised the Second Empire and the moral depths to which Paris had sunk. It was only to be expected that the great project of a tainted regime, entrusted to a man like Haussmann, would be violent and primary, devoid of humanity and sensibility.

The scale of what was accomplished in Paris in the Second Empire is immense. It is difficult to conceive of such a comprehensive overhaul occurring in a built-up city voluntarily, without the help of a tragic fire or earthquake. Such a rebuilding would have indeed been legally and practically impossible without one extraordinarily powerful weapon in the city's arsenal: the power of eminent domain.

The legal structure of eminent domain in France dates from 1807, when a law first established that private property occupying the space of a future public thoroughfare could be appropriated by the government. Although the use of this power was strictly limited, the 1807 law formed the foundation of the legal structure that would be heavily relied upon in the Second Empire rebuilding of Paris.

In 1841, a new law was passed to refine the terms of the exercise of eminent domain. As a matter of practice, expropriations became much more common—it is on the basis of this law that the rue Rambuteau and the other new roads of the 1840s were built.

With industrialization, the need for infrastructure investments was growing, and in 1848, the Constitution of the newly created Republic formally recognized the concept of eminent domain. Article 11 of the Constitution read: "All property is inviolable. However, the State can require the sacrifice of a property for a legally recognized reason of public use, and in exchange for a just and preceding indemnity." It was officially established that the right to property might need to be sacrificed on occasion for the collective good.

On March 26, 1852, a new decree, pertaining specifically to expropriations for Paris, was prepared and signed into law by President Louis-Napoléon Bonaparte. It allowed the government much greater latitude in determining which buildings and lots could be expropriated, although in all cases expropriation continued to require a declaration of public use. If it was impossible to maintain buildings fit for living on the remaining lots, the decree also allowed the public authority to combine what remained into new lots, vastly improving the government's ability to monetize its holdings after a new infrastructure was built.

This was the legal framework that Haussmann found on his arrival, and the one that he used for the next sixteen years. Thanks to these laws, the city of Paris was able not only to build new streets but also to engage in what, in fact, was active real estate development. It would acquire all the lots that a new street would pass through, then reaggregate the frontage lots on the new street and sell them back to the private sector.

The method, often presented as part of the "Haussmann system," was hardly a new idea. In 1791, architect Charles Mangin had suggested exactly this. His idea was to build a new square where the place du Châtelet stands today, and then publicly redevelop all of central Paris piece by piece, using the proceeds from the previous development. "The acquisition and resale of houses and land," Mangin explained, "would yield a continuous profit that would be gathered in a fund for the improvement of Paris and used to pay for the squares and public monuments in the proposed plan."[7]

Haussmann's administration successfully implemented a similar approach, selling back the land it had expropriated at the value warranted for lots along newly created avenues. However, the financial benefit to the city was to be limited by a host of practical and legal factors. In the end, the proceeds from the sale of both new lots and salvaged building materials accounted for about 20 percent of the total cost of the creation of the new roads—enough to offset the costs significantly, but far from enough to allow the works to pay for themselves.

The high level of expropriation costs was a major factor in dampening the profitability of these development operations. The core problem was that the expropriation indemnifications were determined by a jury consisting of property owners, who were likely to be expropriated themselves someday. Egged on by the newspapers, these juries started raising the indemnifications to surprising levels, and found themselves supported by the courts when the city appealed. To Haussmann's dismay, the prices paid by the city began to skyrocket.

Lawyers began specializing in this area, creating a cottage industry aimed at maximizing the payouts decided by the juries. Stories circulated: Upon seeing a newly rich man, a friend asked, "How did you make your fortune?" The reply was, "I was expropriated."

Not all intermediaries were scrupulous. Some prepared fraudulent accounts for expropriated businesses to make the case for inflated indemnities. They would refurbish stores and make sure that on the day of the on-site inspection there was a flurry of shop boys hired for the occasion and that the place was packed with customers, who were, of course, paid for their presence. Parisian ingenuity applied itself with great success to the challenge of indemnity maximization.

None were as successful as those in the know. The prefect's wife, Octavie Haussmann, once naïvely remarked, "Every time a new avenue is decided, it seems we have a good friend who owns land in its path and has to be expropriated."[8]

For the city of Paris, the financial implications were becoming problematic. At these levels of cost, the city budget would not be able to support all the projects that had already been officially announced. A national subscription had just been launched to fund the Crimean War, a distant and expensive conflict that was putting severe strain on the French treasury. The city nevertheless decided to go ahead and issue sixty million francs in new debt to fund its infrastructure projects.

Visitors to Paris are always struck by the extraordinary uniformity of Parisian architecture. This is due, more than anything, to the massive number of buildings built in a concentrated period: more than 100,000 houses between 1852 and 1870.

Another factor is that many of these buildings are of a specific type: the *maison à loyer*, or rental building, a type that positively exploded in the Second Empire. In a growing city with whole neighborhoods undergoing rapid gentrification, those with money to invest—including the Pereire brothers, with their Société Immobilière—vied to snap up prime land for revenue-generating rental properties. The *maison à loyer* became a wildly popular investment vehicle

Architecturally, the *maison à loyer* posed a new and fascinating problem. For the first time, architects were asked to design homes for people they did not know and whose specific needs they could not discuss. The bourgeois home was now to be mass-produced and designed in advance.

Architects responded by producing a new residential typology, what is now known as the "Haussmannian" apartment building. The name is a bit of a misnomer, as Haussmann himself played no part in its conception; it just appeared at the time of what later became known as the Haussmannian restructuring of Paris.

The architecture of the Haussmannian apartment building has its origins in the early ensembles with strict architectural prescriptions: the rue de Rivoli and the place de l'Hôtel de Ville/avenue Victoria. These, together with some later ensembles, such as the place Saint-Michel, acted as powerful examples, widely propagated throughout the profession by architecture magazines. Thus, a sort of "cultural consensus," in the words of architectural historian Pierre Pinon, was arrived at between builders and developers, to observe a set of design principles.[9]

The one important constraint imposed on all who built buildings along the new roads was a covenant to the sales agreement by which the city sold the land to developers. It stipulated that the buildings on each block should have "the same heights between floors and the same principle façade lines" and that the "façades should be in stone, with balconies, cornices and moldings," so that the whole block should form "a single architectural ensemble."[10] The city provided examples of designs, giving developers a sense of what was expected.

There were, at the same time, binding rules for the height, shape, and layout of buildings. Height rules had been in place for Paris for a long time, but they were updated by the decree of July 27, 1859, which clarified the constraints. There were also often layout rules, such as those that stipulated large, shared courtyards in order to maximize the ventilation of the buildings.

These cultural and regulatory factors resulted in the Haussmannian building: a seven-story stone building with a broad front of at least fifty feet and a regular pattern of rectangular windows. The *étage noble,* either the second or third story, was taller than the others and had a wrought-iron balcony, as did the top story. There was an additional story in the *mansarde,* the attic under the characteristically shaped roof, which was covered in slate. The buildings are remarkable for the strong horizontal lines of the balconies and cornices, which continue along a whole block. Inside, the apartments tend to follow a well-defined layout, with an enfilade of rooms along the main front, as well as other common features of apartment design.

The specific architectural features of the Haussmannian building were a direct result of the mass availability of industrially produced building elements, such as iron railings for balconies. The emergence of industries relating to decoration and elegance were core to the identity of the

Second Empire and, by extension, to the aesthetic that governed the building of the new Paris. The architecture of the Second Empire, with large-scale deployment of industrially produced decorative elements, relied on it intensively.

Although there is surprising diversity in the detail of the designs, the Haussmannian building type is instantly recognizable and is at the core of the image of Paris. Already, it was in stark counterpoint with the American way of doing things: A *New York Times* correspondent of the time wrote back about the French ability to achieve a "general effect combining and harmonizing special beauties," as opposed to the "houses and stores of the American city, which everyone builds and paints to suit himself, without caring much for how the whole street will look."[11]

For years, the Palais du Louvre had loomed over the center of Paris, enveloped in a strange dark cloak. The building had been hidden behind an elaborate architecture of wooden scaffolding, punctuated by external suspended stairs. To the poetically minded, it looked like an immense timber cathedral at the heart of the city.

Toward the end of 1856, the scaffolding started to be taken off. The stately new Grand Louvre was gradually unveiled to the city. At its center was a new space, the cour Napoléon, enclosed by new buildings on the north and south sides. Louis Visconti and Hector Lefuel had designed the facades that mirror each other across the courtyard, each with three pavilions decorated with detached columns, sculptures, and pediments, which are connected by arcades surmounted by freestanding sculptures and more sober pedimented windows. To the north and south of the Arc de Triomphe du Carrousel, the long galleries connecting the Louvre to the Tuileries were rebuilt or completed. A new monumental facade defined the Louvre along the rue de Rivoli. The whole ensemble was fine indeed.

To celebrate the end of this huge project, there was, of course, a celebration. On the national holiday, August 15, 1857, Napoléon III saluted the realization of a vision of kings from long ago as a symbol of the continuity of French culture over the ages. The orchestras played and the people danced.

Since its completion in 1857, the Louvre complex remained largely untouched until recently. In 1989, President François Mitterand inaugurated a major expansion, including the building of a glass pyramid at the center of the main courtyard and a large lobby below. The courtyards of the Richelieu and Denon wings were covered with glass roofs and populated with splendid sculptures. Millions of people visit this complex every year, of which, no doubt, only a small proportion appreciate to what extent what one sees is the result of the work of Napoléon III and his architects.

By the mid-1850s, the Second Empire seemed to be going from success to success. The French economy was buoyed by an international environment of growth and industrialization that was, in the words of Eric Hobsbawm, "so extraordinary that men were at a loss for precedent."[12] Politically, the regime was stable and strong. Militarily and diplomatically, recent events had begun to reestablish a track record of victory and prestige. The story of Napoléon III's leadership so far was a nearly uninterrupted series of triumphs.

The new face of Paris was one of these achievements. All those who came to the city were impressed and enchanted by what they saw. As Prince Albert, the husband of Queen Victoria, wrote to his uncle, Leopold I, king of Belgium, "How has all this been accomplished in so little time? That is what no one understands."[13]

But the new Paris was just beginning to take form. It still consisted of only the rue de Rivoli, the boulevard de Strasbourg, and the avenue de l'Impératrice. Even the first wave of projects was not quite complete. The center of Paris, from the Hôtel de Ville to the place du Châtelet, was an enormous construction site. If the undertaking was to go further—much further, as the emperor envisioned—many new projects needed to be planned and funded. As Napoléon III and Haussmann knew, there was a great deal of work still to be done.

At the beginning of 1857, the situation of the French Empire worsened. The national treasury was showing signs of strain from the high levels of expenditure, including the cost of the Crimean War and infrastructure investments for Paris and elsewhere. The political opposition, incapacitated at the time of the coup d'état, was beginning to reorganize. The days of consensus about the projects for Paris were gone—in the drawing rooms and salons one began to hear criticism of the city's new projects and of Haussmann's management of the municipal administration.

Napoléon III was under pressure to take a tougher stance on expenditures and to limit the scope of the works in Paris. He set a course of greater austerity but would not adjourn or even postpone the rebuilding of Paris. On February 16, 1857, at the opening of the legislative session, he made his position clear: "In view of the requirements of the situation, I have resolved to reduce expenditures, without suspending the *grands travaux*."[14]

Eleven

·———·

THE 180 MILLION FRANC TREATY

In the first days of 1858, Georges-Eugène Haussmann, wearing a thick coat, a scarf, and a hat, came down from his apartment inside the Hôtel de Ville. He was accompanied by the head of the Roads Department and the lead city architect, Victor Baltard. Together, they stepped out into the biting winter air to inspect the soon-to-be completed boulevard de Sébastopol and to discuss the preparations for its inauguration.

The distance from the Hôtel de Ville was so short that they had decided to walk. This pleased Haussmann, who had no small pride in his hearty, athletic bearing and disliked being cooped up in his office. On the way, the prefect admired the new place de l'Hôtel de Ville: A place where convicts had once been ripped apart before throngs of onlookers was now an elegant square surrounded by tidily arranged avenues. The Tour Saint-Jacques was isolated at the center of a pretty public garden. Haussmann never tired of contemplating the orderly and modern aspect of what used to be the chaotic center of Paris.

Up to this point in his tenure as prefect, Haussmann had achieved everything that could have been hoped for. He had fulfilled the emperor's instructions with verve, established himself as a member of the senior cadre of the imperial system, and returned the Hôtel de Ville to a respected seat of national power.

To reward him for his achievements, Napoléon III had, in June 1857, arranged for Haussmann to be appointed senator, a promotion in the imperial hierarchy that made him the equal of any member of the city council. Haussmann was mentioned as a possible minister of public works, and even, in the future, as a potential minister of the interior.

Haussmann undoubtedly yearned for the status and privileges that such a promotion would bring. But he also knew that being prefect of the Seine offered him something that no other position could: the chance to build a legacy. The new city would stand, visible to all, for generations, a demonstration of what an enlightened and benevolent leader could achieve for the benefit of his people and the glory of the nation. Haussmann had already invested himself greatly in this undertaking and wanted to be fully and completely identified with its success. He would not consider relinquishing responsibility for the rebuilding of Paris.

So far, Haussmann had built a reputation through his dogged and uncompromising ability to bring the city's long-standing projects to completion, even amplifying their scope and impact. Now, with the boulevard de Sébastopol only weeks away from inauguration, Haussmann's mind was on the many new projects prepared by his staff in the last few years that had not yet concretely begun. Many of these projects had secured their declaration of public use; others had been defined and were ready to begin going through the administrative process. These projects, all inspired by the plan the emperor had showed Haussmann in June 1853, covered a much broader part of the city and would truly begin to remodel the entire face of Paris.

But Haussmann had so far been unable, for financial reasons, to move forward with these plans. With the debt incurred to fund the first set of projects, the city had run out of financial headroom. Taxation would have been a solution, but Napoléon III was categorical: There would be no new taxes on Parisians. Despite all of Haussmann's efforts to find clever ways around the problem, the reality remained. The city was simply not in a position to fund the next wave of projects without the help of the national government.

To Haussmann, a contribution from the national government was entirely justified. Paris was not just any city; it was the capital and heart of France. Its tranquillity, prosperity, and renown were, unarguably, of national interest. But the Legislative Assembly was dominated by representatives from other parts of France, with mostly rural constituents, who did not agree that so much money should go to Paris. Nor did many of the ministers, who were struggling with the financial difficulties of the national treasury. The minister of public works, Eugène Rouher, was not terribly pleased by Haussmann's increasing power and had never been a real proponent of the vision for Paris. The minister of finance, Pierre Magne, was concerned about being remembered as a poor manager of the nation's finances. Overall, after the building of the Grand Louvre and the subsidies already granted to the city of Paris for Les Halles and the new streets of the center, there was little appetite for additional expenditure. Napoléon III continued to give Haussmann his support in principle, but he was not prepared to force this issue through the Legislative Assembly or override the minister of finance.

Haussmann did not for a moment accept that the next wave of projects might need to be canceled or deferred. For him, things were simple: The emperor had presented him with an ambitious vision, one that Haussmann wholeheartedly believed in and that he remained determined to realize. From the outset, it had been evident that there would be tremendous opposition to break down and inertia to overcome. There were some constraints posed by the emperor that Haussmann had to abide by. But for all the rest, he would simply find a way through or around any obstacle that presented itself.

Haussmann had therefore relentlessly pursued long negotiations with the minister of finance and the minister of public works on a funding package for the new projects. The funding agreement was now, finally, approaching the point where it could be submitted to the Legislative Assembly for approval. Never sure if these negotiations would be successful or sufficient, Haussmann had, at the same time, begun working on less orthodox ways of accessing funds. He was prepared to do anything that could not incontrovertibly be shown to be outside the bounds of legality to finance the building of the new Paris.

In the days that Haussmann was working so intensely on the funding for his new projects, the life of the Empire continued. Thursday, January 14, 1858, was a gala night at the Paris Opéra in rue Le Peletier, with a special program in honor of the great baritone Eugène Massol, who was retiring. The emperor and empress were to attend.

At 8:30 that evening, the hall was full. Despite the chilly winter evening air, a crowd milled under the gas lights in the street in front of the Opéra, hoping to catch a glimpse of the emperor. Soon the imperial cortège was spotted descending the boulevard, surrounded by twenty-four lancers from the imperial guard in full dress: sky blue tunics doubled in amaranth-colored cloth, polished-steel breastplates, aiguillettes of gold and red silk, leather breeches, and copper-plated helmets embossed with the imperial monogram. This smart convoy turned into the rue Le Peletier at a brisk trot. Two carriages passed the crowd in front of the Opéra, then the imperial carriage, with mounted officers at its left and right. As the first carriage reached the building's gate and turned inside, the imperial carriage slowed to a walking pace.

Suddenly, a huge explosion rocked the Paris night. People and horses were thrown to the ground; windows on both sides of the street shattered. Another blast resounded from under the horses pulling the emperor's carriage, and then a third, from directly underneath the carriage.

The scene was chaos. Horses collapsed, dead; others bolted, terrified.

Bystanders shouted and ran for cover, or rushed to the bodies writhing on the sidewalk in pools of blood. The imperial guards scrambled, many gravely injured. In the midst of the noise and confusion, the battered imperial carriage stood motionless. No one knew if, inside, the imperial couple was dead or alive.

An injured guard was the first to reach the carriage. With his bloodied face, he peered inside. Eugénie, thinking it was an attacker, screamed, but Napoléon III recognized the soldier. Amazingly, neither the emperor nor the empress was seriously injured. Their lives had been saved by a steel plate that had recently been installed in the floor of their carriage, precisely to protect them from this sort of attack.

The explosion had blocked the right door of the carriage. The emperor and empress could have unlatched the left door, but it opened directly onto the crowd, where the terrorists might still have been lurking. So they waited, trapped inside their carriage, for the imperial guard to gather what remained of the detachment. The lancers came around and shielded the left door, allowing the emperor and empress to exit the carriage and scurry into the safety of the opera house.

Georges-Eugène Haussmann, who happened to have been waiting at the door of the Opéra to greet the imperial couple, took part in the impromptu meeting held in the vestibule. It was decided that the safest course of action would be for the imperial couple to proceed as planned—the last thing the police wanted was to have to escort the couple back out through the carnage and to have the opera crowd come out into the street and discover the scene. So, moments later, having nursed a few superficial cuts, the emperor and empress appeared in the imperial box. They listened to *William Tell* while, just outside, the injured were tended to and the bodies of the dead were carried away.

The minister of the interior and the prefect of police eventually arrived from their respective dinners. Napoléon III, in his understated way, made it clear to them that he was not impressed. But their teams worked quickly: Before the show was over, the emperor was provided with a pre-liminary report. It had already been discovered that the perpetrators were Italian nationalists, angry at Napoléon III's policy to effectively prevent the creation of an Italian state.

Napoléon III was well known for his calm demeanor after the last assassination attempt against him—he had taken the trouble to approach the crowd to ask them to hand the perpetrator over to the police un-harmed. But this time, he was deeply unsettled. As the performance neared its end, he thought things over. He was in contact with Cavour and Mazzini, the political leaders of the drive toward a unified Italian state, and did not believe they thought it was in their interest to threaten him directly. At the same time, this attack was not the haphazard at-tempt of an unbalanced individual. It was a well-organized action by professional agitators. He had very nearly just lost his life.

Before daybreak, police stormed a hotel room in rue du Mont-Thabor, just steps from the Jardin des Tuileries, and captured the man respon-sible for the attack. His name was Felice Orsini.

Orsini was not demented or disaffected. He was smart, capable, and acting not out of impulse or delusion, but for the achievement of precise political objectives. He was a member of the staunch Republican fringe of Italian nationalists, a product of the same underworld of nineteenth-century nationalist insurgency that Napoléon III himself had been a part of in his youth.

Napoléon III had proclaimed his sympathy for the creation of a unified Italian state, but he had de facto been supporting the Pope's temporal powers over the Papal States, a policy vigorously supported by France's Catholics. Orsini had come to see Napoléon III as a traitor to the Italian nationalist cause and resolved to assassinate him, even though Giuseppe Mazzini and the other leaders of the nationalist movement were against it. Orsini had had the bombs made in England and then smuggled into France. He had recruited three accomplices, prepared the assassination plot, and personally thrown the third bomb. Had the steel plate in the floor of the imperial carriage not been so effective, history would remember him as the assassin of Napoléon III.

Even though Napoléon III may have been personally inclined toward clemency for Orsini, he was concerned about a precedent of leniency. Orsini and two of his accomplices were tried, sentenced to death, and executed. The third accomplice was sentenced to life in the French labor camps of Guyana.

In the weeks that followed the attack, Napoléon III fired his prefect of police and minister of the interior and replaced them with no-nonsense members of his security apparatus. He put in place sweeping new restrictions of liberties. He proclaimed that his son, who at the time was just turning two years old, would succeed him if he died, and passed a resolution allowing the empress to be regent. Napoléon III was making a clear statement of his firm intention that the Empire not be compromised, even if he himself were killed.

Haussmann was, of course, disturbed by the assassination attempt. At the same time, it was clear to him that a period of renewed personal authority on the part of the emperor might be a propitious time to make progress on the transformation of Paris.

The agreement between the city of Paris and the national government was nearly ready. It would organize joint funding for a program of nine sets of projects for the capital, with an estimated total expenditure of 180 million francs. The national government would pay sixty—soon reduced to fifty million francs—toward these projects if they were all completed in full, as promised.

The projects included in the 180 Million Franc Treaty covered much of what we think of today as Haussmannian Paris: the avenues converging on the place du Château d'Eau (today's place de la République); t streets that form what we know of today as the Opéra neighborhood; the boulevard Malesherbes; the place de l'Etoile and several new avenues in the area; the avenues converging on the pont de l'Alma on both the Right Bank and the Left Bank; the avenue des Gobelins and the boulevard Saint-Marcel; and the boulevard Saint-Michel, which had been approved three years earlier but which was still unfunded and on which construction had not begun.

Not coincidentally, it was right around this time that the well-connected Pereire brothers expanded their real estate activities. They injected new capital into the company they had used to develop the rue de Rivoli and changed its name to the Compagnie Immobilière de Paris. They quickly bought up land in several of the areas that Haussmann had designated to receive the investments funded by the 180 Million Franc Treaty, especially the new Opéra neighborhood and the place de l'Etoile. With their access to inside information, they stood to make a fortune from the edevelopment of these areas.

Others had gotten wind of events. One day, Charles-Auguste de ⸱ny, who lived in the lower part of the Champs-Elysées, learned that r de Persigny's wife had mentioned something at a party about a ct for the gas lighting of the place de l'Etoile. He rushed to the v of the Interior and was able to confirm that something was ⸱rny and his friend the Countess Le Hon bought tens of thou- ⸱uare feet of land on what would eventually become some of ⸱ost expensive real estate. Unfortunately for them, circum- ⸱ them to sell before they could realize the gain they were

9, 1858, Haussmann was to address the Paris City been several critical junctures already in his ten- dmark moment. He had finally secured a promise

Rue Traversine in the Latin Quarter
(Roger Viollet / The Image Works)

Plan of Paris in 1853
(Roger Viollet / The Image Works)

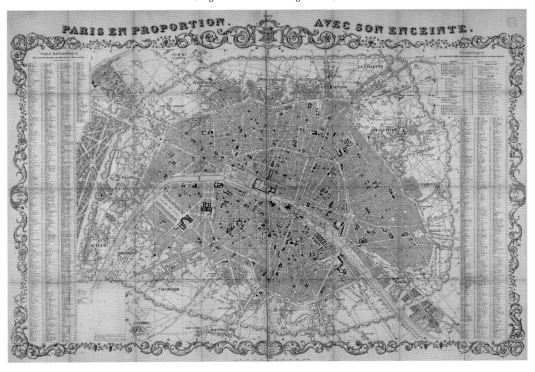

Napoléon III
*(Réunion des Musées Nationaux/
Art Resource, New York)*

Napoléon III's office in the
Palais des Tuileries
*(Réunion des Musées Nationaux/
Art Resource, New York)*

The building of the extension to the rue de Rivoli
(Roger Viollet / The Image Works)

Napoléon III visiting the Grand Louvre construction site
(Réunion des Musées Nationaux / Art Resource, New York)

Victor Baltard
(Bibliothèque Nationale de France)

Jacques-Ignace Hittorff
(Rheinisches Bildarchiv Köln, rba_207 105)

Georges-Eugène Haussmann
*(Réunion des Musées Nationaux /
Art Resource, New York)*

Eugène Viollet-le-Duc
*(Ministère de la Culture / Médiathèque du Patrimoine,
Dist. RMN / Art Resource, New York)*

Boulevard de Sebastopol, 1860
(Roger Viollet / The Image Works)

The Théâtre Impérial du Châtelet by Gabriel Davioud
(Bibliothèque Nationale de France)

A night view of the Palais de l'Exposition for the Universal Exposition of 1867
(Bibliothèque Nationale de France)

The Naumachie of the parc Monceau
(Bibliothèque Nationale de France)

The rebuilding of the Ile de la Cité, 1867

(Roger Viollet / The Image Works)

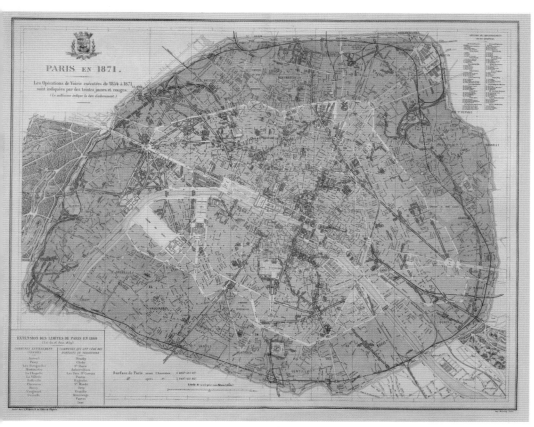

Plan of Paris in 1871, showing the projects of the Second Empire

(Bibliothèque Nationale de France)

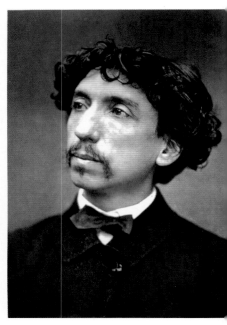

ABOVE: Charles Garnier
(Réunion des Musées Nationaux / Art
Resource, New York)

LEFT: The grand staircase of the
Opéra
(Réunion des Musées Nationaux / Art
Resource, New York)

The Opéra upon completion, 1874
(Roger Viollet / The Image Works)

of funds from the state, but the remainder of what he was asking from the city was much more than had ever been requested. The darkly dressed, distinguished men of the city council listened attentively as Haussmann spoke:

> The enterprise of transforming Paris's street network is not, as some think, a magnificent fantasy of the city administration and the city council nor is it, as some people who are better informed of the origin of our plans believe, the extravagant manifestation of a particular taste of the Emperor for the splendor of his capital. . . .
>
> No one is less inclined than you to dissipate in vain expenditures the wealth of the City, of which you are the stewards. Your convictions had to be strong indeed for you to persevere, without discouragement and without rest, through so many difficulties and displeasures, in the realization of this vast set of projects that, it is true, yield unanimous praise when they are completed, but that encounter such opposition and criticism while they are under way. . . .
>
> The Paris city council has many times proven its intelligent and thoughtful dedication to the greater public good. The importance and the public benefit of the proposed projects are too evident, and the public needs to be satisfied by the State budget too well known for me to have hesitated to propose, gentlemen, for the City to assume the entire expense, if it could support such a burden. But the undertaking would exceed the resources that the City budget can provide. As it is offered to us, the contribution of the State is restricted to its narrowest limits, but I believe it can suffice. The results of the last budgets show that the City, once everyday expenses are taken care of and interest on the debt is paid, can invest 20 million francs a year in the special projects. With a reasonable amount set aside for municipal, religious, health-care and educational buildings, for the increasing needs of the water network and various other infrastructure projects, it follows that a sum of 120 million francs spent, over ten years, from

*budgetary revenue to continue to equip Paris with masterly roads will not
shake its finances. . . .*

    I trust, gentlemen, that you will approve the proposed convention.[2]

Haussmann's trust was to be rewarded.

Not a week later, Napoléon III presented himself on horseback for the
inauguration of the new boulevard de Sébastopol. It was two in the
afternoon, and the spring sun was resplendent. "The day was a holiday,
and one can say without exaggeration that the valid population of Paris
had almost in its entirety come out to celebrate the inauguration."[3]

As the emperor approached, an enormous screen held up between
two Moorish columns was opened like a curtain. The regal new boulevard stretched forward, festooned with colorful decorations sport-
ing the symbols of the regime and full of soldiers standing at attention.
The perspective lines crisply converged toward the place du Châtelet,
with the Seine and the Ile de la Cité beyond. Behind the emperor, the
boulevard de Strasbourg continued straight to the gare de l'Est.

Napoléon III was extremely proud of this new accomplishment.
There was a military orderliness and precision to the aesthetics that
pleased the emperor. The name of the new boulevard itself recalled the
most famous success of the Crimean War, telling the French they could
once again take pride in the might of their nation.

As exciting as the rue de Rivoli had been, it was but one street
through the city center, and, even more important, it was a project
initiated by his predecessors. The boulevard de Sébastopol was completely a Second Empire project. It represented the step from isolated
roads to a network of ordered boulevards, an embodiment of Napoléon
III's vision for the city. It was something he felt confident that no one
but a Bonaparte would have done quite like this.

The date was April 15, 1858, just a few weeks after the Orsini attack. The situation in Italy was heating up, the Empire's finances were in a poor state, and the internal political situation was complex. Although no one challenged his ideas to his face, Napoléon III could hear the swelling chorus of criticism about the growing authoritarianism of the regime and about the cost and usefulness of the works for Paris.

In his speech, Napoléon III brought up the progress of his plans for Paris. He addressed Haussmann and the city council:

> *When future generations will cross our great city . . . they will acquire the taste of beauty through the spectacle of these works of art. . . . But your work, gentlemen, is far from done. You have approved a master plan that must continue what you have so well begun. The Chamber will, I hope, soon vote it, and we shall each year see new arteries open, populous neighborhoods be made more sanitary, rents tend to go down due to the number of new buildings, the working class become wealthier through work, misery diminish through a better organization of charity, and Paris thereby answer more and more to its highest destiny.*[4]

Haussmann, in the section of the audience reserved for the highest dignitaries, smiled with satisfaction. The emperor's praise rang sweetly in his ears. But more important, Napoléon III had directly expressed his wish to the senators and deputies that they endorse the 180 Million Franc Treaty. There could be no doubt that the legislators would eventually approve the agreement.

Haussmann observed the scene and reflected. The skimpy state participation of less than a third seemed to him indecently small. But the agreement, with all its faults, was the requisite condition for the continuation and amplification of the transformation of Paris. Despite his frustration, Haussmann could on this day savor one of his greatest triumphs as prefect of the Seine.

The agreement was signed less than three weeks later, on May 3,

1858, by Pierre Magne, minister of finance, and Eugène Rouher, minister of agriculture, commerce, and public works, on behalf of the French government and by Georges-Eugène Haussmann on behalf of the city of Paris. Later that month, on May 28, 1858, the 180 Million Franc Treaty was officially adopted by the Legislative Assembly.

With the treaty enacted, the prefecture staff worked with renewed vigor at preparing the expropriations, public-works contracts, and other administrative steps required to proceed with the huge new wave of projects.

Privately, however, Haussmann continued to be concerned about funding. For a city the size of Paris, the upcoming projects were a true large-scale bet on the future. The city's share of the investment would be 130 million francs, compared to total recurrent revenues of only 80 million francs in 1859, with, by then, significant municipal debt. And while Haussmann had publicly asserted that the budget of 180 million francs would be sufficient for the planned projects, he already knew this would not be the case.

With all the foot dragging and various obstacles he had encountered in the preceding months, Haussmann had long realized that the ordinary institutional channels would yield only a portion of the investment he felt was warranted. So he went directly to the emperor to make the case for the creation of a special fund that would give the city flexibility in the timing and in the use of funds raised. In reality, his intention was to use the funds to raise additional moneys in a much less transparent way. Haussmann prevailed, and on November 14, 1858, an imperial decree established the Caisse des Travaux de Paris.

The Caisse des Travaux de Paris operated outside the city accounts. It was to be the vehicle for the payment of all expenditures related to the new thoroughfares, whether for expropriation or for contracting. It would receive revenues related to the projects, from the sale of materials or from the sale of land along the new roads. Over the eleven years it operated, from January 1859 until December 1869, the Caisse des Travaux de Paris received revenues of 365 million francs and spent a total of 1.2 billion francs.

The difference was to be funded by the city. But the Caisse des Travaux de Paris also had the ability to issue its own securities, under guarantee of the city of Paris. The quantity of this off-balance-sheet funding—as we would think of it today—did not need to be approved by the Legislative Assembly, as it was not considered municipal debt, nor even by the minister of finance, only by the city council. It started at 30 million francs, but Haussmann later managed to get it increased to 100 million francs. Although this was not an unsubstantial help, it was only a small step compared to Haussmann's next idea.

Most of the urban projects of the Haussmann administration were conducted by concession. The specifications would be written by the city Roads Department and contractors would bid. The winning contractor would pay the expenses out of pocket and receive payment from the city on delivery of the completed project.

Haussmann's idea was that, instead of payment on delivery, the contractors would receive vouchers for future payment attracting interest at a rate of 5 percent. Ordinarily, the contractors would not have accepted paper instead of payment, but the clever part of the idea was that since the vouchers were guaranteed by the city, the contractor could sell them to a third party and thereby monetize them without delay. It was a roundabout way to get financial institutions to advance the funds for the projects, against future reimbursement by the city, without the need for borrowing, which would have required the approval of the Legislative Assembly.

The third party that supported this arrangement was the Crédit Foncier de France, conveniently run by Haussmann's old friend from

Burgundy, Louis Frémy. The Crédit Foncier had been created in 1852 to make inexpensive mortgages broadly available in France, but almost from the outset, it had been involved in other activities, primarily lending to municipalities for their urban-development projects. The most significant counterparty of these activities, by far, was the city of Paris.

By the early 1860s, concessions had become the norm for the city of Paris's projects. By then, contractors had experience with the expropriation process and were comfortable incorporating these costs into their bids. They were also much more effective than the public administration at reaching negotiated settlements with owners, thereby avoiding the costs and delays of systematic recourse to the courts. The payment in vouchers guaranteed by the city, generally sold by the contractor to the Crédit Foncier, became the standard modus operandi. For Haussmann, it was a magnificent vehicle: It allowed him to access hundreds of millions of francs off balance sheet without disclosure and without approval. By 1867, the covert debt run up in this way would reach 463 million francs, with 86 percent of it held by the Crédit Foncier.

Jules Baroche, the president of the state council, had a burly physique but the decidedly unthreatening face of a lapdog, with drooping cheeks and enormous sideburns. A leading Paris lawyer in the 1840s, he had been part of the conservative opposition to King Louis-Philippe. He had served as President Louis-Napoléon Bonaparte's minister of the interior from 1850 to 1851 and then, after the coup d'état, moved to the state council, which he presided for ten years, starting in 1853, before serving as minister of justice during much of the 1860s. Unsentimental and effective, he was a precious ally for Napoléon III.

Baroche was a punctilious legalist. In addition, he disliked Georges-Eugène Haussmann, whom he saw as an extravagant self-aggrandizer, and had no interest in the transformation of Paris. On December 27, 1858, under the leadership of Baroche, the state council delivered a judgment that reversed several years of practice by the city of Paris and would considerably raise the cost and administrative complexity of the *grands travaux*.

The state council's decision was that landowners were to retain ownership of the portions of lots not required for a new public infrastructure and that they should be fully indemnified not only for the portion of land that was expropriated but for all the buildings affected, even if these stood on land retained by the owner. For Haussmann, the decision was a catastrophic misjudgment. It meant that landowners would be fully indemnified for all losses but would still be allowed to retain land that would soon have frontage on a magnificent new avenue, and that would therefore increase tremendously in value. The decision eliminated the city's mechanism of partial self-financing through the sell-back of the re-aggregated lots along the new streets. It was, from Haussmann's perspective, a vicious strike against the vision for Paris.

Haussmann fought back. But the whole matter seemed abstract to Napoléon III, who never focused on the issue enough to understand it. Since Baroche was a key person in the implementation of imperial policy, Napoléon III never challenged him on this subject. Haussmann was forced to accept defeat.

Another major legal setback followed a year and a half later. In a decision dated June 12, 1860, the court of appeals established that the indemnification of tenants must take place at the time of expropriation of the proprietor, even if the tenants were to be allowed to continue to benefit from their leases. This was important because, with the projects of the 180 Million Franc Treaty spread over ten years, the city's policy was to expropriate properties in advance, taking advantage of market conditions, and let leases run out by nonrenewal rather than by eviction in order to minimize costs. The decision of the court of appeals put an end to this practice, forcing the city to indemnify tenants as soon as the expropriation was handed down. Haussmann described the decision as a "true disaster" that would have "incalculable consequences."[5] The city had to comply, generally choosing to defer expropriations, and therefore buying the properties at a much higher value.

Despite these setbacks, as the decade of the 1850s came to a close, Haussmann's multiple mechanisms to ensure large-scale funding for the building of the new Paris were in place. They would prove formidably effective until they finally unraveled, bringing their architect down with them.

Twelve

THE NEW CITY EMERGES

As the projects of the 180 Million Franc Treaty began to be built, the full extent of the new Paris began to appear. Four major squares, each with its own background and characteristics, encapsulate the tremendous and multifaceted building activity under the Haussmann administration.

The place de l'Etoile—the site today officially named place Charles-de-Gaulle—was not a new creation. But it is, for the historian of cities Pierre Lavedan, Haussmann's "one urban masterpiece."[1]

The place de l'Etoile was already a major entry point into Paris, occupied by the Arc de Triomphe and the Ledoux-designed pavilion for the personnel in charge of duty collection at the city border. The prefect's contribution was the idea of creating an entire urban composition around the monument; it would consist of a large circus with twelve avenues radiating out like the spokes of a wheel. Five of the streets existed, but Haussmann painstakingly arranged for the remaining seven to be created, at just the right angles to reach the desired level of symmetry and order. The result is a striking urban form, especially if one goes up to admire it from the top of the Arc de Triomphe, as Haussmann always recommended one do.

For the architecture of the place de l'Etoile, Jacques-Ignace Hittorff proposed a scheme consisting of low buildings linked together by an arcade. Haussmann, preferring freestanding monumental structures and a design that catered more to the needs of vehicle circulation, rejected the plan. Hittorff persisted, presenting an amended design with no arcade but with buildings much lower than those Haussmann had in mind, and managed to secure the emperor's assent on the basis that the lower buildings would do more to underscore the grandeur of Napoléon III's uncle's monumental arch—an obviously unassailable argument. Haussmann, who continued to dislike Hittorff's ideas as much as he disliked their author, was vanquished. The rest of the houses would be built, over time, to Hittorff's design. The most Haussmann could do was to get petty revenge by placing three rows of trees in front of the buildings, in an effort to hide the facades of Hittorff's buildings.

Despite being the fruit of such discord, the place de l'Etoile has an undeniable unity and compositional power. It has become a remarkable emblem of Second Empire urban design.

The place du Château d'Eau, today's place de la République, is, at 300 yards by 130 yards, one of the largest squares in Europe. Its origins stem from the emperor's vision of a grand square at the center of new working-class neighborhoods in the north and east of the city. As it turns out, the square was built in a different location and with a different layout than the original idea. There is no better illustration that there was no master plan for Second Empire Paris, only intentions that evolved over time.

Napoléon III had pictured the great new square at the intersection of a huge cross formed by two new streets, one leading from the place de la Bastille to Père Lachaise Cemetery and the other leading from the

Grands Boulevards to the place du Trône (today's place de la Nation). In other words, it was imagined roughly where the place Léon Blum stands today. The long side of Napoléon III's cross, leading to the place du Trône, was initially planned to branch into the Grands Boulevards a little to the south, so as not to disturb the top of the boulevard du Temple, which was a favorite promenade spot for Parisians, an area where there were many theaters and much street entertainment.

After reviewing the plans for the area, Haussmann concluded that it would be better to have the new avenue lead directly to the top of the boulevard du Temple, at the site of a preexisting square named place du Château d'Eau, positioned at a kink in the Grands Boulevards. Barracks had been built on this square in 1854, and Haussmann felt that connecting the new street to the square would facilitate troop movements between the barracks and the large military center at the Vincennes Fort. Far from a drawback, Haussmann saw the fact that his plan would entail the destruction of the theaters—for him a nest of vice—as an added benefit. So when the decree for the new avenue, which received the name avenue du Prince-Eugène (today's boulevard Voltaire), came out on August 29, 1857, it connected straight into the place du Château d'Eau, along the front of the barracks, wiping out the top of the boulevard du Temple and its seven theaters.

Haussmann's decision radically changed the nature of this bit of Paris. He expanded the square and made it the point of convergence for new avenues. From a lively, human-scaled stretch of the Grands Boulevards, which Parisians had enjoyed for generations, it became a massive intersection of major arteries. Initially, there was no specific plan about how to manage the space where all these arteries come together. That was left for later, while the city focused on building the streets themselves.

The crossing of the canal Saint-Martin was a more pressing problem. The broad new avenue du Prince-Eugène would have to cross the canal either at grade with a drawbridge or rotating bridge or else over a fixed bridge with a steep incline. Neither of these solutions was satisfactory.

Haussmann turned the problem over and over in his mind until he found a solution: Instead of raising the street, he would lower the canal. On July 9, 1861, a decree was passed, approving repurchase of the concession for the canal Saint-Martin for 12.3 million francs. This allowed the city to build extra locks on the canal, lowering the water level by twenty feet. The avenue du Prince-Eugène could therefore cross at grade, without the slightest disturbance. The emperor took his horse to go see for himself how it would work, and he was delighted with Haussmann's ingenuity. The clever solution would allow the creation of a straight, uninterrupted artery of nearly two miles through the east of Paris.

The creation of the avenue du Prince-Eugène in 1860 had caused the destruction of seven theaters on the boulevard du Temple. Rather than reinstate them in the same area, Haussmann saw an opportunity. He decided to rebuild the theaters on the new place du Châtelet, a bold step to bring cultural institutions to the city center and give form to this square.

The site of the modern-day place du Châtelet had been, for many years, occupied by the Grand Châtelet, a fortified tower protecting the northern end of the pont au Change, which gave access to the Ile de la Cité, Paris's institutional center. The hulking structure of the Grand Châtelet had been completely demolished at the beginning of the century, under Napoléon I. When the boulevard de Sébastopol was built, it was decided that this, its southern end point, would be entirely redesigned.

Haussmann was frustrated by what he saw as a terrible planning mistake made by his predecessors. Had the boulevard de Strasbourg been built to end just a few yards to the west, its extension, the boulevard de Sébastopol, would have been in perfect alignment with the pont au Change, with a view of the dome of the Sorbonne. Instead, the boulevard de Sébastopol ran directly into the Seine, just east of the bridge. The design of the place du Châtelet would have to deal with this unfortunate lack of foresight.

The city architects and engineers came up with a typically elegant solution. The boulevard de Sébastopol would run along one side of the new place du Châtelet, with a symmetrical arrangement on the other side. The pont au Change would line up neatly with the center of the square. The architecture of the square would underline its order and symmetry. It would be a fine urban composition.

But there was a significant problem with the large fountain already occupying the place du Châtelet, which unfortunately did not line up with anything. Although moving it was an engineering challenge and would cost a significant sum of money, Haussmann decided to displace the Palmier fountain in order to line it up with the pont au Change and the center of the future square. On April 24, 1858, nine days after the inauguration of the boulevard de Sébastopol, the fountain was lifted, transported, and set in its new position, where it stands today.

It would, however, still be a while before Parisians could admire the new layout. The scaffolding was not taken off the fountain until the following New Year's Day. And even then, the pont au Change, which was being rebuilt, was still under construction. On August 15, 1860, the bridge opened. On that day, finally, one could drive uninterrupted from the gare de l'Est to the Ile de la Cité, a distance of nearly two miles. With this achieved, the structure of the place du Châtelet was in place.

The architect selected to design the two new theaters on this square was the same one who had presided over the moving of the fountain. He had already been noticed for his work at the Bois de Boulogne and would go on to design many more buildings and public places for Paris. Gabriel Davioud would turn out to be the architect with perhaps the single greatest impact on the urban landscape of Second Empire Paris.

Davioud's father had been a low-ranking civil servant who died when his son was still a boy. Davioud's mother had raised him on her own, working hard to give her son a good education and to instill in him a strong work ethic. The boy attended drawing school and, talented and diligent, entered the Ecole des Beaux-Arts in 1842, at the age of seventeen. In 1849, when he first entered the Grand Prix de Rome competition, he won the second prize. With his mother experiencing financial difficulties, he decided not to try again for the first prize, as one typically did, and instead dedicated himself to his career in the city of Paris's administration.

In 1853, Davioud was assigned to work on the Bois de Boulogne. He built dozens of kiosks, chalets, and café stands. He also designed the entrance gates and restored several houses, together with the old windmill of Longchamp Abbey. In recognition of the quality of his work, Davioud was promoted to chief architect of the division.

All his life, Davioud remained an exceptionally hard worker, somewhat effaced behind his designs. He had no desire for cosmopolitan glory and was uncomfortable in the limelight. But he had a tremendous passion for his craft. Even today, he is not among the more famous architects of the period, although his imprint on Paris is immense: "He is the one who most powerfully contributed to giving the capital an image so familiar that we cannot imagine that it could have been different."[2]

Davioud designed the Théâtre Impérial, on the west side of the place du Châtelet, and the Théâtre-Lyrique, on the east, as variations on a theme, two compact blocks facing each other across the square. The main fronts are dominated by a center portion of large arched bays, framed on either side by solid masonry corners. The style of the two theaters is a restrained classicism, with ornament but without sculptures, with design details giving each building a distinct character. The structures are a pure continuation of the French tradition of theater design, inspired by the great architects of the late eighteenth century, Victor Louis and Charles de Wailly, but transposed to appeal to the tastes of the Second Empire.

The Théâtre Impérial du Châtelet was inaugurated on April 19, 1862, with Empress Eugénie in attendance. With a capacity of 2,500, it was the largest theater in Paris. Known for its remarkable acoustics, it was also used as a concert hall. Over the years, Tchaikovsky, Grieg, Richard Strauss, Debussy, and Mahler all conducted in this hall. It continues to function today as the Théâtre du Châtelet.

The Théâtre-Lyrique was inaugurated later in the year, on October 30. It was a leading opera house throughout the 1860s, premiering major works by Gounod, Bizet, and Berlioz. Today, the building houses the Théâtre de la Ville.

The place Saint-Michel, the first Second Empire square to be built on the Left Bank, continued to demonstrate the new art of urban life envisioned for the modern Paris. This square was, in fact, built literally on top of the old, messy world it was to replace.

The boulevard Saint-Michel, the new north-south axis through the Left Bank, was part of Napoléon III's original colored plan and had been declared of public use back in 1855. Construction, though, had been delayed until the early 1860s. By then, the rebuilding of the pont Saint-Michel, the bridge connecting the new boulevard to the Ile de la Cité, was nearly complete. There naturally arose the question of what to do with the space where the street and the bridge would meet.

Historically, the site had been occupied by a small square, the place Saint-Michel. This square was just a space around a fountain between the houses opposite the bridge, connected to the surrounding neighborhood by small, crooked streets. Entirely insensitive to the history and character of the place, Haussmann decided to demolish the whole area to create a much larger and more modern square. Gabriel Davioud was selected as architect.

The design needed to resolve an awkward street layout, as the boulevard Saint-Michel was on a skewed axis compared to the pont Saint-Michel. Davioud's idea was to create a triangular place with a monumental fountain at the back, facing the bridge. Two symmetrical streets would follow the sides of the triangle, one of these being the start of the boulevard Saint-Michel. To give the composition the appropriate cachet, Davioud set detailed architectural prescriptions for the buildings facing the place. He himself designed the fountain, with its stone basins, pink marble pillars, and giant pediment, as well as the building it backs up against. The sculpture *Saint Michael Slaying the Demon,* by Francisque Duret, was hoisted into the niche.

Although the fountain was not well received by the critics at the time, it has become a familiar and popular urban icon. This well laid-out, thoughtfully designed ensemble was an important example of the quality of urban space that the Second Empire was undertaking to create.

The public places and the many new streets being created across the city were only one aspect of the *grands travaux.* The city as a functioning entity went through deep changes in many other ways. Far from being only a monumental or circulation scheme, the rebuilding of Paris was a giant step toward providing the amenities to better meet the everyday needs of citizens in a time of massive demographic, social, and economic change.

The country as a whole was in transformation, with deep economic mutations and greatly increased internal mobility. In the years of the Second Empire, no less than 7 percent of the French population moved from the country to the cities.[3] The population of Paris alone increased by close to one million people, with many of the new arrivals coming from the poorest regions of France. These people overwhelmingly established themselves in the new neighborhoods of the north and east, joined by some of those displaced by the rebuilding of the city center. The new, larger, working-class neighborhoods generated by these dynamics were the locus of a whole new type and scale of social problems.

The ills of the new industrial city—illegitimate births, prostitution, suicides, criminality, riots—were considerable. There were growing needs to be addressed in the areas of indigence, illness, mental illness, and policing. And, of course, the growing population had ordinary needs when it came to the areas of administration, education, sanitation, and so on. The Second Empire administration took these needs seriously and sought to implement policies and to build facilities to meet them.

The maintenance of social stability and the upholding of Christian values were seen by authorities as essential in the midst of such social changes, leading the government to build a host of new churches. These were not only the monumental churches, such as La Trinité and Saint-Augustin, or the churches that had already been started in wealthy neighborhoods, such as Saint-Vincent-de-Paul and Sainte-Clotilde, but everyday churches to serve the spiritual needs of all classes of Parisians. In the fast-growing northeast alone, four churches were built: Saint-Ambroise, Saint-Jean-Baptiste de Belleville, Notre-Dame de la Croix, and Saint-Joseph. Three more were built in northern parts of the city: Notre-Dame de Clignancourt, Saint-Eugène, and Saint-Bernard. And five churches were built across the south of the city: Saint-Pierre de Montrouge, Saint-François-Xavier, Notre-Dame des Champs, Notre-Dame de la Gare, and Saint-Lambert. These churches reflected an impeccable conservative taste, with nods to the Gothic, Romanesque, and classical heritage of France. They became important landmarks in each of their neighborhoods, symbolizing the Empire's moral values and its ambition for Paris. Other religions were not forgotten: Structures were built for the capital's Protestants, a group to which Haussmann himself belonged, and two synagogues were built for the Jewish population.

Napoléon III believed that parks would play an important role in increasing the health and morality of the working class. This was why he was so attached to the development of the Bois de Vincennes, the working-class counterpart to the Bois de Boulogne, which opened in 1865. He also wanted small parks, similar to the "squares," or private communal gardens, he had seen in London, but open to the general public. The first garden of this type was the one surrounding Tour

Saint-Jacques, along the rue de Rivoli, opened in 1856. The head of the Department of Parks and Promenades, Adolphe Alphand, and his team created twenty-three more of these little parks in every part of the city, from the Batignolles to Montrouge and from Grenelle to Belleville. They are still referred to as *squares*, with the French pronunciation.

The Second Empire presided over a large-scale drive to build a whole infrastructure of urban facilities: town halls for each arrondissement, barracks for the imperial guard, churches, hospitals, hospices, universities, high schools, middle schools, and primary schools. A few notable examples of the many practical, everyday buildings built under the Haussmann administration to serve the needs of a modern city are the Sainte-Anne asylum, built in 1867 by Charles-Auguste Questel; the Santé Prison, built by Emile Vaudremer in 1868; and the massive new slaughterhouse built in La Villette in the late 1860s.

Despite these efforts, many contemporaries saw the transformation of Paris as a social regression. Overall, the lives of Parisians, and especially the upper and middle classes, improved during the years of the Second Empire, but there was a constant arrival of new inhabitants—close to 700,000 in twenty years—replenishing the numbers on the bottom rungs of the social ladder.[4] With the recapture of the center of the city by the bourgeoisie, the poorest elements of society, those with the most children and the most precarious positions, were relegated to the distant neighborhoods near the fortifications.

Historically, Paris had been composed of many small, extremely dense neighborhoods, often with an identity defined by some dominant economic activity. Although there were rich and poor areas, many of Paris's *quartiers* had quite a bit of heterogeneity, and were, in any case, in close proximity to one another. The rebuilding of Paris changed that, putting the rich with the rich and the poor with the poor. Some considered that this created a "dangerous separation of society's classes . . . , imprudently breaking the old equilibrium."[5] It certainly greatly changed the life of workers, who used to live in the same neighborhoods as their places of work and now often had a walk of an hour or more to get to work. They now lived surrounded by other working-class people, and on Sundays they stayed in their distant neighborhoods and drank in the cabarets.

The failure to improve sufficiently the living conditions of the Parisian working class, despite the emperor's professed personal interest in such matters, was a great missed opportunity of Second Empire policy. The government largely restricted itself to measures exempting the poor from certain taxes and limiting the price increases of basic goods like bread and meat. For the rest, public and private philanthropy served as a decidedly imperfect safety net.

After the experiments of the early years, workers' housing was left entirely in private hands. The result was considerable hardship for the working class. Rents went up faster than salaries—3 percent annually between 1856 and 1866. The apartments were small and often unsanitary—in the outer arrondissements, it was rare to have heating or any means of cooking. Proprietors imposed draconian conditions on their tenants. Complaints about housing were recurrent and strident throughout the 1860s. For the populations of the outer arrondissements, the fact that there were paved roads, street lighting, and churches did not make up for the difficulties of daily life. A large number of Parisians felt that they had simply not benefited from the changes taking place in Paris.

Like Napoléon III, Haussmann had little knowledge of architecture and was not particularly sensitive to its aesthetics. He fancied that he had an artistic side—in his youth he played the cello and in old age he wrote poetry—but in reality his artistic views were basic, highly conservative, and not particularly well informed. This did not prevent him from authoritatively expressing them and confidently imposing them on the emerging city. He loved monumental buildings, preferably with a dome, and grand perspectives carefully laid out in their axes. He preferred architecture of a simple classicism, without innovation or audacity. As one architectural historian cleverly wrote, Haussmann "was a man of much common sense but less than common sensibility."[6]

Haussmann, in fact, never professed that architectural beauty was a primary concern of the transformation of Paris:

> The positive services rendered hide behind the splendor of the layout and of the perspectives, or rather, the beautification of the city and the grandeur of the effects produced result from utility itself, deeply understood. Superficial minds easily mistake this: because the works already accomplished in Paris open picturesque perspectives for strollers and gives a grandiose appearance to certain parts of the old city that were hitherto unsightly, they imagine that magnificence and pleasure are the goals of the City's undertakings. . . . What is good, in the highest meaning of the word, is naturally beautiful, and the very character of serious art is to give excellent shape to what is truly good.[7]

The administrators and architects of the Second Empire nevertheless succeeded in building a city with tremendous architectural character. This was in part due to the sheer scale of the undertaking and the straightforwardness of the approach, but it was also due to the compositional principles employed. Haussmann systematically sought simple, clear layouts and endeavored to punctuate perspectives with an architectural element. Both Napoléon III and Haussmann associated beauty with order and appreciated linear axes and continuity of expression in the buildings along them.

At the same time, the Second Empire did not replace the preexisting city completely. Instead, the new designs created connections within the historical fabric. The result is a plan that is full of imperfections. There are streets that don't quite connect as one would want them to, links that seem obvious on a map but for some reason were never made.

These imperfections allow the urban fabric of Paris to avoid the monotony that a similar composition would have in a greenfield site. In the words of Pierre Pinon, "[T]here is no Haussmannian city without the old Paris."[8]

The work of the Second Empire's architects naturally also contributed to the quality of the environment. But this contribution did not rely on the spectacular architecture of showy monuments. Instead, the environmental quality of Paris is the result of a large mass of everyday architecture across the city, produced at a consistently solid—and only intermittently exceptional—standard. The second half of the nineteenth century was a great period in Parisian history for minor public buildings: arrondissement town halls, churches, markets, theaters, et cetera. It is through the design of these more modest buildings, the creation of urban amenities like schools and firehouses, and the construction of many run-of-the-mill apartment buildings that architects played a large role in the development of the identity and character of Paris.

The architecture of the Second Empire was stylistically diverse. In fact, part of the difficulty some have with the work produced stems from the impossibility of categorizing it in a single style. When one considers the historical dynamics, it is readily apparent that there was such a great deal going on, culturally as well as technologically, that it is difficult to imagine a uniform style of expression. With the Industrial Revolution, metal as a material for architecture was emerging, and civil engineering was fully established as a field. As long-distance travel became faster and safer and as means of graphic reproduction became highly accessible, the set of cultural referents of both architects and their clients broadened. With new advances in archaeology, knowledge of antiquity and of its breadth of forms of architectural expression expanded. And, as all this was happening, the diversity of architectural clients exploded from the narrow world of the court and church to politicians, civil servants, new institutions, and private citizens.

From this came a flowering of architectural expression that included

the metal structures of Baltard, the Greek-inspired iconoclastic classicism of Hittorff, the intellectually rigorous modernism of Viollet-le-Duc,
the rational elegance of Labrouste, the classically inspired exuberance of
Garnier, the grand institutional classicism of Lefuel and Duc, and the
more restrained and urbane neoclassicism of Davioud, among others.

The architects who designed and supervised the building activity of
Second Empire Paris were themselves extremely varied in origin and in
character. But the role they were able to play was, in all cases, under-
pinned by a formalized training system for architects in France, a firmly
established environment of high cultural standards, and a profession
structured to support the design and building of major public buildings.
The Ecole des Beaux-Arts played the central role in this system, preparing aspiring architects through a pedagogy structured around the Prix
de Rome, which was awarded in the spring of each year.

The role of architects in public administrations was equally important. For many years architects had been attached to the Crown in order
to assume responsibility for the building, expansion, and maintenance
of royal properties. Although the exact form of these positions changed
with the political vicissitudes after the Revolution, the idea of a corps of
architects primarily attached to major public buildings continued. The
city of Paris followed the same model: When Haussmann became prefect, he was presented with a flock of architects now reporting to him,
including a number of winners of the Prix de Rome.

Haussmann typically had turbulent relationships with architects. He
believed he understood matters better than they did, and he genuinely
did not grasp that the process of drafting and resolving design problems,
far from being a subordinate task of execution, is core to architectural
design. It is no accident that he most appreciated architects, like Davioud,
who would pose no challenge to his ego, and he was utterly incapable of
working with those, such as Hittorff, who were willing to stand up for
the value of their profession.

Haussmann was profoundly hurt and never forgave the fact that Victor

Baltard voted against his election to the Académie des Beaux-Arts on December 7, 1867. Baltard, a lucid, logical spirit who, as a professor at the Ecole des Beaux-Arts, played an important role in the profession by that time, knew that, whatever Haussmann's other qualities, he did not have a developed artistic sensitivity and simply did not understand the craft of the architect. On that basis, it was impossible to give Haussmann his vote. Haussmann was elected nonetheless.

Thirteen

·————·

AN EXPANDED CAPITAL AND
A NEW MONUMENT

Every day, in the dark hours of early morning, the *maraichers,* growers of fresh produce, converged on Paris, traveling in horse-drawn carts and pushing handcarts. They arrived at the entry points to the city and waited in line to pay the *octroi,* the tax for bringing goods into Paris.

Louis XIV had had the city walls of Paris pulled down in the seventeenth century. But since 1782, there had been a new wall—really more of a fence—built around the city to prevent evasion of the *octroi.* That barrier, marked by the customs pavilions designed by Claude-Nicolas Ledoux, still formed the border of Paris in the 1850s.

The *octroi* collection points posed a real problem of convenience. Each time one wanted to reenter the city, one had to stop, queue for a time routinely as much as half an hour, and state whether or not one had anything to declare. Personal vehicles were usually not inspected, but the nuisance was still considerable. With the upgrading of the Bois de Boulogne and the creation of the avenue de l'Impératrice, fashionable people on their promenades constantly had to cross through the Etoile checkpoint, which was one of the busiest.

The urban areas growing outside these checkpoints had become a real concern to the administrators of Paris. François-Jules Devinck, the chocolate entrepreneur on the city council, summarized the sentiment: "[A]n industrial city, composed of eighteen distinct municipalities, has established itself as a dangerous belt around the capital, benefiting from its schools, its hospitals, its theaters, of all the advantages of its neighbor, without paying the *octroi* or contributing to the costs."[1]

Prefect Haussmann was also concerned about the development of the suburbs. The new workshops and factories sprouting up all around Paris paid no tax on their raw materials. No tax was paid on the building materials used for the construction of new buildings in the suburban zone. And the residents did not pay the *octroi* on what they consumed. Nevertheless, new roads, water-supply and sewers systems, and street lighting would need to be built in these fast-urbanizing areas.

Haussmann also had a more ideological concern. Like most of the city council members, he believed that the development of large-scale heavy industry, with all the unskilled workers it would attract, should not be encouraged in Paris or its vicinity. Subjecting an area to the *octroi,* thereby imposing an extra tax on fuel and raw materials, was a surefire way of eliminating heavy industry near Paris.

Since the 1840s, Paris had been surrounded by a massive new fortification situated between half a mile and a mile beyond the city limits, encompassing the city and its immediate suburbs. Moving the city limits to this new physical border made intuitive sense. In 1853, the Siméon commission had purposefully included the whole territory within the fortifications in its urban plan, stating, "[I]t is obvious that sooner or later these towns will be incorporated into Paris."[2]

Haussmann agreed, and he preferred for it to occur sooner rather than later. In 1856, he tried to start the annexation process. He called a subset of the city council together and presented his arguments. But the council members, with little appetite for a measure as unpopular as imposing the *octroi* on the suburbs, balked. Disappointed, Haussmann resigned himself to shelving the idea for the time being.

After the 180 Million Franc Treaty was signed, with the national government's contribution pared back to fifty million francs, Haussmann, who was still seeking to resolve the impossible dilemma of funding the *grands travaux,* returned to the idea that the only way to increase revenues without new taxes was to grow the tax base by physically expanding the city.

He went to the emperor and the new minister of the interior, the same Claude-Alphonse Delangle who until then had been president of the Paris City Council, and who had been against the annexation in that capacity. Haussmann made a well-reasoned case. In addition to being fair and logical, he said, expansion was the only way to secure funding for the infrastructure needed for the rapidly growing city.

Haussmann maneuvered astutely. He brought the issue up to the city council tentatively, saying that no action would be taken immediately. This was a ruse. In reality, the process moved forward at breakneck speed.

Once the idea became public, the inhabitants of the affected areas and their elected representatives clamored their opposition. Numerous industrial facilities had been established outside the city precisely because there was no *octroi.* As one deputy explained in the parliamentary debate, the fact that the peripheral area within the city was largely empty, while the area immediately outside the limits of the *octroi* was densely occupied, said everything one needed to know about the benefits of being outside rather than inside the city limits. Furthermore, expanding the city would not fundamentally solve the problem: It was easy to foresee that as soon as the new geographical limit for the *octroi* was set, new industrial activities would spring up just outside this zone.

Haussmann countered with arguments about the benefits of becoming part of Paris, namely the building of streets and provision of urban amenities of much higher quality. Despite the promises, the municipal councils of seven of the affected towns voted against the expansion plan. The public consultation yielded more than four thousand responses, the respondents either protesting against the plan or requesting changes. The government took little heed and continued to claim that the plan enjoyed massive popular support. One material concession was made to the businesses of the newly annexed territory: There would be a ten-year transition period, during which they would be exempt from the *octroi* on fuel.

The international environment helped Haussmann's cause. By the spring of 1859, France had sided with the king of Piedmont-Sardinia, and war with Austria seemed inevitable. The nation's attention was grabbed by the escalation of hostilities. The expansion of Paris was rushed through the Legislative Assembly and the Senate with only the briefest of debates. The Annexation Law was signed by Empress Eugénie, acting as regent while her husband was in Italy to supervise the theater of operations. The date for the expansion of Paris to the fortifications was set for January 1, 1860.

War broke out before summer. Napoléon III led the French army to victory at the Battle of Magenta and triumphantly entered Milan on June 7, 1859. The allied French and Piedmontese armies achieved another major victory at Solferino on June 24. But Napoléon III was prudent: Concerned by the prospect of getting ensnared in the conflict, he offered the Austrians an armistice.

On August 14, 1859, the eve of the national holiday, Napoléon III returned triumphant from the Italian campaign. Haussmann recalled the celebration:

> *I will never forget the truly triumphal entry of the Army into Paris, with the Emperor at its head . . . and the moving succession of flags and can-*

nons seized from the enemy, of prisoners captured on the battlefield. . . .
I had had bleachers placed all around the square [place Vendôme], in
which the Empress and her court, surrounded by the great dignitaries of
the Empire, took their places before the Ministry of Justice; and the repre-
sentatives of all the bodies of the State and other authorities on either side
in full costume; in the others the elite of Parisian society, fighting one
another for the best spots, and in front ladies in grand dress throwing
flowers to the soldiers. What a grand spectacle! What enthusiastic and
triumphal ovation! We were certainly at the apex of the Imperial Power.[3]

With the new year, the expansion of Paris went into effect. Overnight, the city grew from thirteen to thirty-three square miles and gained 400,000 new inhabitants, taking its population from 1.1 million to 1.5 million.

Thirteen towns outside the city limits had a portion of their territory consolidated into Paris. Eleven towns were dissolved and completely subsumed into Paris. Belleville, with a population of 55,000, was the largest of these, followed by les Batignolles-Monceau (44,000 inhabitants) and Montmartre (33,000 inhabitants). The others were Auteuil, Passy, La Chapelle, La Villette, Charonne, Bercy, Vaugirard, and Grenelle.

Haussmann described the annexed area as "a compact belt of suburbs built at random, covered by an inextricable network of narrow and tortuous roads, of alleys and dead ends where nomadic populations with no real connection to the land accumulate with prodigious speed and without efficient monitoring."[4] But in reality, the annexed territory was extremely diverse, and despite the urbanization of the Second Empire and after, these areas retain their distinctive character. These villages hidden away inside Paris, with their picturesque side streets and charming relics, continue as a source of great delight for Parisians today.

The best-known example is Montmartre, which has in certain places retained the character of a village center on a hill overlooking, and separated from, Paris. Auteuil and Montrouge were also massed little villages, although without the same striking topography. In Vaugirard and Charonne, the street layout is still as established by the seventeenth-century gardens, vegetable patches, vineyards, and rural domains of the nobility. La Villette was similar, with many hostelries along the two major roads that crossed it, but it was transformed early in the nineteenth century, when the canal was built, bringing early industrial installations. Les Batignolles, Javel, and Bercy had all also developed significant industrial facilities by the 1860s. On the heights to the northeast, Belleville was popular for establishments serving wine and stewed rabbit and for its festivities. It was only later that it grew into the populous bastion of the French working class. Other areas within the new city limits remained completely undeveloped. The whole twentieth arrondissement was a "veritable Parisian Siberia," the place du Trône (today's place de la Nation) surrounded by vacant lots.[5]

A new arrondissement structure—the one still in force today—was established at that time. The twelve oddly shaped arrondissements that existed prior to 1860 were replaced by twenty compact arrondissements fanning out clockwise from the center—the perfect structure for a rationally administered modern city.

The expansion presented the opportunity to dismantle the Fermiers généraux wall, including the pavilions built by Claude-Nicolas Ledoux at each of the checkpoints. Four of these pavilions remain today, at place Denfert-Rochereau, place de la Nation, place Stalingrad, and place de la République Dominicaine, at the entrance to the parc Monceau.

In 1853, when the property of former king Louis-Philippe and his family was confiscated by the French state, a sizable estate northwest of Paris was among the assets to be turned over. The ownership status was, however, legally complex, a situation resolved with the help of the Pereire brothers.

Their help was, as one might suspect, not a matter of philanthropy. The Pereires had been interested in the area since the opening of their train line into the gare Saint-Lazare in 1837. By 1853, they had developed avenues on either side of the tracks, creating a boulevard that now bears their name. They and other speculators avidly bought land in the vicinity of the former royal property—the future parc Monceau—and devised all sorts of development plans. The incorporation of the entire area into Paris was the long-awaited opportunity to move the development plans into the operational phase.

In 1860, the city of Paris signed a far-reaching agreement with the Pereire brothers. The city agreed to sell two-thirds of the former park to the Pereires for development. In exchange, the Pereires and the other landowners would give the city the land needed for a set of new avenues through the neighborhood: boulevard Malesherbes, avenue de Villiers, avenue de Wagram, place Wagram, and place Pereire. The city had already decided to inflect the boulevard Malesherbes so that it ran right along the new development, providing a stylish artery straight from the city center to the new neighborhood. The city would also, of course, build the park itself. This was a notable example of public-private urban development long before it became theorized and rediscovered in recent decades.

The transaction allowed the development of a large new urban area, overcoming the complications of multiple property owners and without capital outlay by the city. But it was negotiated directly between the city and the Pereires without transparency, oversight, or due process. This way of conducting business could only arouse suspicion, especially in the fast and loose times of the Second Empire.

By now, Haussmann had many detractors among the opponents of the imperial regime. But the prefect's most powerful enemy was within the Second Empire governing elite. His name was Achille Fould.

Fould was not one of the idealistic, modernizing members of the

Second Empire cadre, such as Victor Persigny, Emile and Isaac Pereire, and Napoléon III himself, who all had been raised with Saint-Simonian* and Bonapartist ideas. On the contrary, Fould was conservative with respect to both his ideology and temperament, a supporter of the July Monarchy closely aligned with conservative interests, such as those of James de Rothschild.

Fould was an elegant man, with rich dark hair parted on the side and a thin chin-strap beard. His features were coarse but attractive; he had thick, expressive lips and a nose that looked like those of a roughly modeled clay sculpture. He was Jewish, like his exact contemporary Emile Pereire, but came from the opposite end of the social spectrum: He had grown up in a posh part of Paris and, as the son of a prominent banker, had attended the best schools. While his older brother took responsibilities in the family bank, Achille entered politics, becoming a deputy in 1842. In 1848, he joined Adolphe Thiers in supporting Louis-Napoléon's presidential campaign. Fould gradually gained the president's confidence, and in 1849, Louis-Napoléon appointed him minister of finance.

After the Second Empire was established in late 1852, Fould rose to become the most important person in the regime after the emperor. He had a steady hand in financial affairs, always able to reassure the banking community and ensure the success of government bond issues. Fould became indispensable to Napoléon III and his influence gradually extended to every area of policy. He eventually moved to the position of minister of state, with a broad portfolio of responsibilities that included theaters, museums, libraries, and archives—it was in this capacity that he had authority over the Louvre expansion.

Fould was no proponent of Persigny's theory of "productive expenditures." On the contrary, his view was that the government was spending far beyond its means. Unable to substantially curb the emperor's

---

* The current of political and social thought inspired by the ideas of the count de Saint-Simon.

spending, Fould nevertheless tried to limit the number of generously remunerated free riders and vocally opposed what he saw as unnecessary projects, foremost among which was the rebuilding of Paris. Naturally, this made him the sworn enemy of Haussmann, Persigny, and another powerful Second Empire figure, Count Alexander Walewski.

Count Walewksi was, on the surface, a Polish-Italian nobleman who had spent his life in France. But, as everyone in Paris knew, he was in reality a great deal more than that.

In 1806, Napoléon I had spent some time in Warsaw, where he met a beautiful Polish countess named Marie Walewska. He pursued the countess and they began an affair, which in May 1810 produced a son. Although it would not become relevant for many years, the young Count Alexandre Walewski was therefore the biological cousin of another boy growing up in a different part of Europe, Louis-Napoléon Bonaparte.

Walewski escaped Russian-occupied Poland at the age of fourteen and moved to France, where he undertook a military career, wrote some not very successful plays, took part in various diplomatic intrigues, and tried his hand at politics. Most of all, he became a central character in the worldly Parisian life of the July Monarchy, achieving distinction as a founding member of the infamous Jockey Club in 1832 and later as lover of the famous actress Rachel.

In 1846, with the help of Adolphe Thiers, Walewski found his professional calling: diplomacy. He became the French ambassador in Florence, followed by postings in Buenos Aires, Florence again, Naples, and London. In May 1855, Waleski was appointed minister of foreign affairs, a role that allowed him to preside over the treaty that ended the Crimean War. Walewski may not have had the brilliant intellect of other top cadres of the Second Empire, but he was reasonable and dependable. And, unlike Morny, he did not constantly get caught up in shady financial schemes.

In 1860, Walewski found himself without a role. He coveted Fould's position of minister of state and the residence in the Palais du Louvre that came with it. Walewski's wife had an even more ardent desire for these comforts, and, as the court was well aware, the beautiful Countess Walewska had a very special form of access to the emperor. In the words of Prosper Mérimée: "For some time, our friend [Fould] was disliked because he held the purse strings tighter than those who liked to pick in the purse would have liked. A beautiful lady who, it is said, has already picked a great deal, wanted for her husband the place of our friend. Since she often had her hand in a place where one does not encounter resistance, she ended up having her way."[6]

At the council meeting of November 22, 1860, Napoléon III stunned his ministers by announcing the appointment of Walewski as minister of state, together with measures to allow for more meaningful parliamentary debate. He offered Fould the position of minister of finance, but Fould stormed off, piqued as much by his sacrifice to Walewski as he was upset by the concessions to parliamentarism. Fould retired to his home in Tarbes, at the foot of the Pyrénées. He was bitter and depressed. It appeared his career was over.

The changes of November 22, 1860, were a victory for the "productive expenditures" camp. Persigny and Walewski returned to the government, and Morny, to whom Napoléon III had offered a ministerial position, stayed on in the critical role of president of the Legislative Assembly, his position reinforced.

This situation presented the perfect opportunity for Haussmann to clarify his status. He was, on paper, subordinate to the minister of the interior. In practice, however, he went directly to the emperor whenever he felt it necessary, something the ministers of the Interior and their respective staffs did not appreciate in the least. When he was minister of the interior, Adolphe Billault had once formally called Haussmann to order on this point, but Napoléon III had ignored the complaint.

Haussmann had grown impatient with the need to constantly seek approvals from those he called the "bureaucratic pygmies" of the Ministry of the Interior when his programs already had the direct support of the emperor. He therefore presented the emperor with a proposal that would have made him minister for Paris, and threatened to resign if it was not accepted, whatever the consequences on the transformation of Paris, which was now in full swing.

Napoléon III was prepared to accept the request, but the ministers were vociferous in their opposition. What was unacceptable to them was that having a minister for Paris would imply that their own authority did not apply to the capital city. A compromise was finally reached, giving Haussmann increased delegated authority and allowing him to attend the council of ministers, but stopping short of giving him the title or rank of minister. It was not quite what Haussmann had hoped for, but he proclaimed himself satisfied nevertheless. Although he continued nominally to report to the minister of the interior, in practice he was accountable to no one but the emperor.

Haussmann later also gained the right to attend meetings of the state council whenever matters of the city of Paris were discussed. Together with his positions as senator and quasi-minister, this allowed him to be present in every major decision-making forum except the Legislative Assembly. Whenever the matters of the city of Paris came up in any of these, Haussmann was an impassioned and unabashedly partisan advocate for his own cause.

With his power solidly established, Haussmann decided to adorn himself with a title. His maternal grandfather, Georges Dentzel, the former governor of Vienna, had been made baron by virtue of his service to France under Napoléon I, but the title had fallen in disuse since the death of Dentzel's son. Haussmann decided to claim it. So although he was by no means of noble extraction and his claim to the barony was dubious, he became, from then on, Baron Haussmann. In December 1862, Napoléon III granted Haussmann yet another distinction, making him a Grand Cross of the Legion of Honor. These honorifics meant a great deal to Haussmann, who would continue collecting titles of purely ceremonial orders, from Sweden to the Ottoman Empire, for the rest of his life.

Prefect Haussmann entertained lavishly, maintained a luxurious household, and, through his wife, gave generously to philanthropic causes. His status was reflected in his two official residences: the prefect's apartment in the Hôtel de Ville and the Château de Longchamp in the Bois de Boulogne, which Haussmann used as a weekend retreat and to entertain in the summer months. In 1861, after the death of his father-in-law, Haussmann also inherited a fine property outside Bordeaux, the Château de Cestas, in addition to the country property he already owned in the Lot-et-Garonne. With power, titles, and fine properties, the prefect of the Seine had gathered all the trappings of Second Empire success.

What began as Napoléon III's favor to a mistress, appointing her husband to the coveted position of minister of state, turned out to have consequences in an area that one could have presumed to be unconnected to ministerial politics and, even more so, to the goings-on in the emperor's bedroom: the building of a new opera house for Paris. And yet, it would lead to an abrupt change of events, with, it is fair to say, considerable repercussions on architectural history.

The development of the place du Châtelet had provided Paris with two large modern theaters. But the greatest institution dedicated to lyrical art, the Académie Impériale de Musique—the official name of the Opéra de Paris—was still housed in a temporary structure in the rue Le Peletier, built in 1821 after the destruction by fire of the previous opera house.

The building of a permanent opera house was a long, slow process. By 1847, Prefect Rambuteau had selected the site, on the east side of the place du Palais-Royal, between the Louvre and the Palais-Royal. The opera house would accompany the extension of the rue de Rivoli, along with the new north side of the Louvre, contributing to the revitalization of the city center. But this scheme was not to be, for the revolution of 1848 cut Rambuteau's tenure short. When the rue de Rivoli extension was built a few years later, the new opera house was no longer part of the plan. The site Rambuteau had intended was instead used for the Grand Hôtel du Louvre.

Charles Rohault de Fleury, one of the most well-known Parisian architects, had been appointed as the Opéra's official architect in 1846. Since that time, he had conducted many studies of various sites around Paris for the new building. Other architects, also vying for the chance to build the Opéra, did the same. For a while, the idea of building on the place de la Concorde seemed to be in favor. There was another plan to build on the boulevard des Italiens, near the site of where the Le Peletier opera house stood, with a grand new north-south avenue connecting it to the square we now know as place André Malraux, at the bottom of today's avenue de l'Opéra.[7]

Later, Rohault de Fleury began promoting a new site, the one where the building would eventually be built. It was located off the boulevard des Capucines, right at the spot where the new street leading to the city center from the gare Saint-Lazare reached the Grands Boulevards. A decree for an extension of this street, the avenue Napoléon, which would form a connection onward to the Louvre, had been published on May 3, 1854. The convergence of streets at the proposed site created an awkward layout, one that a new monument could help to resolve. Most important, there was land available to build a big opera house and a whole neighborhood around it.

The Orsini attack on the life of the emperor in 1858 gave new urgency to the building of a new opera house. It reminded everyone that the structure in rue Le Peletier, notwithstanding the fact that it was supposed to be temporary, had been in service for more than thirty years and was inadequate in many ways, not least in ensuring the security of important guests. Rohault de Fleury produced multiple designs of potential layouts for the new site on the boulevard des Capucines, and gradually he gained the support of Achille Fould, the minister who had responsibility for the Opéra, as well as of Prefect Haussmann.

The Pereire brothers had started buying land in the area in 1853. In 1859, they expanded their company and bought up more property around the future place de l'Opéra, well before the layout of the square and its designation as the site of the new opera house were publicly known. The two brothers, playing real-life Monopoly in Second Empire Paris, began the construction of another hotel, the Grand Hôtel de la Paix, even larger than their previous Grand Hôtel du Louvre. This hotel, which opened in 1862 and was again designed by the Pereires' architect, Alfred Armand, had eight hundred rooms and all sorts of amenities, including electric lighting and one of the world's first hydraulic elevators.

An imperial decree dated September 29, 1860, made it official: The new opera house would be built as the centerpiece of an urban composition at the top of the avenue Napoléon, at the crossing of the boulevard des Capucines. Charles Rohault de Fleury prepared the design for the crowning work of his career, the large-scale project that would ensure his fame for future generations. The city also commissioned Rohault de Fleury to design the facades of the other buildings on the square, so as to compose a harmonious ensemble.

In November 1860, only two months after the publication of the decree establishing the site of the new opera house, Rohault de Fleury was ready with his design for the new building. His Opéra had a central body with curved wings on either side. It was a grand composition, in the great French tradition of theater design.

But that same month, Rohault de Fleury's dream of going down in history as the architect of the Opéra was to meet its cruel fate. Achille Fould, the minister of state with whom Rohault de Fleury had been working on the new opera house, was replaced by Count Walewksi. The story of the Opéra was about to take a major unexpected turn.

Now responsible for the project for the new Opéra, Walewski was aware of several designs competing with Rohault de Fleury's. He was also under pressure to give the commission to the architect favored by the empress, Eugène Viollet-le-Duc. Walewski halted the growing polemic and relieved himself of the burden of this decision by taking the unusual step of launching a competition for the design of the coveted project. It was through this process that an unknown young Parisian architectural genius emerged to the world: Charles Garnier.

Charles Garnier came from a working-class family living in the rue Mouffetard; his father was a blacksmith and his mother a lace maker. His parents gave him a basic education and allowed him to take drawing classes. At fifteen, he started working for an architect, and when that studio closed, he was accepted in the studio of Hippolyte Lebas, one of the most reputed architects in the city. In 1842, at the age of seventeen, Garnier was admitted to the Ecole des Beaux-Arts. His artistic vocation was clear to him; as he later said upon seeing the Parthenon for the first time, "There is no hesitation to be had between the arts. One must be God, or else an architect."[8]

Garnier first entered the Prix de Rome competition in 1847, but he did not win the coveted prize. The following year, with all of Paris upside down in turmoil because of the revolution, Garnier competed again, working on the program for a "National Conservatory for Arts and Sciences." His cleverly articulated design, with the large, finely executed renderings that were de rigueur, won the first prize, earning Garnier a much sought-after fellowship at the Villa Medici in Rome. He immediately left to study the architecture of ancient Rome and Greece, sending exquisite submissions back to Paris.

When Garnier next set foot in Paris, in 1853, it was a very different place. There was now an emperor and ambitious new construction projects under way in the center of the city. Despite this, Garnier, even with his Grand Prix de Rome and his talent, was unable to gain commissions.

He had health problems, including a bout of depression, and ended up working for the city of Paris on menial projects. He designed an apartment building on the boulevard de Sébastopol for a speculator. Some days, he believed he would achieve great things; other days, he was without hope. He waited for an opportunity worthy of his talent and ambition to present itself.

On December 29, 1860, as most people were preparing to celebrate the New Year, the announcement of the Opéra competition was made. The deadline to submit the *esquisse,* or sketch, was impossibly short, barely over a month. This did not bother Garnier, who was accustomed to swift design and intense drafting. He threw himself headlong into the *charrette*—the word architects used to describe an all-out sprint to produce a set of drawings—even though he knew his chance of winning was negligible.

In early February, 171 designs were submitted for the Opéra competition. The jury chose five finalists. To general surprise, neither Rohault de Fleury nor Viollet-le-Duc were included. The only famous architect among the five was Joseph-Louis Duc, who withdrew because at the time he was in charge of the important works on the Palais de Justice in the Ile de la Cité. Three of the remaining architects were in their mid-thirties: Garnier, his good friend Léon Ginain, who had won the Grand Prix de Rome in 1852, and Alphonse-Nicolas Crépinet. The jury, composed of illustrious architects determined to put the architectural quality of designs above issues of affinity, notoriety, or nepotism, had virtually ensured that the most prestigious architectural commission of the era would be granted to an architect who was not yet well established.

Garnier's project was ranked last of the five. He suggested to Ginain, who had come in first, that they combine their efforts, but Ginain turned him down. So Garnier reworked his project to improve it as much as he could in the little time he had.

The final submissions were received and the members of the jury reviewed, analyzed, and discussed the projects. On May 29, they were ready to announce their decision.

That morning, Garnier received a visit from Alphonse de Gisors, one of the members of the jury. Gisors told Garnier the conclusion the jury had reached: "You considerably improved your project, whereas Ginain weakened his. Your plan is remarkable in its simplicity, clarity, logic and grandeur. The jury admired the design in three distinct parts: public foyer, hall and stage, as well as the outer loggia, the staircase, the originality of the façade, and especially the side façades."[9] He gave the young man the news that he had dreamed of hearing: Garnier had been selected to built the new home of the Opéra de Paris.

Garnier had an unforgettable physical appearance: a strangely shaped head with more of a beak than a nose, leathery skin, dreamy, inquisitive eyes, a wispy down-turned mustache with a *mouche*,* and a canopy of wild brown hair that seemed as if it had never once received the services of a barber.

Garnier smoked incessantly. He loved the witty company of architects and other artists and, was an exuberant participant in the cultural life and pleasures of Paris, often leading his friends in ribald songs around the dinner table late at night. He was a gifted writer, who composed many impertinent ditties and several plays. But along with periods of prodigious productivity, he also had spells of lethargy and depression. He became the most famous architect in France, a figure so often drawn and painted that he was recognized in the street. He was the prototype of the Romantic artist.

After winning the competition, Garnier immediately established a

---

* What would be known today as a "soul patch."

studio and threw himself into the design of the Opéra. He hired a team of nine architects and draftsmen and had a temporary structure built right on the construction site, with a balcony allowing him and his staff to observe the progress firsthand. Inside the studio, he set up long drawing tables and decorated the walls with bits of classical ornament. This became the heart and soul of the site, visited over the years by many distinguished people, including both the emperor and the empress.

Garnier was a warm and generous man. He showed concern for his employees, staying abreast of their personal issues and helping them resolve them. Although he was unmistakably in charge, his studio had a collegial atmosphere. Rather than issue instructions, Garnier preferred to talk through challenges, using his intuition and rapid intellect to help a collaborator reach the best solution. He could be difficult to work with, because his mind moved quickly and he always expected his collaborators to understand what he was thinking, even if he had not yet explained it. Nevertheless, the studio was permeated by a spirit of friendship and intellectual energy.

Day after day, in the little wooden structure, through sketch after drawing after model, the plan for the new Opéra began to come together, while, around it, the excavations began.

Fourteen

AN EMBATTLED PREFECT

On Tuesday, August 13, 1861, the day of the opening of the boulevard Malesherbes, the official government newspaper, *Le Moniteur*, proclaimed that the new artery "belongs to this vast set of useful works that is not the least of the titles of the Emperor's government to public gratitude."[1] In reality, the transformation of Paris had become considerably more controversial than at any time in the past.

The creation of the boulevard Malesherbes was not a new idea. It had originally been decreed in 1808 by Napoléon I as part of an urban composition surrounding the église de la Madeleine, but even though a plan was eventually laid out, construction had never begun. In 1852, the plan was resurrected in order to "improve the flow of traffic, which has had a tendency to increase, between the rich and much-frequented area around the Madeleine and the Monceau barrier."[2] Implementation was, however, immediately suspended while the city focused on the preparation of the 1855 Universal Exposition. It was resumed after the conclusion of the 180 Million Franc Treaty and was ready to receive traffic by the summer of 1861.

Nearly a mile in length, the boulevard Malesherbes created a new connection from the center of the city to the outlying area of Monceau, now in the midst of development. It had entailed the removal of a hill occupied by miserable hovels, the infamous Petite-Pologne. At the same time, it crossed some of Paris's poshest streets, the rue de la Ville-l'Evêque, the rue Lavoisier, and the rue de Rumfort. For the first time, the *grands travaux* affected the richest of Parisians.

In the weeks before the boulevard's inauguration, there had been a vigorous polemic about the new street. The press noted that the street, "which only twenty years ago would have cost little, has become extremely expensive as it must use land now occupied by elegant and comfortable buildings."[3] But the real issue involved more than the cost. In effect, the city was expropriating old aristocratic families of the Saint-Honoré neighborhood and demolishing their *hôtels particuliers* in order to allow the Pereire brothers and their newly moneyed associates to reap huge profits by developing the Monceau plain at the far end of the boulevard. The wealthy inhabitants of the affected area were unhappy and made themselves heard. Haussmann noted that, while the overturning of neighborhoods full of working-class homes, stores, and workshops for the rue de Rivoli and the boulevard de Sébastopol had gone without major complaint, "this year, when we needed to only disturb the habits of people privileged by fortune . . . we received language of unprecedented violence."[4]

The timing was right for a polemic. In June and July of 1861, the talk of the town had been the arrest and trial of Jules Mirès, a Second Empire banker accused of financial misdeeds. It was a surprising development, because Mirès, who also came from Bordeaux's community of Portuguese Jews and had been an associate of the Pereire brothers, owned two newspapers that were unfailing vehicles of government propaganda and was thought to be protected by the regime. The word on the street was that the "Mirès affair" involved payments to senior officials and members of the Bonaparte family and that the full truth would never be known. It was the first time that someone close to the regime had been officially accused of corruption.

Mirès was indicted, together with a senior government official, Count Henri de Siméon—the same Count Siméon who had led the commission on the planning of Paris back in 1853. The trial was full of dramatic twists, but in the end both Mirès and Siméon were pardoned. Around the same time, Charles-Auguste de Morny, whose reputation for dubious dealings was universally known, received the title of duke. All this gave the impression that the emperor was condoning, if not encouraging, rampant corruption among those in his entourage.

Because of Mirès's involvement in real estate projects and his past association with the Pereires, his tribulations inevitably led to questions about the real estate dealings of the city of Paris and the role of the ubiquitous Pereire brothers, who were providing funds to the city, closing transactions on behalf of the city, developing the city's land, and even running the buses. It seemed the Pereires were involved in everything the city of Paris was doing.

The suspicions against bankers were fueled by the brazen display of their wealth. The Pereires had a magnificent *hôtel particulier* at 35, rue du Faubourg Saint-Honoré, today the offices of the embassy of the United Kingdom. They surrounded themselves with the finest works of art in a luxurious decor. In the words of one guest, "[g]old streams through, the chandeliers blaze, the carpets are as thick as the moss of the woods."[5]

Prefect Haussmann was, of course, at the center of the suspicions. Known to be close to the Pereires and Morny, he was associated by public opinion with the environment of easy money and insider deals. In a world where unscrupulous profits, heady speculation, and graft were the norm, one would have to be quite credulous, the thinking went, to believe that the projects of the city of Paris, all concluded behind closed doors, were any different.

The attacks in the press were such that a Saint-Simonian writer, with a patina of impartiality from having opposed the coup d'état and gone into exile, was drafted to publish a pamphlet defending both the administration of the prefect of the Seine and the Pereires' Compagnie Immobilière de Paris. The essay, repeating many of the official arguments concerning the *grands travaux,* asserted:

> *All the actions of the Seine Prefecture were legal. They were subject to legal and administrative control by French institutions that present such a perfect model that they are everywhere the object of admiration and even imitation.*
>
> *The Compagnie Immobilière is not a monopoly. It owes the position it occupies to the use it was able to make of its liberty and its capital. . . . The company has conducted its work so as to justify the success it has achieved: it deserves encouragement and cooperation, instead of the attacks it has been receiving.*[6]

It is safe to bet that not a soul was convinced by this transparent exercise in propaganda.

The ceremony for the inauguration of the boulevard Malesherbes was another opportunity for large-scale self-congratulation. Napoléon III, wearing the uniform of a general of the French army and riding in an open calèche, descended the newly completed boulevard, which was festooned with Venetian masts and decorated with small trees, a row of soldiers standing at attention on either side. In the tent set up for the event, filled with dignitaries, the speeches rang triumphant. But there was also a great deal of self-justification and, from time to time, indignation. The champions of the *grands travaux* were on the defensive.

Haussmann spoke first. He reminded the audience of the fifty-year history of the project for the boulevard Malesherbes. He brought up the seventeen fine houses built in the way of the boulevard in the last decades in order to, characteristically, place the blame on the earlier administrations, which had allowed them to be built, rather than on his administration, which had demolished them. Still, he explained, these demolitions were a small sacrifice in comparison to the benefits brought by all the new buildings to be erected along the new boulevard and the development of the Monceau plain, "not a new neighborhood, [but] a new city that is being founded."[7] He underlined the sacrifices that Parisians were making all across the city, in the east, south, and west; "In all directions, the exuberant population of Paris will soon find new neighborhoods, larger than many cities, and will be able to spread itself among them according to its need and taste."[8]

Haussmann addressed another persistent criticism: that he was building only for the richest classes. Yes, he conceded, "on the high-priced land along the main thoroughfares that everyone visits we see only houses of this type." But the fact that they were being built in such numbers by private developers meant that there was demand: "[L]uxury houses will certainly stop going up as soon as it is true that the city has enough of them."[9]

Haussmann accused his detractors of not going to see for themselves the areas where the new homes for the working class were being built. He presented statistics of houses built and rental prices. He could not argue against the increase in rental prices, but he asserted: "[T]he campaign of public works for Paris, far from having caused the high rents of which the population complains, had and continues to have the effect of tempering the increase in rents by stimulating construction in many places and by generating a competition that cannot fail, in the end, to turn to the advantage of tenants."[10]

Haussmann then turned to yet another front of the attacks, the allegation that he was bringing the city of Paris to financial ruin. For someone with such a love of numbers, it is striking that he gave no information regarding the overall cost of the *grands travaux* or the amount of funding secured. He limited himself to generalities, reassuring the audience that the city's accounts were sound and properly managed. He gave some irrelevant figures from the previous year's budget and, to ward off rumors of insolvency, defiantly divulged that, at the moment he was speaking, the city had a positive balance of thirty million francs on its account with the treasury.

Haussmann concluded his speech with a vintage piece of grandiloquent Second Empire pandering:

> *The supreme praise we can confer upon the nephew of Caesar [that is to say, the Emperor Augustus] is to have embellished the seat of the Empire. . . . Our descendants, who will gather the fruits of Your Majesty's constant solicitude for matters regarding Paris, will note that, in our country as well, the nephew of Caesar [referring here to Napoléon III, nephew of the "modern-day Caesar"] renewed the Imperial city, but primarily to increase the well-being of his subjects, and by his perseverance in this laborious enterprise . . . Your Majesty has earned the merit of our time and of posterity.*[11]

The object of such ear-ringing sycophancy climbed to the dais next. Napoléon III declared that "the opening of yet another avenue is no longer remarkable today." He explained that he would not have held a ceremony were it not to publicly support the work of the city council and the prefect of the Seine. He acknowledged the controversy: "The improvements to the capital, once finished, will cause admiration; but during their execution, they generate criticisms and complaints. That is because it is impossible, in this type of undertaking, not to harm certain interests. The role of the administration is to manage the interests, without deviating from the way forward."[12]

Haussmann was pleased at what he heard, a public testimony of support and encouragement for the transformation of Paris. Unfortunately, the speech was about to take a turn that would be much less agreeable to the prefect.

Napoléon III turned to the situation of Paris's poor. He commended the city for the measures taken to decrease the cost of water, to reduce rental taxes on the poorest households, and to limit price increases for bread and meat. He noted the creation of churches, schools, and public health facilities throughout the city. But more needed to be done. He expressed his desire that the city "decrease, as much as the finances will allow, taxes on goods of first necessity."

Haussmann was dismayed. He had explained to the emperor how much the city's tax revenue was needed to fund the transformation of Paris. He had tried to convince him that the least to be expected was that Parisian citizens pay something for the tremendous improvements they were already benefiting from. He had also presented technical arguments: Since the *octroi* was a fixed amount per item, not adjusted for inflation, the tax was already, in effect, decreasing each year. He had explained that the taxes collected by the national government had increased dramatically thanks to the growth of Paris but that this money was not being shared with the city to reinvest in Paris. All this had fallen on deaf ears. By making this statement publicly, Napoléon III was signifying to Haussmann that there would be no further discussion on the subject. Haussmann was being instructed to cease debate and comply.

Haussmann had already found it difficult to finance the projects for Paris without the new taxes he had proposed. He had struggled mightily to secure funds from the central government and had even resorted to unorthodox financing mechanisms that required all the creativity of his financier friends. The mandate to decrease taxes on Parisians would make the impossible equation he was facing even worse.

The evening of the inauguration ceremony was the opportunity for Parisians to discover the new boulevard Malesherbes and the parc Monceau.

Although there were only sparse buildings along the boulevard, the first structures aroused enthusiasm. "Who would have suspected that two rows of houses, decorated with colonnades of encrusted marble and sculptures, would arise as if by magic above the eddies of dust and heaps of rubble that passersby observed with curiosity from the place de la Madeleine to the rue de la Pépinière?"[13] The boulevard Malesherbes instantaneously became a prestigious Paris address.

At the midpoint of the boulevard, there was a construction site, only barely begun by the time of the inauguration. It was for the new église Saint-Augustin, located at the point where the direction of the boulevard changed. For this job, Haussmann had chosen Victor Baltard, the architect of Les Halles, who had done work on many of Paris's churches. Placing the église Saint-Augustin on the small and oddly shaped site so that the dome would be in the axis of both boulevard Malesherbes and avenue Friedland was a tricky task for Baltard, but he achieved a significant work of architecture, notable for its elaborate and refined metal structure, invisible from the outside.

The highlight of the inaugural evening was, incontestably, the parc Monceau, brightly lit and decorated for the occasion. After passing through the elegant wrought-iron gates of the park, one was immersed in a delicate world of vegetation, unlike anything that existed in the city. Wide paths ambled between lush lawns, without even a hint of the strict order of the French style of garden design. Exotic plants and flowers abounded, artfully arranged in the topography. A pond led to a romantic colonnade, the imagined relic of the world of an ancient poet. A little farther on, there was a small pedestrian bridge, a cave, and a little waterfall. The whole space contained pavilions and furnishings in the finest contemporary taste.

The park was the pride of Adolphe Alphand, the head of the Department of Parks and Promenades, and his architect, Gabriel Davioud, who was responsible for the various pavilions, railings, and other architectural details. The parc Monceau was hailed as the greatest achievement yet of the Haussmann administration. It was the precise embodiment of how elite Second Empire society wanted to see itself.

. . .

As Haussmann had said in his speech, construction was indeed under way on all sides of Paris. In particular, the *grands travaux* were in the process of comprehensively restructuring some of the city's most historic neighborhoods on the Left Bank.

Just south of the Ile de la Cité, occupying a dense territory less than a mile long and about half a mile wide, lies the Latin Quarter. Around the numerous religious institutions and the University of Paris, the Latin Quarter provided a fertile intellectual environment. It was here, for example, that the eighteenth-century philosopher Denis Diderot lived most of his life, editing the *Encyclopédie* and drinking away many a night in the neighborhood taverns with his friends Friedrich Melchior Grimm and Jean-Jacques Rousseau. A veritable world unto itself, the Latin Quarter had established equally rich traditions in weighty matters of learning and in much lighter affairs of unbridled student revelry.

By the early 1860s, the projects of the Haussmann administration had begun to overturn this quaint world forever. The boulevard Saint-Michel plowed its broad furrow through the neighborhood north to south, erasing dozens of historic streets from the map. The boulevard Saint-Germain began to run perpendicular, starting from the east. The orderly layout of broad arteries and well-aligned modern apartment buildings replaced the urban fabric of narrow medieval streets and densely packed houses, irremediably destroying the character of the historic Latin Quarter.

Although some bitterly decried the brutal wholesale destruction of Paris's past, it was an almost anecdotal aspect of the Left Bank works that caused the most political strife for Haussmann. As part of his plan for the boulevard Saint-Michel, Haussmann wanted to lop off a small section of the Jardin du Luxembourg and redirect the rue de Médicis. Assuredly, this was a fairly minor transgression in the context of the mass destruction under way, but it became a major issue because it affected the official residences attached to the Palais du Luxembourg, seat of the Senate.

Suddenly, Haussmann was embroiled in a bitter battle with the leaders of the Senate, who were determined to defend the material comforts associated with their positions. The issue actually came up for discussion before the Senate in plenary session and the emperor himself was asked to arbitrate. Although Haussmann got most of what he wanted, the episode consolidated the dislike of the prefect among a faction of senators, who were prepared to act against him as soon as they were given the opportunity. The opportunity was, in fact, rapidly approaching.

In September 1861, Achille Fould, the former minister of finance, still in his self-imposed retreat in Tarbes, broke his silence. He sent the emperor a lengthy memorandum entitled "On the State of the Finances." It was, in summary, a comprehensive indictment of the Empire's financial policy.

> In reviewing the financial situation, it is easy to foresee that unless a significant change is made, we will find ourselves before serious difficulties. Public debt and the Treasury overdraft have both increased considerably. To cover the expenditures, credit in all its forms has been resorted to and the resources of special institutions under state jurisdiction have been used.
>
> . . .
>
> During the last discussion of the budget, it was concluded that the national debt is likely to reach, by the end of the year, close to one billion francs, a number that is certainly not exaggerated. The Legislative Assembly and the Senate have already expressed their concerns on this subject. That sentiment has penetrated business circles, which foresee a crisis that will be all the greater because the local governments and private companies, following the example of the national government, perhaps too hasty in pursuing a goal of improvement and progress, have thrown themselves into very considerable expenditures.[14]

The text was a direct attack on the government, and specifically on Ministers Walewski and Persigny, as well as on Prefect Haussmann. Napoléon III surprised everyone again by replying publicly to Fould: "You brought out a danger before my government . . . with such lucidity and you supported your opinion with such convincing arguments that I have decided to completely adopt your ideas."[15] It was rumored that Napoléon III's intention was to bring Fould back to the government, while at the same time retaining Walewski and adding Haussmann, who would be minister of public works, with responsibility for the administration of the city of Paris. Fould initially refused, then began to entertain a compromise.

The *New York Times* correspondent wrote of the backroom dealings:

> *I know on good authority that Mr. Fould did at first make many conditions with the Emperor, which he subsequently consented to waive. Now he tells his intimate friends that he shall get rid of Count Walewski, Mr. Haussmann, the famous Prefect who has pulled down half Paris, and others, and that the Emperor only stipulates for a little time to break their fall. This may be so, but these men show very strong at Court yet, and it is very difficult to guess what may be done from one day to another by a man like the Emperor.[16]*

As much as Fould may have been opposed to Haussmann, whom he considered fiscally irresponsible to the point of being a threat to the regime, Fould's real enemy was still Count Walewski. The *New York Times* correspondent described the fighting: "The cabal against [Fould] is making herculean efforts, and it is backed by the Empress and Countess Walewski. The vermin which has been preying on the vitals of the State for so many years, is fighting for the dear life, and will die hard."[17]

Fould was reappointed minister of finance on November 14, 1861, in a government that maintained Walewski as minister of state, with

Haussmann continuing in his role as prefect. Among the ministers, Fould had strong allies in Jules Baroche and Eugène Rouher. They were certain to make things as difficult as possible for Haussmann and his expensive ambitions.

Despite their vast personal differences and the many antagonisms among them, Persigny, Morny, Walewski, and Haussmann shared a general ideology drawn from the core of the Bonapartist project itself. Men like Fould, Baroche, and Rouher were different. They were great apparatchiks who had made themselves appear indispensable to the Empire's stability, but they did not have a visceral belief in the historical destiny of Napoléon III's rule. In the opinion of their enemies, by seeking to efficiently maintain an orderly status quo rather than using their power for transformational purposes, they were undermining the imperial vision itself.

The emperor, wanting to make the best use of the competence of all these men, did his best to maintain a delicate balance. But Fould had come to be seen by the financial community as the guarantor of its interests, giving him an unassailable position. In 1863, Fould forced the former finance minister, Pierre Magne, out of the government and then stayed in position as Persigny, Walewski, and Delangle were all replaced. Haussmann continued, but he had become extremely isolated.

With the passage of time, Napoléon III had become less personally engaged in the transformation of Paris, distracted as he was by the internal politics of the Empire, weighty issues of diplomacy and war, and other passions, such as sexual dalliances and the writing of his *History of Julius Caesar*. But he remained committed to the vision of the new Paris and was unfailingly supportive of Haussmann. One observer summarized the situation: "[T]he hostility of Fould, . . . of the other ministers, of the state council, of the appeals court, of the court of accounts, and of course the insufficient control of an unelected city council, none of this was enough to stop the prefect, because Napoléon III supported him."[18]

Haussmann was controversial and, at times, a political liability to the emperor, but he was diabolically effective. Furthermore, he had one tremendous quality that the emperor valued above all: his loyalty. Haussmann's attachment to the emperor was not born of convenience or opportunism, but of deep conviction, rooted in family tradition. Never, from the moment he was first appointed as prefect of the Var until the end of his prefectoral career, did Haussmann do anything but serve Napoléon III with complete, unreserved diligence.

For all his arrogance, Haussmann maintained a filial, almost servile relationship with the emperor. He never gave the slightest sign of calling Napoléon III's wisdom into question. At most, he sometimes felt that the emperor was too softhearted, that he hesitated to put his foot down, as Haussmann would have liked:

> The Emperor possessed the calm strength of will, as perseverant as it was patient, which achieves anything with time. But he also had such a measured and polite way of expressing what he wanted and of dealing with objections brought to his ideas that many let themselves be caught in the hope of changing his intentions. True, His Majesty long meditated on a project before fixing it in his mind; but when he had made it his own with conviction, those whose views it troubled only had one effective resource: to win time, which his extreme gentleness generally made easy.[19]

Haussmann also had another quality that was important to the emperor. In the midst of all the political battles, and despite the expedients he used, Haussmann never lost his conviction that he was doing the work required for the betterment of society. He deeply believed that a well-organized and industrious public administration could bring about order and progress. He had always been confronted by people, such as Berger and now Fould, who did not understand this vision and could therefore only be an obstacle to forward movement. There were others, obsessed by their narrow self-interest to the point of being blind to a broader vision. Haussmann was altogether different. Although his views, even for the time, were decidedly not progressive, he remained a man who believed that human industry would bring about a better future, that each generation has a responsibility toward its descendants. For him, anyone who stood in the way of this great enterprise was to be eliminated or overcome.

In the first years of the Empire, there had been no room for opposition. Unanimity reigned, proclaimed in the flowery language of officialdom and enforced by means fair and otherwise by the minister of the interior and the prefects in every *département*.

The 1857 legislative elections had been the first sign of change. The officially endorsed candidates were heavily advantaged—they alone were allowed to hold campaign meetings and they received the overt support of the government-sanctioned press. Despite this, three Republican candidates were elected in Paris and in Lyon. These three broke from the Republican dogma in place since the coup d'état by deciding to take the oath of loyalty to the Empire and occupy their seats in the Legislative Assembly. Jacques Louis Hénon, Louis Darimon, and Emile Ollivier became the first Republican deputies of the Empire. In off-cycle elections the following year, two more Republicans were elected, both lawyers: Jules Favre and Ernest Picard.

Over the years to follow, the five Republican members of the Legislative Assembly used their eloquence and intelligence effectively to make inroads against the regime. They avoided attacking the Empire or the emperor directly, instead pursuing every issue likely to appeal to public opinion or to divide the rest of the Legislative Assembly. This group, soon dubbed "the Five," were the advance scouts of the return of France to democracy.

The Five adopted a disciplined approach. They identified four issues to bring up again and again. One of these was the "immoderate enterprises of municipalities without brakes or controls" in Paris and Lyon. They, of course, detested Haussmann, with his conservative, even reactionary, political views and his authoritarian personal style. More importantly, they saw the political benefit in attacking the prefect. He was the personification of a dictatorial, centralized rule over the capital city that was undertaking a complete reconstruction of Paris without transparency or consultation. The prefect of the Seine represented the excesses of the Empire, but he was, at the same time, distant enough from the emperor to leave himself vulnerable to attack.

Ernest Picard had already positioned himself as an opponent of the prefect, using the unpopular expansion of Paris as a campaign theme. In speeches before the Legislative Assembly in 1861, Picard criticized the transformation of Paris, attacking not the urban vision, but the means: the expansive use of expropriation, the opacity around the transactions, and the size of the debt incurred. Picard denounced the "mysterious dictatorship that picks apart neighborhoods if it doesn't simply destroy them, without producing a statement of its assets and liabilities, while divestments and adjudications are conducted contrary to law."[20]

Picard led a campaign of relentless criticism of the prefect over the following years. Haussmann was immensely irritated, but he did not believe the ramshackle opposition was a serious threat to him. He continued his work, as certain as ever of its value to human progress and of the strength of Napoléon III's desire to see it completed.

As the 1863 elections approached, the imperial machinery kicked back into gear to ensure the victory of the official candidates. It succeeded in rural areas but not in the big cities. Somehow, the citizens of Paris were not grateful to the government that made it the "most tranquil, the richest and the most beautiful big city in the world," as the campaign rhetoric reminded them.

Thirty-five nongovernment candidates were elected to the Legislative

Assembly. The opposition was still relatively small, but it was a talented group that now included the Republican Jules Simon, the conservative Pierre-Antoine Berryer, and Napoléon III's erstwhile ally, Adolphe Thiers.

The government came under fire from all sides. The Republicans, of course, attacked the lack of individual liberties, the restrictions on the freedom of the press, and the fact that Paris and Lyon were not administered by elected officials. The conservatives attacked the government's foreign policy and the financial irresponsibility of the regime—Berryer had reached the conclusion that the Second Empire had, in the space of twelve years, amassed a cumulative deficit equal to that of the previous fifty years of French history, despite the windfall of 285 million francs of revenue from railway concessions. And of course there were still the Bonapartists, who criticized Fould and Rouher for managing the economy with the hand brake on. Armand Béhic, an industrialist who became minister of agriculture, commerce, and public works in July 1863, joined this camp and entered into open conflict with Fould within days of his appointment.

Haussmann continued to be one of the favorite targets of the parliamentary opposition, led by Picard and Simon. He attracted outrage and ridicule for a speech in which he said, in substance, that, in the absence of new taxes, the best way to balance the budget was through "productive expenditures"—in other words, more spending. In another speech, he provoked the wrath of the opposition by using the term *Parisian nomads* to refer to new migrants to the city.

Despite the controversies and the political attacks, Prefect Haussmann had built a large and effective administration and populated it with capable men who served him as he liked, "with conscientious fidelity, with absolutely irreproachable zeal."[21] He had scrapped with the prefecture of police, the Ministry of the Interior, and other administrations to give the prefecture of the Seine unshared dominance of the management and development of the capital city. He was at the apex of his personal power.

Haussmann's life was entirely dedicated to his work. He would be at his desk with the day's newspapers read well before the rest of the staff arrived and he would not leave in the evening before all his work was completed. His relationships with coworkers remained formal; his closest friends were men like Frémy, with whom he could discuss the inside politics of the Empire over drinks and cigars. His pleasures, too, were related to the office he occupied, with long, formal dinners, confidential visits with ministers and bankers, and evenings in a private box at the Opéra. One suspects that even when he took young mistresses from the ballet and the theater troupes, his actions were due to social conventions as much as to the carnal pleasures such liaisons attended. He laid claim to a certain sensuality, but his writings nearly never hint at any sentiment of tenderness or affection. Toward his wife it seems he felt only respect for her family, pedigree, and role in maintaining her husband's social and political position. Obsessed as he was by his status, his daughters were a source of significant anxiety, especially the younger girl, Valentine, who allegedly went so far as to have an affair with the emperor before her father could get her betrothed to someone suitable.

In March 1864, Haussmann received an honor rarely bestowed within one's lifetime: One of Paris's main arteries was named after him. After considering to name what is now known as the boulevard Saint-Michel after him, it was decided to give Haussmann's name to the new boulevard that passed near the location of the house where the prefect had been born—a house destroyed, it was noted, by the *grands travaux* themselves. This street, of which only the first portion had been built at the time, has kept its name to this day, while many other Parisian streets named after prominent figures of the Second Empire have been renamed. The name of Napoléon III himself is only carried by a small square in front of the gare du Nord that hardly anyone knows has a name at all.

One journalist summarized a sentiment that was certainly in line with the regime dogma, but which many Parisians genuinely felt: "Paris will owe to Mr. Haussmann improvements that no one before him had dared undertake, or almost imagine. It is a justice that we must render him, and that we could not render him too often. Men of such character, of such perseverance, are rare and, to recognize it, the usual practice is to wait until they are dead."[22]

Haussmann was a remarkable administrator who imprinted his personality on the whole enterprise of the building of the new Paris. As Eugène Rouher, his government colleague and frequent opponent, said of him, "Haussmann has everything in large: qualities as well as faults."[23]

Fifteen

RAZING THE CRADLE OF PARIS

Many centuries ago, Paris fit on an island. On that island, Parisians established a market, built places of worship, and created the first institutions of government. Even after the city expanded to the mainland, the Ile de la Cité remained the beating heart of Paris.

Today, it is nearly impossible to conceive what the Ile de la Cité was once like. Staid institutional buildings and open spaces have replaced crowded houses on little squares and dead-end lanes. The lawyers, judges, and clerks of the courts, the bureaucrats and officers of the police headquarters, the doctors, nurses, and patients of the Hôtel Dieu, and the tourists filing into Notre-Dame and the Sainte-Chapelle have replaced the shopkeepers, matrons, idlers, and the ragtag children who ran through the narrow, crooked streets.

The teeming, impenetrable Ile de la Cité exercised a fascination on Parisians of the nineteenth century. It was celebrated by the lovers of all things Gothic, like Victor Hugo, who wrote a veritable ode to the medieval memory of the island in his 1831 novel, *The Hunchback of Notre Dame*. On the other hand, the Ile de la Cité was feared as a reputed den of vice and criminality. Eugène Sue's immensely popular novel, *The Mysteries of Paris,* published in serial form in 1842 and 1843, gave a darkly terrifying view of the lowlife of the island.

On the Ile de la Cité stood the cathedral, Notre-Dame de Paris, at the time the city's most iconic building. The graceful structure dominated the island, looking down on the houses huddled around it like a shepherdess over her flock. But the cathedral was in a terrible state. For many years, there had been no maintenance. The masonry was deeply damaged, pinnacles and gables were broken, the glasswork was degraded, and many of the sculptures adorning the building had been stolen.

The battered state of the monument struck many of France's intellectuals as a shame and an outrage. So in 1842, a group of writers and artists, including Victor Hugo, Alfred de Vigny, and Jean-Auguste-Dominique Ingres, signed a petition requesting action to bring Notre-Dame back to its former glory. A committee was formed to coordinate a comprehensive restoration of the structure. Among the members of this committee was Prosper Mérimée, the inspector general of historic monuments.

Mérimée is best known today as a writer—he wrote, among other things, the story upon which the opera *Carmen* was based. As inspector general of historic monuments, his work consisted of inventorying and studying historic buildings and doing what he could to protect and preserve them. Mérimée was an important catalyst in the early development of architectural restoration in France, helping to raise awareness of France's architectural heritage and to cultivate a generation of architects with the requisite knowledge of architecture, archaeology, and history to maintain and restore it.

The Notre-Dame committee organized a competitive selection process in which several teams of architects presented their credentials and proposed approach to the restoration of the cathedral. In 1844, the committee selected the team of Jean-Baptiste-Antoine Lassus and Eugène Viollet-le-Duc to lead the renovation.

By this time, the thirty-seven-year-old Lassus was well on his way to establishing himself as an important member of the first generation of architects in France specializing in historic preservation and restoration. Viollet-le-Duc, on the other hand, was barely thirty and had only one project to his credit: the restoration of the basilica in Vézelay, Burgundy. The son of an administrator of royal residences, he came from an artistic and literary family, which had given him quite a bit of exposure to France's luminaries from the youngest age. One of those who remembered him as a boy was Prosper Mérimée, the man who not only launched Viollet-le-Duc's career by giving him the Vézelay commission when he was only twenty-five, but who helped him win the Notre-Dame competition and who would continue promoting his fortunes in the years to come.

Lassus and Viollet-le-Duc shared an understanding of architecture that was rooted in a deep opposition to the tradition of the Ecole des Beaux-Arts. Lassus had started at the school in 1828 but soon rebelled against its culture and left to study with Henri Labrouste. Viollet-le-Duc had shunned the school altogether and learned architecture through his own research and travels and through experience on the job as a draftsman.

Part of the reason the Beaux-Arts system was held in disregard by these architects was because of its devotion to the cult of classical antiquity, to the detriment of other building traditions, specifically the Gothic. Lassus was one of those who believed that not only did Gothic architecture have intrinsic qualities but that it was of special value in France as a great building tradition native to the country, an expression of the national genius and not reliant on the importation of foreign tastes and concepts.

Each step one makes in a Gothic church modifies the perspective and changes the aspect of the monument for the observer. One's spirit suddenly flies up to a world of marvels. One is struck by the unity, and yet each part, each detail presents a new combination, a disposition as ingenious

as it is unexpected, so that each step provides the pleasure of a discovery.
Inspiration has triumphed over all practical obstacles and opened the
doors to a new world.[1]

Animated by this spirit, Lassus and Viollet-le-Duc threw themselves
into the work of restoring Paris's prestigious cathedral. They began by
conducting an in-depth historical and archaeological study of the building. They then started the actual restoration, but funding was tenuous,
so the work advanced in fits and starts.

After the wedding of Napoléon III and Eugenia de Montijo—which
took place in the cathedral—the project continued on firmer footing.
An important factor in the new impetus was the support of the empress,
not surprising, given that Eugénie was known for her strong Catholic
sentiments. But there was another, more fortuitous connection between
the new empress and the project to restore the crumbling cathedral.
Prosper Mérimée had been friends with Eugénie's parents for many
years, without the slightest idea that the little girl he used to dangle on
his knee would one day become empress of France. After the marriage
of Napoléon III and Eugénie, Mérimée became a central figure of the
imperial court, ideally placed to promote the restoration of Notre-Dame.
More broadly, he used his privileged position to spearhead the first serious campaigns, under the Second Empire, to protect and restore France's
architectural heritage.

Notre-Dame had already seen many changes and additions in its close
to six centuries of existence. Lassus and Viollet-le-Duc therefore confronted an issue many preservationists face, that of what, among the
many modifications over the years, to keep, or, in some cases, to reinstate. They ended up removing the eighteenth-century decoration of the
choir to restore its earlier, medieval character. They decided to maintain
the twelfth-century rose windows in the thirteenth-century nave, despite the anachronism.

They did a great deal of reconstruction. For example, they knew from drawings that a spire had existed atop Notre-Dame in the past. So they rebuilt one that was as faithful as possible to the images they had studied. Since much of the cathedral's ornamental sculpture was missing, they had it reconstituted, where necessary by extrapolation from contemporaneous cathedrals where the sculptures had been better preserved, such as Chartres, Amiens, and Reims. Many of the sculptures adorning the facade of Notre-Dame are therefore not originals, but reconstitutions. The architects injected some entirely new ideas: The famous chimeras at the top of the facade, for example, were a creation of Viollet-le-Duc. The architects were, on the other hand, uncompromising in their use of the same materials and techniques as were used by the original builders, eschewing new resins, cements, and artificial materials.

The restoration was complete by 1864. Paris finally again had a cathedral worthy of the capital of France, a symbol of the country's religious and historic identity. Today, while most visitors imagine that they are seeing the building as it always stood, they are in reality seeing its interpretation and reconstitution through the eyes of nineteenth-century architects. Notre-Dame, as unlikely as it may seem, is in large part a monument of the Second Empire.

Ideas and projects for the Ile de la Cité had percolated throughout the 1840s. One of these was to turn the island into a sort of Gothic sanctuary, a place where one could experience the island of the fifteenth century as described by Hugo. Another was to pull down the old neighborhoods to open lines of sight onto the main monuments and build new structures that reflected modern taste.

The radical transformation of the Ile de la Cité started inconspicuously. In 1858, the city administration undertook the widening of the street that crossed the island from north to south between the pont au

Change and the pont Saint-Michel, both of which were being rebuilt. Along this street, on the north side of the island, was the wholesale flower market. Prefect Haussmann felt that the site of the flower market was the perfect location for a new building to house the commercial court, which occupied an unsuitable space on the upper level of the stock exchange. He expanded the expropriations to make room for the building, for a new flower market to its east, and for an open space to the south. The demolition of the first significant portion of the old Ile de la Cité was under way.

One reason why Haussmann liked the site was that it was situated right in line with the boulevard de Sébastopol and he could therefore use it to mark the perspective with a great architectural feature. Napoléon III agreed, and suggested that the new structure be modeled after a building he admired, the Palazzo della Loggia in Brescia, Italy. The architect, Antoine-Nicolas Bailly, began working in accord with these recommendations and delivered the new commercial court, including a dome in the axis of the boulevard de Sébastopol, in 1865. Haussmann was particularly proud of the result. He would be disappointed to know that traffic on the boulevard de Sébastopol now runs the other way, so that drivers cannot admire the alignment of the dome as he conceived it.

Haussmann continued with the destruction of the old neighborhoods of the Ile de la Cité. Soon the administrative process was under way to expropriate the houses south of the commercial court site to make room for new headquarters for the Paris Guard and Fire Brigade—not a coincidental choice for a neighborhood that many people considered the epicenter of Parisian criminality. The building, which is still today occupied by the Paris police, was built starting in 1862 by the little-known architect Victor Calliat. It is a massive and not particularly remarkable building. One marvels that so much land at the heart of Paris would be dedicated to a building that brings so little to the urban landscape.

• • •

At a reception in March 1863, Napoléon III was introduced to a forty-year-old scientist who had just made the remarkable discovery of a new kind of microorganism that causes infectious diseases—what we now call bacteria. The scientist's name was Louis Pasteur.

Napoléon III was fascinated. He read Pasteur's papers and met the scientist again to discuss his ideas. He invited Pasteur to Compiègne to give biology lectures to his guests over tea. The interest was lasting: Napoléon III supported Pasteur's research until the end of the Second Empire.

Pasteur's findings revolutionized hospital care. They established the importance of separating patients and sterilizing medical equipment. The implications on hospital design were far-reaching: There would now be separate wards, preferably with well-ventilated open spaces in between.

Napoléon III, Haussmann, and Armand Husson, the director of the Assistance publique, the relatively newly created Parisian public health authority, were keen to implement these concepts. It was decided to rebuild Paris's historical central hospital, the Hôtel Dieu, as a model of the new ideas.

The hospital would be rebuilt on the Ile de la Cité, near its historic site. The old buildings along the river in front of Notre-Dame would be destroyed, allowing for the enlargement of the parvis, the open space in front of the cathedral. The neighborhood to the north, forming the whole central portion of the island, from the rue de la Cité to the rue d'Arcole, would be leveled to make room for the new hospital. Napoléon III wanted construction to begin without delay—he was keen that the building of the hospital, the "asylum of the suffering," begin before that of the Opéra, a "temple of pleasure."[2]

Emile-Jacques Gilbert was appointed architect. He put forward the project of a neo-Gothic structure, as was in vogue at the time, with cross windows with mullions and transoms. Napoléon III rejected the idea; he wanted a resolutely modern structure.

Gilbert returned to the drawing board and conceived a four-story hospital with a series of parallel wings, divided by courtyards, on either side of a large central courtyard. The different parts of the building were connected by covered galleries. The design was, like much of the architecture of urban amenities of the period, of a straightforward classical style, without excessive exuberance.

After the death of Gilbert, responsibility for the project passed to his son-in-law, Arthur-Stanislas Diet, another laureate of the Grand Prix de Rome. A debate ensued about the height of the building and the insufficiency of the open spaces. One story was lopped off the project and then another off the actual building as it neared completion, concessions to the doctors, scientists, and civil servants now obsessed with light, air, and open spaces. While Haussmann was delighted that the site on the Ile de la Cité had excellent exposure, he was dismayed by the height reductions, which brought the capacity of the hospital down from eight hundred beds to only four hundred and therefore made the whole project, in his view, uneconomic. The building was not completed until 1878.

To the west of the area cleared and rebuilt by Haussmann stands the Palais de la Cité, the seat of the French kings from the twelfth century to the fourteenth, now known as the Palais de Justice for its role as the epicenter of the French court system. Planning for an expansion of the complex had begun in the 1830s, but the designs of the site's architects, Joseph-Louis Duc and Etienne-Théodore Dommey, were not approved until 1847. Construction began soon thereafter, with the bulk of the work conducted from 1858 to 1865.

The expansion and restructuring of the Palais de Justice caused the destruction of structures on the edges of the complex and of others inside the complex not considered to have historic or architectural merit. In what we see today as a strange paradox, Duban and Lassus were therefore at work painstakingly restoring the architectural jewel of the Sainte-Chapelle just as Duc and Dommey were overseeing the destruction of irreplaceable historic structures all around it, including the residential quarters of the Palais de la Cité.[3] To take their place, Duc designed new buildings "of majestic coldness, appropriate, one thought, to the justice rendered in them."[4]

The most problematic addition was the western end of the complex, meant to form the new grand entrance to the courts. The interior of Duc's hall is beautiful and won him the acclaim of his peers. Outside, Duc built a facade that is well composed, if heavy, which one can imagine fitting in harmoniously in a park or some other large space. The facade is, however, completely out of proportion with the neighboring place Dauphine, with its seventeenth-century redbrick houses with limestone quoins. The effect is compounded by the insanely extravagant staircase, which looks more the work of a pastry chef than that of an architect. In fairness to Duc, his plan was to pull down the whole western end of the Ile de la Cité and replace it with a composition in harmony with his new structure. The houses across a narrow street from the new behemoth were indeed soon destroyed, but the rest of the charming, intimate place Dauphine was preserved, leaving Duc's facade looking today like a graceless, overdressed guest intruding on an intimate dinner party.

There is no more breathtaking illustration of the Second Empire's transformation of Paris than the before and after images of the Ile de la Cité. In fewer than ten years, a veritable hive of human activity, with a complex organic structure of houses and little streets, was cleared away and replaced by large open spaces and boxlike institutional buildings. The population of the island fell from fifteen thousand in the 1850s to five thousand at the end of the century, to less than two thousand today.

Lest the idea that Haussmann actually relished the destruction be taken for an affectation, here are his own words: "As a young Law student . . . I would walk along the old Palais de Justice, with, on my left, the ignoble heap of thieves' dens which used to dishonor the Cité and that I later had the joy of razing, from top to bottom."[5]

The island that made Paris definitively lost the character and rich-
ness forged over centuries. One lucid observer wrote that "la Cité, the
cradle of Paris, will soon only be a memory, after which it will only be
a name."[6] That is indeed exactly what happened.

Sixteen

THE BEGINNING OF
THE FALL

In the course of 1865, controversy flared again. At issue this time was Haussmann's plan to cut off large parts of the west and south of the Jardin du Luxembourg in order to develop them. In particular, he intended to sacrifice the part of the garden known as the *pépinière*—the nursery. Years later, with this place long gone, Guy de Maupassant wrote a lovely short story entitled "Menuet," an ode to this "dear garden of bygone days, with its labyrinth of paths, its smell of the past and the graceful detours of its hornbeam hedges."[1]

The mostly upper-class residents of the Luxembourg neighborhood were appalled by the plan and not in the least intimidated by the powerful prefect. Despite the fact that the project had already been officially decreed, they gathered a petition of over twelve thousand signatures and submitted it directly to the emperor. The opposition press got involved. In March 1866, when the emperor came to attend a performance at the nearby Théâtre de l'Odéon, he encountered a crowd shouting "Sack Haussmann!"

The minister of the interior prepared a report on the matter for the emperor. The Senate weighed in with its opinion. The Legislative Assembly discussed the issue. And finally on August 14, 1866, a new decree was published with a significantly watered-down version of the project. The amputation of the western part of the park was thrown out. But the new street crossing the southern portion of the park, today's rue Auguste Comte, was maintained, as was the idea of developing the section of the park to the south of that street. As it happened, the project was completed only years later. Instead of handing the whole area to private developers, as Haussmann had intended, the city ended up earmarking a number of lots for the institutional buildings that occupy the area today.

The avenue de l'Observatoire, which crossed the southern portion of the park, was transformed into a promenade, a costly affair that Haussmann considered one of his finest achievements. Again, Davioud was in charge of the design. This park is famous for its sculptures and fountains, especially the southernmost fountain, which has at its center the last work of the sculptor Jean-Baptiste Carpeaux, a friend of Charles Garnier who had contributed to the sculptures of the Opéra.

In 1865, after some delay to find a contractor willing to take the concession, the western-most section of the boulevard Saint-Germain was finally started.

The eastern end had been built in conjunction with the boulevard Saint-Michel. Then, instead of continuing through the most historic portion of the route, in the heart of the old Left Bank, work began at the other extremity.

The new segment went through the faubourg Saint-Germain, for some time now Paris's most prestigious *quartier.* Home of the genuine nobility, it was full of splendid *hôtels particuliers,* with a spirit of tranquillity entirely opposite to the chaos of the Ile de la Cité, Les Halles, or the faubourg Saint-Antoine. The new artery eliminated *hôtels partic-*

uliers in part or in whole and took considerable land from the generous gardens that gave these properties their charm.

By the end of the 1860s, the two ends of the boulevard Saint-Germain were finished. The path between them was obvious, and plotted out by the city's staff, but for the time being, the project was not taken any further.

With the boulevard du Prince-Eugène and the covering of the canal Saint-Martin finished and work on the other major projects of the 180 Million Franc Treaty completed or well under way, the administration returned to the problem of the new, hugely expanded place du Château d'Eau—the future place de la République. An imperial decree dated February 11, 1865, established the definitive perimeter of the square and appointed Gabriel Davioud to produce a design.

No sooner was it laid out than the square became an urban design headache. Its vast scale, the numerous traffic entry points, the huge pedestrian islands lost in the midst of it all—only made worse when the square was used as a tram stop and then a massive Métro hub—posed a problem that would plague generations of urban designers. The best schemes—which remained unbuilt—reversed the huge open expanse of the square by building the center back up with theaters in a bid to reestablish a human scale and bring some life and animation back. One hundred fifty years later, the Paris municipality is still struggling with this space, which has recently been comprehensively redesigned.

On the northeast side of the square, next to the barracks, Davioud designed and supervised the building of a department store, the Magasins Réunis. Parisians had recently seen a number of these new stores, which sold a broad assortment of goods, go up: the Bon Marché and the Grands Magasins du Louvre in the 1850s, and the Samaritaine and the Printemps in the 1860s. But these were all located in rich, central

neighborhoods. Building a department store in a working-class neighborhood was to take a real chance. The Magasins Réunis ended up failing
commercially and the building was reconverted. Today it is a hotel,
with commercial space on the ground floor.

On the northwest side of the square, where the fountain had previously stood, Haussmann and Davioud imagined a great new cultural
facility, what they called the Grand Orphéon, a music hall with the
enormous capacity of ten thousand spectators. The Grand Orphéon
was intended to "initiate the masses to knowledge of all the master-
pieces of our repertoires, and thereby contribute to their artistic and
literary education."[2] Haussmann was attached to this idea, conceived as
a working-class counterweight to the Opéra. The project did not get off
the ground before the end of the Second Empire, and the governments
thereafter did not have the means to fund it, so it was never built.

The place du Château d'Eau is a powerful example of the strengths
and weaknesses of Second Empire urbanism. Haussmann boldly created a major square and decisively contributed to the fluidity of circulation across a significant portion of northeast Paris. But as he did so, he
created a space of poor urban quality and destroyed forever the unique
environment of one of the most appreciated stretches of the Grands
Boulevards. As one of the participants in a project for the square in
the 1870s wrote, "This life, this animation, this prosperity has been
destroyed. . . . The immense square that, by day, is as sad as a vacant
lot and, by evening, stays dark and deserted . . . has isolated everything that surrounds its immense perimeter."[3]

By the mid-1860s, it became clear to Haussmann that the projects funded
by the 180 Million Franc Treaty would be both late and significantly over
budget. At the same time, he was eager to start a number of projects he
had not been able to include in the 180 Million Franc Treaty. Declaring
that the time had come to make one last push to complete the *grands*

travaux, he requested approval for the biggest bond issue in the city's history. After the 50 million francs raised under Berger, the 60 million raised early in Haussmann's tenure, and the 130 million raised in 1860 to fund the 180 Million Franc Treaty, Haussmann was now asking for no less than 300 million francs.

The money was needed, according to the public pronouncements, to provide the new arrondissements with streets and squares on a par with those now in the center. There were also some projects for the historical arrondissements and new public facilities to be built, such as churches and the new Hôtel Dieu. Haussmann explained that the city, with its own resources, would be able to do this work within ten years, but borrowing the funds would allow it to complete the whole program within five. What was not mentioned publicly was that the city of Paris needed a substantial part of the new money to pay for the overruns of the earlier projects.

The discussion before the Legislative Assembly was contentious. Pierre-Antoine Berryer was the most vocal opponent of the proposal:

> *I maintain that nothing shows the need for this borrowing. I say that if the city, through its own faculties, is able to execute the works it desires within ten years, it is not good that it resort to borrowing. The city needs to return to measure and to wisdom. . . . I consider this debt as a veritable calamity and it is for that reason that I oppose it.*[4]

The proposed bond issue, decreased to 250 million francs, nevertheless passed comfortably, 181 votes to 51. Thiers, Berryer, Favre, and Picard were among those who voted against.

Haussmann had presented the bond issue to the Legislative Assembly as fully prepared—Emile Pereire, who was the banker arranging the transaction, was even present during the parliamentary debate. Haussmann had cavalierly negotiated the terms of the issue directly with Pereire, without consulting other banks and bypassing the Ministry of

Finance. Not even to be consulted for a bond issue of this size was un-
fathomable to Achille Fould, who began to voice his complaints to Napoléon III. In January 1866 and again a few months later, he told the
emperor that he had proof of accounting irregularities in the city's
books. "The city has no budget, because we do not know precisely either
the resources or the needs."[5] Still, Napoléon III would not reprimand or
challenge his prefect of the Seine.

Haussmann had not divulged anything yet about the cost overruns on
the projects of the 180 Million Franc Treaty. But the readers of the *Journal des débats politiques et littéraires* had become accustomed to the articles
on the municipal debt of Paris by a certain Léon Say. Say parsed the
publicly disclosed information on the city accounts and wrote article
after article combatting the financial management of the city. Haussmann and Devinck answered his articles in long, technical rebuttals, but
Say persisted.

Far from being an Opposition rabble-rouser, Say, the grandson of
famous free-market economist Jean-Baptiste Say, had worked in a major
Parisian bank, served on the Boards of Directors of several companies,
and had written a technical book on French credit policy in the eighteenth century. Say's doctrine was simple: reduce expenses, work off
the debt, and decrease taxes. In December 1864, he had written an article stating that in the current era of prosperity, the city of Paris need
not and should not incur additional debt. The city's surplus should be
used to markedly decrease the *octroi,* which would stimulate enterprise.

In addition to the articles that continued for the next three years, Say
published two books on the financial situation of the city of Paris. He,
more than anyone outside the prefect's administration, understood the
issues with the city's budget, and he most decidedly did not agree with
how things were being done. His work would spur an ever-increasing
investigation into what exactly was going on with the city's accounts.

· · ·

The projects launched in the second half of the 1860s, after the money from the 180 Million Franc Treaty ran out, were entirely financed by the city. They were what Haussmann called the "third network." They included the Boulevard Haussmann, the extension of the rue Lafayette, the boulevard Saint-Germain, the extension of the rue de Rennes, and the avenue des Amandiers (today's avenue de la République). They also included new streets for the territories annexed in 1860, such as the rue des Pyrénées through the former towns of Belleville and Charonne and the rue Caulaincourt in Montmartre.

The new projects outside the urban core contributed to one of the distinctive characteristics of Paris: the maintenance of a high level of urban density over a broad area.

Paris had adopted regulations allowing building heights corresponding to a six- or seven-story apartment building, what one can reasonably climb on foot. In other words, the city was implementing pretty much the densest system of land occupation achievable before the widespread use of elevators.

For the administration, the technical matter was how to ensure the achievement of this high-density development across a large area. The original approach, taken under Berger, was to offer tax breaks in exchange for immediate development of an entire area. For example, the 1851 law for the extension of the rue de Rivoli exempted buildings from property taxes for twenty years if they were erected immediately. Haussmann disliked this, loath as he was to leave tax revenue on the table. He implemented a totally different approach, wherein the city negotiated the immediate development of the plots on the street corners, or sometimes used a public building to indicate the urban structure, and then let the area fill in over time. For decades, one could see in a number of neighborhoods perfectly finished streets with Haussmannian buildings at the corners, while the other plots remained completely vacant.

The result is that, while in most cities the population density drops off quickly as one leaves the central core, in Paris the dense urban fabric covers the entire city and extends in some places into the suburbs. Paris has a population density of more than 80 people per acre, not so far from Manhattan's 112, despite the fact that Paris has nearly twice the land area of Manhattan. The population density in Paris is many times greater than that of other American downtowns, which have around twenty people per acre, or fewer. The high number of residents, in turn, requires a commensurate amount of services to maintain this population: cafés, restaurants, bakeries, grocery stores, and so on. This extremely compact urban environment is an essential part of Paris's character.

Another policy that played an important role in Paris's appearance was the systematic planting of trees along the avenues. Rambuteau had initiated this practice in the 1830s. Haussmann continued it, systematically planting rows of trees five meters from the building alignment wherever there was room. He particularly loved chestnut trees, which accounts for their large numbers. Since Napoléon III preferred open perspectives and unobstructed facades, Haussmann sometimes had to employ ruses to get trees planted on the thoroughfares. But he did, with the result being that Paris appears as a city with quite a bit of greenery, even though, other than the two large parks on its edge, the amount of park space is quite limited.

In the summer of 1866, international tensions again monopolized the nation's attention. France held its breath as the two other Continental powers, Austria and Prussia, faced off. On July 3, after only a couple of weeks of war, the Prussian army imposed a crushing defeat on the Austrians at Königgrätz. It was a disaster for the French, whose diplomacy was based on having the Prussians get bogged down in the conflict, which would both weaken the Prussian military and allow France to achieve territorial gains on its northeast border as arbiter of the peace. After Königgrätz, it was clear that Prussia was the dominant power in the German-speaking world and that momentum was on the side of Kleindeutschland, a unified Germany that would exclude Austria.

In a way fully characteristic of the Second Empire, cultivating a constant ambiguity between reality and fiction, Paris celebrated the Peace of Prague in August 1866 as a great event. The illusion of a role for France was maintained by the fact that Venetia was ceded to France, even though it was understood that France would immediately turn the territory over to the new Italian Republic. In reality, the cycle of errors and misjudgments that would lead France to the cataclysmic defeat of 1870 was under way.

Furthermore, the French people did not know it, but their leader was seriously ill. Napoléon III had suffered from multiple ailments for some time: rheumatism, anemia, and liver problems. In 1865, his health started to decidedly deteriorate. A recurrent pain in his lower abdomen intensified each year, finally becoming debilitating and seriously impairing his ability to rule the nation at what was to be a critical juncture.

Seventeen

GLAMOUR AND DECAY

In the winter of 1867, thousands of workers were busy on the Champ-de-Mars fastening rivets, lifting plates of glass, hauling soil, and planting trees. They were preparing a new Universal Exposition, much larger than the one held in 1855. As usual, everything was late, but when it came together, it promised to be quite something.

Napoléon III's idea was to use the 1867 Universal Exposition as an opportunity for the comparative observation of industrial practices in different countries and to showcase ideas from around the world to improve the lot of the working class. He appointed Frédéric Le Play to be commissioner of the exposition. Trained as a mining engineer, Le Play had dedicated his career to the statistical and field study of the labor economy; today, he is considered a pioneer of sociology.

Napoléon III and Le Play were naturally aware of the nascent movement in favor of a socialist revolution. As the exposition was being prepared in Paris, the International Workingmen's Association, of which Karl Marx was an early and active member, was planning its second international conference in Lausanne. In the days before the exposition,

Marx was in Germany, correcting the proofs of the first volume of *Das Kapital,* which would be published in September.

Napoléon III and Le Play, of course, had a markedly different outlook from that of Marx and his followers. They envisioned that workers themselves would be sent to the exposition to share ideas and techniques. In this way, they hoped to co-opt workers into a movement that would improve the conditions of the working class without fundamentally contesting the capitalist system.

With Paris about to play host to the world, France was going through several forms of crisis.

On March 17, two weeks before the opening of the exposition, Adolphe Thiers grimly warned his colleagues in the Legislative Assembly that "we cannot afford to commit a single error more."[1] He was referring to the regime's repeated foreign policy mistakes. In the Crimea, Rome, Poland, and Mexico, France had gradually alienated every potential ally: neither England, nor Russia, nor Italy, nor Austria—which France had actively contributed to weakening—could be counted upon to do anything to hinder the increasingly assertive Prussia should war break out. Nor did France act with care toward this new foe: In early 1867, Napoléon III made a clumsy attempt to buy Luxembourg from William III of the Netherlands, something sure to provoke the anger of Wilhelm I. In the weeks before the opening of the exposition, France and Prussia were teetering on the edge of war.

The French economy, which had enjoyed a fantastic run, began to falter. A weak harvest coincided with market concern about the level of the deficit. Eugène Rouher, at the head of the government, was spending public funds to prop up banks and industrial companies. Napoléon III was considering a new public subscription of one billion francs to relaunch the economy.

The regime was also experiencing a weakening of its hold on the nation.

Napoléon III tried to put in place a controlled process of liberalization, hoping for a transition toward a more democratic Empire that he could pass on to his son. In January 1867, he announced to the country that he had started to implement measures to "give the institutions of the Empire their full development, to further extend public liberties."[2] The right of the Legislative Assembly to call on ministers was reestablished and the grip on the press was loosened. Strangely, Napoléon III left the same people as before in charge of this new policy. The exception was Achille Fould, who was in poor health, and finally left the government. He died only ten months later.

Very few people knew the details of the emperor's health, but everyone could see he was but a shadow of his former self. His doctors were now quite certain that he had a stone somewhere in his urinary tract and feared that his condition was quite serious. They wanted to conduct an exploratory operation, but that in itself carried considerable risks. So nothing was done, other than prescribe the emperor tincture of opium. As a result, when he was not in constant pain, Napoléon III was immensely drowsy. There is no doubt that his state of health had an impact on the repeated tactical errors by the French leadership.

The 1867 Universal Exposition was the supreme celebration of Napoléon III's reign and the triumph of his magnificent capital, which had been fully transformed. It was the iconic pinnacle of the Second Empire, and, as far as sheer exuberant self-belief, perhaps of French history itself. Or maybe it was just the pinnacle, as one observer wryly noted, of the "incurable vanity that makes the French proclaim themselves greatest in the world in just about anything."[3] It was certainly the last time that France could, with even vague credibility, believe it was the greatest country on earth.

In the words of Emile Zola:

The great season of the Empire was beginning, which would make Paris the abode of the world, decked and full of music and song, where one

would eat and fornicate in every room. Never a reign at its height had
called the nations to such a colossal junket. Toward the blazing Tuileries,
in a magical apotheosis, the long parade of emperors, kings and princes
began, from the four corners of the earth.[4]

In reality, the opening of the exposition was not grand. The weather
was terrible and nothing was ready. As a result, there was no speech or
ceremony, just a walk by the emperor and empress past crates in various stages of unpacking.

The dreary rain continued throughout the whole month of April.
Then the weather gradually improved, the gardens were completed, and
late exhibitors, such as the Chinese and Japanese, were ready. The crowds
began to grow.

The centerpiece of the exposition was an enormous oval single-story
building designed by the engineer Jean-Baptiste Krantz. Composed entirely of metal and glass, the 1.5-million-square-foot structure startled
Parisians, who saw it as a radical departure from the neoclassical architectural canon. It was hard to comprehend, as there was no main facade
and the architecture never put itself forward—the only place from
which you could really understand the building was the roof, a portion
of which was open to the public, providing a spectacular view of Paris.
The building looked entirely designed for function, yet it had a strange,
otherworldly allure, due not least to the reddish hue of the oxidized
metal elements. Some were enthralled by the "iron coliseum" in this
"new cosmopolis, the Rome of industry and art."[5] Others did not know
what to make of it. Théophile Gautier said it looked like "a monument
built on another planet, Jupiter or Saturn, according to a taste we do not
know and with colors to which our eyes are not accustomed."[6]

The building's organizational scheme was simple: The paths leading to
and from the center of the oval were each dedicated to a country; each of
the seven concentric galleries was dedicated to a theme. Around the
whole outer edge ran a huge succession of eating and drinking establish-

ments of all types. Immediately inside that ran a broad and ample gallery for machines and tools, featuring a suspended walkway and a clever sheet-metal structure that a then unknown engineer named Gustave Eiffel had helped to design. In the innermost of the concentric galleries was the exhibition on the history of labor, containing tools and products from the Iron Age to the early nineteenth century, with a section featuring new ideas for the "physical and moral improvement of the population": practical clothes, furniture, model homes, and materials for the education of children and adults. At the center, there was a garden.

As a result of the layout, there were no grand vistas and perspectives, just an endless succession of novelties to discover at every turn. Yet the scheme was so simple that visitors did not get lost. In terms of the practical experience it attended, the building was a great success.

Even those who had visited the 1862 International Exhibition in London were impressed with the quantity and quality of items on display in Paris. There were all sorts of things: industrial equipment, carriages, photographs, musical instruments, furniture, pottery and porcelain, jewelry, artillery and ammunitions. Visitors discovered the new elevators by the Otis company, reinforced concrete—first patented that year—a steam-powered car, carriages with convertible roofs, and the enormous fifty-five-ton Prussian Krupp cannon. British and American visitors were surprised by the progress made by French steam-powered machinery, and generally by the quality of the French displays. Other nations excelled in specific areas, for example "the unartistic savages of the New World" won the Grand Medal for musical instruments, thanks to Mr. Steinway of New York, "an event that has astonished the Parisians even more than if the Prussians were to march up the boulevards this afternoon, with Bismarck at their head."[7] In the art exposition, the French reasserted their supremacy, but the show featured the first significant presence of American artists, such as James McNeill Whistler and Winslow Homer.

The main building was surrounded by elaborate gardens, which charmed the visitors. "If the French have a talent for anything it is for making exquisite gardens," noted the *New York Times*. "The plants and flowers exhibited by the many floraculturists in this land of flowers and the adjacent kingdoms is alone worth seeing."[8] The park contained beautiful Russian, Swiss, German, and Austrian pavilions, all made of wood, and a French building showing off exquisite French carpentry. There was a British building of "elaborate ugliness," as well as an American building of "simple ugliness." One could visit a Chinese tea pavilion, an ensemble of Egyptian palaces, Turkish baths, Russian izbas, a Kyrgyz yurt, and the replica of the summer palace of the bey of Tunis, which would later stand in the parc Montsouris until it was destroyed by fire in 1991. Flying above it all was a hot-air balloon.

Visitors got an unprecedented taste of the immensity and diversity of the world, thanks in large part to the new technology of photography. Displays showed the peoples, crafts, and architecture of the huge territories held by Britain and Russia, as well as those of Tunisia, Egypt, Turkey, China, and Japan. The British had a spectacular display of photographs of Indian architecture.[9] Visitors were fascinated by the Tunisian and Indian pavilions in the gardens. It was inevitable that all these exotic stimuli would launch in France and in Europe a multidecade wave of architectural designs, which encompassed everything from neo-Mauresque pavilions to facsimile Chinese pagodas.

Thanks to Haussmann's fourteen years of effort, France's capital was hands down the most glamorous and exciting place in the world. It was truly at this moment that Paris gained the reputation of being the Queen of Cities, a status that it still enjoys today. As Europe consolidated into nation-states, there was talk of the whole Continent some day forming a single nation. Victor Hugo wrote in the first chapter of the monumental *Paris-Guide* that accompanied the exposition: "Before having its people, Europe has its capital."[10]

The *New York Times* correspondent shared his enthusiasm for the experience Paris offered during the exposition:

From 5 to 6 o'clock on Sunday, when the vast crowd was pouring out of the Exhibition, closed by a signal from the great bells from Prussia, the scene was wonderful. The steamers, omnibuses, American street railway and cabs of Paris can carry 11,000 persons an hour. This was only a fraction of the multitude, but the day was as fine as possible, and they swarmed all the avenues, and the graded ascent of Trocadéro, and gradually dispersed over Paris. A little later, the avenue of the Champs-Élysées was filled with almost as large, and a far more splendid crowd returning from the Bois. At night every theatre, ball, garden, and music hall was filled; for the people are coming now in great pleasure trains from all parts of France, and lodgings are not only filling up, and carriages and omnibuses occupied, but the streets and all public places show that not only Paris but France is en fête, with Kings and nations for her guests. And amid it all, I did not see one ragged or filthy person, like the thousands seen every day in London, nor one person intoxicated, nor one beggar, nor one person whom I had any right to consider "a woman of the town plying her vocation." Neatness, order, decency are everywhere; and if there is anything else in Paris, it does not make its appearance in public.[11]

The new avenues, the elegant new buildings, the expanded and restored Louvre and Notre-Dame, the splendid parks and gardens, the profusion of modern conveniences, and innovations like the brand-new *Bateaux-Mouches,* which transported visitors along the Seine, and the new railway line, which took travelers around the circumference of Paris to the Champ-de-Mars, dazzled visitors. Nor had the Grands Boulevards lost their magic: They "are not only the head and the heart of Paris, they are the soul of the world. Paris without boulevards would be the universe in mourning," commented one observer."[12]

From April to October, there was an uninterrupted parade of royalty.

First came the king of Greece, then the king and queen of Belgium, then the prince of Prussia, followed in June by Alexander II, czar of Russia, and, a few days later, by Wilhelm I, king of Prussia. And on it went until October.

Prefect Haussmann was kept busy showing the dignitaries around and organizing receptions and dinners at the Hôtel de Ville. The greatest fete was the banquet offered on October 28 for the visit of Emperor Franz-Josef of Austria, King Ludwig II of Bavaria, Queen Sophie of the Netherlands, and, of course, the emperor and empress of France. The menu was interminable, with foie gras, crayfish, turbot, pheasants, truffles, woodcocks, roe deer, and many more dishes, all accompanied by a selection of France's finest wines. Adolphe Alphand later wrote, "More powerful than a minister, [Haussmann] was in the full splendor of his success in 1867, when he received at the Hôtel de Ville, in memorable celebrations, all the sovereigns of Europe."[13]

The city was overtaken by unbridled revelry. As one writer noted, "It is not the pleasurable occupations that are lacking in Paris. What is lacking is the hours of the day to even taste them all."[14]

A guide for British visitors advised a visit to a *bal masqué* in the grand hall of the Opéra:

> To witness the scene in perfection, the visitor should wait until 12 or 1 o'clock, when the company is fully assembled and the votaries of the dance are in full activity. On entering the vast salle at such a moment, the effect is scarcely imaginable, the gorgeousness of the immense theatre, the glitter of the lights, the brilliancy and variance of the costumes, the enlivening strains of the music, the mirth of the crowd, and, above all, the untiring velocity with which the dancers whirl themselves through the mazes of the waltz, polka, and mazourka present an appearance of bewildering gaiety not to be described. . . . After the hour of supper, when the champagne begins to exhibit its exciting effects, the scene naturally be-

comes still more warm and lively; but, though noisy and boisterous, the
immense throng is generally remarkable for its good humour.[15]

Helpfully, the author adds, "It will be easily conceived that if a visitor
should take the ladies of his family to witness this extraordinary display,
he must take them to a box as mere spectators, for to mingle with any of
these too vivacious groups would be something worse than indiscretion."

Visitors from the provinces also felt the intoxication of the capital.
Guy de Maupassant described the effect the city had on one of his protagonists, a merchant from La Rochelle:

You know what two weeks in Paris are for a businessman from the prov-
inces. It puts fire in your blood. Every night the shows, brushing against
women, a continuous excitation of spirit. One becomes mad. One ends up
seeing nothing but dancers in leotards, actresses with deep décolletés,
round legs, ample shoulders, all of it almost within reach. One leaves
with one's heart fully shaken, one's soul titillated.[16]

The spirit lasted through the days of the exposition and beyond: "In
a Paris still drunk with pleasure and power, the hour was one of a kind,
an hour of faith in good fortune, the certainty of a luck without end."[17]

Napoléon III had not given up on the cause of workers' housing. At his
request, the section of the 1867 Universal Exposition dedicated to the
living conditions of the laboring class had models, drawings, and proto-
types of homes comprised of three rooms, a kitchen, and, in the words
of the emperor, "all the desirable commodities."[18]

Napoléon III commissioned architect Eugène Lacroix to build in the
rue de Monttessuy, a street alongside the site of the exposition, an actual
model of affordable, modern homes for workers. The overriding concern

was that the model be economically realistic, so Lacroix crammed in eight apartments per floor on four floors (not counting the ground floor) and reduced the courtyards to a minimum. The project demonstrated that it was indeed possible to profitably build decent housing for the masses in the city, although the outcome was unremarkable in terms of quality or innovation. Three of the four original buildings still stand today, although considerably remodeled.[19]

The approach illustrated by this project caused real concern for some of the industrialists and administrators concerned with social issues, including Le Play himself. The fear was that such dense forms of housing would aid the propagation of socialist revolutionary ideas, rather than hinder it. Many believed that the key to avoiding the negative influences of drink, vice, and revolution on workers was, on the contrary, low-density housing, ideally with a garden the worker could tend to.

Napoléon III designated another site, this one across Paris, in avenue Daumesnil, to be used to exemplify a lower-density model. Forty-two workers' houses were designed, each with two stories above the ground floor, and the then revolutionary technology of reinforced concrete would be employed in their construction. The four-hundred-square-foot apartments were considered large for workers' homes and were rationally designed. During construction, an additional floor was added to each house. Napoléon III made a visit to the finished buildings on February 13, 1868. These houses also still stand today.

Napoléon III funded an unusually progressive project to have workers themselves participate in the design process. The experiment was, however, a disappointment. It produced exactly the same type of dense apartment building as had been built in the rue de Monttessuy, similar to what private-sector developers were already building at the time. It seemed that more than innovation, what workers wanted was the replication of existing bourgeois models.[20]

Napoléon III's action in favor of workers' housing left some tangible results, but they were insufficient to have a material effect on the city.

The more significant realizations were those of private industrialists in the major manufacturing centers, like Jean Dollfuss in Mulhouse and Eugène Schneider in Le Creusot; these took the form of low-density workers' garden communities. In Paris, the bulk of the workers' housing created at the time consisted of low-quality, high-density rental complexes built for profit.

Napoléon III was a visionary and an idealist, not an executor. In many areas, he found skilled individuals to execute and improve on his vision—Persigny for conspiratorial politics, Haussmann for the rebuilding of Paris, and Ferdinand de Lesseps for the building of the Suez Canal. Workers' housing was an area in which he had a sincere interest. But looking back from a historical perspective, it is impossible to see his action in this domain as anything but an enormous missed opportunity.

After the luxurious parc Monceau, it became politically important to Napoléon III—and therefore to Haussmann—to build a park for the working population of the rapidly growing nineteenth and twentieth arrondissements. There was a steep piece of land in that area known for its clay terrain, its cesspool, and its convenience as a hideout for criminals. This unpromising location became the site of Paris's most spectacular park, the parc des Buttes-Chaumont.

Starting in 1864, Alphand's Department of Parks and Promenades again surpassed itself. A lake was dug in the center of the park, with an astonishingly high promontory surrounded by water. Atop this, Davioud built a small rotunda with a beautiful view of Paris, connected to the tops of the adjoining hills by charming bridges over a precipitous drop. The park features picturesque vegetation, paths, rambling lawns, a grotto, and a hundred-foot waterfall. It was inaugurated, to great excitement, during the 1867 Universal Exposition.

The south was now the only part of Paris without a park. Prefect Haussmann chose the Montsouris hill as the location for a park to serve the population of the thirteenth and fourteenth arrondissements. Again, there would be a lake, a grotto, a waterfall, and all the other features of the Second Empire parks. The parc Montsouris was inaugurated in 1869, even though construction continued for another nine years. It still serves Parisians of the southern arrondissements today.

On the evening of Friday, April 12, 1867, the place to be in Paris was 7, boulevard Montmartre. That was the address of the Théâtre des Variétés, where Jacques Offenbach's new opéra bouffe, *The Great Duchess of Gerolstein,* was opening, with Hortense Schneider in the starring role.

Giuseppe Verdi was back in Paris, putting the finishing touches on *Don Carlos* for the Paris Opéra. Charles Gounod was about to open *Romeo and Juliet,* and Georges Bizet was preparing *The Fair Maiden of Perth* for later in the year. But the prince of musical entertainment in 1860s Paris worked in a much less serious vein. He was Jacques Offenbach, whose work had a verve, playfulness, wry, transgressive humor, and downright silliness that were perfect for the epoch. His music provided the sound track for the Second Empire.

Offenbach, like the architect Hittorff, was from Cologne, in modern-day Germany. His father was the cantor at the synagogue, and Jacob, who learned music from a young age, became a highly gifted cellist. When he was fourteen, his father used his savings to send him to Paris, the musical capital of Europe and, notably, one place in Europe where being Jewish would not be a hindrance to his career.

Jacob, now Jacques, gradually became known in the salons of Paris. An emphatic, romantic figure, he was sometimes called "the Liszt of the cello." He then started composing little one-act operettas, and in 1858, he staged his first four-act opéra bouffe, *Orpheus in the Underworld.* In 1864, he produced the wildly successful *The Beautiful Helen.*

Offenbach was an unforgettable character. He veritably bubbled with energy and mischievousness. His French was laden with a thick

Jewish-German accent which together with his exuberant style created an irresistible comic effect. A showman, he put on grand productions with spectacular music, costumes, and scenery. More than anyone before, he and his librettists injected humor and satire into their pieces. The critics were generally derisive, but the public loved it. The pieces were full of fabulous, unforgettable melodies that left audiences humming for days. Offenbach's opéras bouffes were the musical embodiment of the Second Empire joie de vivre.

The Great Duchess of Gerolstein was a tremendous success. Napoléon III went to see it on April 24 and returned a few days later with the empress. Every night, the audience included some of Europe's most illustrious people: the Prince of Wales, who would later become King Edward VII; the czar of Russia, Alexander II, and his son, Grand Duke Vladimir; Otto von Bismarck and Helmuth von Moltke; King Ludwig II of Bavaria; King Luís I of Portugal; King Charles XV of Sweden; and the viceroy of Egypt, Ismail Pasha, who enjoyed the show so much that he returned almost every night during his stay in Paris!

Although people loved the music and libretto, what most came to see was the star of the show, Hortense Schneider. She was a superstar. The Paris public adored her verve, as well as her bodily attributes, which were generously displayed during the performance. Her blue boudoir was the social center of Paris: "[H]er court was as closely followed as that of the Tuileries, but a lot more fun!"[21] She counted, among her long list of lovers, the Prince of Wales, the future Edward VII. In fact, she so liberally bestowed her charms on European royalty that Parisians, always on the lookout for an off-color pun, dubbed her the "Passage of Princes," after a recently opened pedestrian gallery off the rue de Richelieu, in the second arrondissement.

In the spring of 1867, a twenty-six-year-old aspiring painter named Auguste Renoir set up his easel on the quai Malaquais, near the pont du

Carrousel. He was part of a group of young artists known as the "Intransigants," who had resolved to "represent things according to their personal impressions rather than the generally accepted rules."[22] They were, according to a contemporary critic, "for the most part without originality or talent"[23] and had for that reason, it was commonly accepted, been unable to have their work shown at the annual state-sponsored exhibitions of fine arts. In a few years, they would start organizing their own shows, which would cause controversy but also bring them some recognition. One critic would mockingly call them "Impressionists," coining the name that would forever designate them.

This emerging group of artists was attracted to the outdoors, where they would try to capture the light, movement, and colors of the world in situ. They usually painted pastoral scenes and would become famous for depictions of the countryside of Fontainebleau, Argenteuil, Bougival, and Normandy. But since he was in the city, staying nearby in the rue Visconti, Renoir decided to paint an urban scene. In the painting he started that day, we see—as in other paintings from the same years by Jongkind, Lépine, and Monet—the landscape of the old Paris. But off in the distance, behind the pont des Arts and the Institut de France, we see the apparitions of the new city in the form of Davioud's twin theaters in the place du Châtelet. The Impressionists' encounter with modern Paris would prove immensely fertile.

The Impressionists hardly invented the genre of urban landscapes. But the combination of their sensibility and the artistic potential latent in the urban environment of Paris after the *grands travaux* led to something unique. The unforgettable paintings that resulted include Monet's views of the boulevard des Capucines and later works in and around the gare Saint-Lazare, Sisley's view of the canal Saint-Martin, Renoir's lively portraits of life at the Moulin de la Galette and elsewhere, and Caillebotte's depiction of the Grands Boulevards on a rainy day.

All of these images of the city as rebuilt in the middle of the nineteenth century are iconic, but the pictures that have had perhaps the greatest impact in forming the representation of Haussmannian Paris came from an artist born half a world away who, until the end of the century, had shown no interest in Parisian cityscapes. Between 1893 and 1903, Camille Pissarro produced a series of panoramas of modern Paris seen from vantage points high above the streets: the place du Havre, the boulevard Montmartre, the place du Théâtre-Français, the avenue de l'Opéra. They show the highly ordered architecture of the buildings, the broad streets with their bustling traffic, the sidewalks with the streetlights, newspaper stands, and alignments of trees. Scenes of the vibrant, living city, whether on an ordinary working day or a day of celebration, under sun, rain, or snow—these have become the definitive images of timeless Paris in the collective unconscious.

While Paris was engulfed in the excitement of the exposition and the entertainment that surrounded it, Prefect Haussmann had a source of great concern in the Legislative Assembly.

As part of the liberalization measures announced by Napoléon III in January, the Legislative Assembly and Senate were discussing a new law concerning municipal councils. The intent of this law was to expand the remit of municipal councils and increase their independence—it would not affect Paris and Lyon, however, which did not have an elected mayor or city council. The idea of changing the status of Paris and Lyon was never seriously entertained, but the debate became an opportunity for the Opposition to bring up the issue of the prefect of the Seine's lack of accountability. Although not directly related to the law under debate, there was a long discussion in the Legislative Assembly on the city of Paris's funding mechanisms. From the discussion emerged a consensus that, as Léon Say had been arguing for close to three years now, the issuance of vouchers entitling the holder to future payments by the city constituted a hidden form of debt. Since any new debt contracted by the city required approval from the Legislative Assembly, the city was, according to this analysis, in violation of the law.[24]

Haussmann, of course, fought back, explaining that, according to the letter of the law, these commitments were legally accepted deferred payment plans for a period not surpassing ten years and therefore were not debt. But in the fall, Haussmann lost the argument. The court of accounts ruled that the payment scheme constituted debt. The city of Paris was therefore forced to fix the situation by entering into negotiations with the Crédit Foncier to transform the covert debt into ordinary debt. On December 2, 1867, the city council approved a first agreement with the Crédit Foncier for repayment of 398 million francs' worth of vouchers guaranteed by the city in annual installments over forty years. On July 10, 1868, the city council approved another agreement with the Crédit Foncier for repayment of 67 million francs corresponding to contractor' fees, land-acquisition costs, and interest, to be paid over thirty-nine years. These new agreements were, of course, subject to approval by the Legislative Assembly, which meant, for Haussmann, the prospect of more hostile debate.

On August 15, 1867, on the national holiday in the midst of the exposition, the scaffolding on the new Opéra de Paris was removed to reveal the main facade of the building to the public.

Some were enthusiastic. Théophile Gautier wrote:

The Opéra is the temple of modern civilization, it is the culmination of art, luxury, elegance, all the refinements of the haute vie. *The fortunate of society who frequent it are discerning and wish to find there the sumptuosities of their palaces and their hôtels. It must be both charming and grandiose, coy and pure, fashionable and classic; the problem is not easy to solve; M. Garnier has succeeded in this almost impossible task.*[25]

Others did not see it that way. One pamphlet called the new Opéra a "vast chimney-front." It vituperated: "[T]he architect wanted it to look very grand and very rich by summarizing all the architectural styles from the Pharaohs to our time."[26]

There was plenty of commentary about the new facade around Paris, but in architectural circles the Opéra and its designer had become the focal point of an acrimonious debate. On one side there was Eugène Viollet-le-Duc and his allies; on the other were the upholders of the system of the Ecole des Beaux-Arts, of whom Garnier was now a particularly prominent representative.

Although Viollet-le-Duc and Garnier had known each other for many years—as a young draftsman, Garnier had worked for Viollet-le-Duc—the two men had always been on opposite sides. Garnier was the gifted product of the Beaux-Arts culture who revered antiquity, while Viollet-le-Duc was the self-taught renegade who had never wanted to set foot in the Ecole des Beaux-Arts and held as his ideal the French genius of the medieval era. Garnier felt that a building should reflect the refinement and values of the culture behind it; Viollet-le-Duc took his inspiration from the constructive rationality of the Gothic cathedral and the Greek temple but abhorred historical imitation.

Viollet-le-Duc, who had been introduced at court by Prosper Mérimée, had become a favorite of the imperial couple. In 1857, he had been put in charge of the restoration—which later turned into a rebuilding—of the Château de Pierrefonds, an impressive medieval castle ten miles from Compiègne, a project followed closely by Empress Eugénie. He had been invited to sojourn in Compiègne, where he played the role of the perfect courtier, participating in the writing and performing of the little plays that the court so appreciated and dashing off lovely little sketches that delighted the empress.

In 1863, to the surprise of many, Viollet-le-Duc had been invited by the government to teach a course at the Ecole des Beaux-Arts. The conflict between the two factions of architectural thought flared as

Viollet-le-Duc sought to deliver a groundbreaking set of lectures on the premises of the institution that most staunchly upheld the classical French tradition, but was prevented from doing so by a group of students. Instead, he published his thoughts in a book entitled *Discourses on Architecture,* the first volume of which came out that same year. Despite the author's association with the restoration of medieval heritage and his deep knowledge of architectural history, the book made clear that Viollet-le-Duc was a modernist, against the blind reuse of historical architectural vocabulary and in favor of the use of knowledge to help each era express itself through the art of building:

> *It has taken the confusion of modern times and a long series of false doctrines to bring us to the state of anarchy and contradiction that we observe today in our buildings. But it is certain that out of this transitory state will come the methods that belong to our century and our society. People of goodwill and without bias should seek to put an end to this chaos. If we want to consider the works of the past as belonging to the past, as rungs we will climb to reach an understanding of what fits with our social state; if we proceed by analysis and not by thoughtless imitation; if we look through all the debris of distant times to find applicable procedures and are able to say why they are applicable; putting aside antiquated teachings, we will have opened the road and we will be able to travel it ourselves.*[27]

This was the moment that architectural historian Sir John Summerson considered the birth of modern architecture.[28] The ideas of Viollet-le-Duc traveled around Europe and the United States and are credited as an important influence in the work of pioneers of modern architecture such as Hendrik Petrus Berlage and Victor Horta, as well as that of the unclassifiable Catalan genius, Antoni Gaudí.

Viollet-le-Duc turned his energies to catalyzing the opening of an independent architecture school, outside the authority of the Ecole des

Beaux-Arts. A number of important figures, including Emile Pereire, Michel Chevalier, and Emile de Girardin, offered their support, and the minister of education, Victor Duruy, provided the required authorizations. The Ecole Centrale d'Architecture opened in 1865 with an innovative educational model and continues to operate today,* while the architecture section of the Ecole des Beaux-Arts was closed in 1969.

All the while, Viollet-le-Duc, who had still not come to terms with his early elimination in the competition for the Opéra, criticized Garnier's work, saying it had too much decoration, basic design errors, and misguided technological choices. Garnier generally focused on his work rather than rebutting the naysayers, but he was not without an ego and was not one to be cowed.

On one of her visits to Garnier's studio, the empress herself waded into the debate. Having some notions of the rationalist precepts, she asked Garnier why the columns were doubled, observing that the ancients did not double their columns. Garnier had no doubt that only Viollet-le-Duc could be behind this question. "Nor did the Ancients move about by railway," he is said to have responded.[29]

Although there is no question regarding Garnier's prodigious talent, the view of most architectural historians today is that the effect of his positions on the profession was ultimately detrimental. By emphasizing individual expression, he opened the path for a generation of architects who would imitate him artificially, without his compositional skill and extraordinary ability to embrace a work of art in its totality. The result was a proliferation of grand, empty facades of overbusy eclecticism in cities around the world.

The visitors to Paris for the 1867 Universal Exposition saw not only the facade of the Opéra but also the splendid new neighborhood that surrounded it. At its center was the place de l'Opéra, surrounded by

---

* The current name of the school is the Ecole Spéciale d'Architecture.

the buildings composed by Rohault de Fleury to go with a design for the Opéra that was never built. Around the square, a whole new network of streets had been built, along with buildings of great elegance, including the huge, modern, and luxurious Grand Hôtel.

The avenue Napoléon, the street that generated the whole neighborhood, was itself not built: Facing the new facade of the Opéra, there was the first stub of the avenue, leading straight into the houses of the butte des Moulins, a working-class neighborhood still to be cleared away. After years, during which the new avenue had not seemed to be a priority, the preparatory studies for its realization had just been launched.

The Opéra neighborhood is emblematic of the urban intentions of the Second Empire. "It is perhaps the only place where the theory of Haussmannism—that of the urban transformation to which the prefect lent his name—was applied in all its rigor. It is at any rate one of those where the effect of the change made itself the most felt. So we must not be surprised that, despite the fact that it was realized late in the Second Empire, it is the very model of the regeneration of urban centers to which the nineteenth century aspired."[30]

Mark Twain, on the tour that would yield *The Innocents Abroad,* visited Paris in July 1867. Twain's account of Paris is suitably exuberant. He stayed in the Grand Hôtel du Louvre and, as would be expected, went to the exposition, to the Louvre, to Versailles, to Notre-Dame, and the other predictable sites. He left hilarious accounts of a cancan, of a trip to the barber, and of the *grisettes*—the working-class girls known for their easy morals—who were a great disappointment. What is less expected is that Twain visited the faubourg Saint-Antoine:

> All through this Faubourg St. Antoine, misery, poverty, vice, and crime
> go hand in hand, and the evidences of it stare one in the face from every
> side. Here the people live who begin the revolutions. Whenever there is

anything of that kind to be done, they are always ready. They take as much genuine pleasure in building a barricade as they do in cutting a throat or shoving a friend into the Seine. It is these savage-looking ruffians who storm the splendid halls of the Tuileries occasionally, and swarm into Versailles when a king is to be called to account.

But they will build no more barricades, they will break no more soldiers' heads with paving-stones. Louis Napoleon has taken care of all that. He is annihilating the crooked streets and building in their stead noble boulevards as straight as an arrow—avenues which a cannon ball could traverse from end to end without meeting an obstruction more irresistible than the flesh and bones of men—boulevards whose stately edifices will never afford refuges and plotting places for starving, discontented revolution breeders. Five of these great thoroughfares radiate from one ample centre—a centre which is exceedingly well adapted to the accommodation of heavy artillery. The mobs used to riot there, but they must seek another rallying-place in future.[31]

At this time, a trio of other Americans began a visit to Paris. Although not as well known as Twain, they would come to have a great influence on American culture. In September, the twenty-two-year-old Robert Peabody and the twenty-year-old Charles McKim arrived in Paris, joined in October by Francis W. Chandler.

The young architects followed in the footsteps of Richard Morris Hunt, who in 1846 had become the first American to study architecture at the Ecole des Beaux-Arts and had gone on to work in the studio of Hector Lefuel, participating in the design of the new Louvre. Hunt, who returned to New York in 1855, would become one of the most prominent American architects of the nineteenth century, designing many houses in New York and Newport, as well as buildings on Ivy League campuses and the Fifth Avenue facade of the Metropolitan Museum of Art. He constituted the first great link between French architectural culture of the mid-nineteenth century and the United States.

McKim, Peabody, and Chandler studied in the studio of Honoré Dau-
met until they gained admittance to the Ecole des Beaux-Arts. They took
full advantage of the city, playing baseball in the Jardin du Luxembourg
and skating on the frozen lake of the Bois de Boulogne. They traveled to
Rouen to see the Gothic architecture there, as well as to the resort town
of Trouville, on the Normandy coast, and to London. They drank in
everything they could in this effervescent environment for students of
art and architecture

Back in the United States, McKim and Peabody, in their respective
practices, would go on to build American monuments like New York's
Pennsylvania Station, the Boston Public Library, and Boston's Custom
House Tower. Chandler would become a professor and the head of the
Architecture Department at the Massachusetts Institute of Technology.
All were durably influenced by the time spent in Napoléon III's Paris
and by their immersion in the Parisian architectural world.[32]

In the fall of 1867, French public opinion was shaken by a tremendous
financial scandal: the collapse of the Crédit Mobilier.

The bank created by the Pereire brothers in 1852, in the heady early
days of the new regime, had financed much of the rebuilding of Paris, in
addition to numerous railway lines, the mines of the Loire, a transatlantic
ocean-liner company, and many more ventures. By the end of the 1860s,
the company had subsidiaries in Italy, Spain, and the Netherlands, was
funding the Russian railway, and was underwriting the Ottoman Bank.

The company's stock prices had gone through major fluctuations, rising to 1,750 francs after the initial public offering, in December 1852,
before decreasing to 430 francs in April 1854, and then recovering again
to reach an all-time high of 1,982 in March 1856. The ups and downs
continued until the mid-1860s, when the downward trend became evident. By October 1867, the shares traded at only 140 francs.

Small holders had become convinced that the Crédit Mobilier was a prudent investment, even indispensable for any portfolio. "Decreases in the share price were nothing. Everyone involved knew that when the Crédit Mobilier went down, it was, like a balloon, only to bounce back higher."[33]

The truth was that market trades were playing an increasing role in the company's activities, compared to actual investments. There was little disclosure, so investors knew little about what the company was really doing. By this time, more than an industrial financing vehicle, the Crédit Mobilier resembled a hedge fund.

By the fall of 1867, the investors in the Crédit Mobilier had lost a total of 581 million francs compared to the issue price of the shares, and a staggering 1.4 billion francs compared to the highest price. The company was restructured with government loans and sixteen million francs of fresh equity capital, which would allow it to fend off bankruptcy for a few more years. Emile and Isaac Pereire were forced to resign.

The collapse was an all-out catastrophe for many small investors who had their life savings invested in Crédit Mobilier shares. For the country as a whole, the insolvency of a company that had once been perceived to be as strong as the government itself was deeply troubling. The original founders, however, did not fare too badly. One source estimated that they made 400 million francs, including 150 millions francs for the Pereire brothers.

The Crédit Mobilier scandal was only the most striking illustration of the surprisingly brazen determination to benefit as quickly and fully as possible, even if collapse was inevitable. Despite the glitter on the surface, many observers could see the decay below. Count Alexander von Hübner, who had been the Austrian ambassador during the 1850s, later wrote that 1867 was the year when "the princes and the peoples were able to see the state of demoralization, of presumption and of carelessness of the French government and Europe understood that it could fear, perhaps in the near term, a new eruption of the revolutionary volcano in France."[34]

The *New York Times* correspondent had exactly that fear:

The great mob of Paris is growing every year to such an extent as to give serious concern to those charged with its direction, independently of any other question than mere size, for not only is it more reckless and more impressionable than the London mob, but it is more vicious and worse disposed by being governed despotically. I do not know how much the Government is alarmed at this immense and growing element of danger, but I confess that as I see it swelling from year to year, and see the government continue blindly in the same despotic measures, I tremble for the day of trouble that will surely come.[35]

Later, after this world had clamorously collapsed, Maxime Du Camp wrote to a friend, "Yes, you are right, we are paying for the long lie in which we lived, because indeed everything was fake: a fake army, fake politics, fake literature, fake credit and even fake courtesans."[36]

·———·

Eighteen

THE LAST FIGHT

When the readers of *Le Temps* opened their newspapers on December 20, 1867, they saw a front-page article entitled "The Confession of the Prefect of the Seine." The piece was signed by Jules Ferry, a young lawyer close to the Republican opposition who was gaining notoriety as a journalist.

In a calm yet forceful tone, Ferry analyzed a report published a few days earlier by the city administration that outlined the progress of the *grands travaux* and the financial situation of the city. For the first time, wrote Ferry, the public had real insight into the city's accounts. The criticism of Haussmann's exorbitant powers and lack of oversight had always been countered by the claim that the prefect was achieving great outcomes at a reasonable cost. Now Haussmann had been forced to divulge that this was not the case, that the program of works had incurred costs far greater than had ever been admitted.

The coming year, 1868, would mark the end of the ten-year period for the realization of the projects of the 180 Million Franc Treaty. Haussmann would have to publish their final accounts. He would also soon have to disclose the cost of the *grands travaux* to the Legislative Assembly for the approval of the renegotiated Crédit Foncier debt. For these reasons, the prefect came clean. He reported that the original estimate of 180 million francs had ballooned to 410 million. This meant that instead of the 130 million francs that had been requested and approved by the city council, the city would need to pay a whopping 360 million francs.

Ferry's view was that the "first network"—in other words, the projects for the city center like the rue de Rivoli and the boulevard de Sébastopol, started in 1848–1852 under the Republic, had met a real need and aroused no controversy. The "second network," the projects of the 180 Million Franc Treaty, had been approved by the official bodies of the Empire, so they were not subject to criticism per se, but their management certainly was, since the final cost was now projected to be more than twice the original estimate. The "third network," the "personal network of Mr. Haussmann," was entirely objectionable: It had never been officially approved by any governing body and the cost was now estimated to be 300 million francs.

Ferry wrote that the sudden revelation of these previously undisclosed costs inevitably led to the questioning of Haussmann's stewardship: "If the prefect of the Seine had reason to suspect, in 1864, the colossal error that tainted his calculations, what would one think of his candor? If, on the other hand, he had no suspicion, . . . what should we think of his vigilance, of his wisdom, of his foresight?"[1]

Haussmann read the *Le Temps* article, like thousands of other Parisians. As usual, he prepared an extensive rebuttal full of figures and references to jurisprudence, together with claims that Ferry had misunderstood various subtleties of public administration.

Ferry followed up with another provocatively titled article on December 31. He did not let himself get dragged into the confusing minutia of accounting treatments and legal rulings. Nor did he indict the fact that the costs had gone up—how could it be otherwise when the *grands travaux* were themselves causing speculation on real estate in

Paris and thereby driving up property prices? While Haussmann was not guilty of the overruns themselves, he was responsible for having failed to anticipate or disclose them.

And in addition to that, it was now known that precisely at the time he was—or should have been—aware of the cost overruns, he had secretly begun a new wave of projects. In 1866, Haussmann had declared, "The City is not now any more ready for a new program of construction as it is for a relinquishment of resources. We need to resist new undertakings of any importance as energetically as a premature reduction in taxes."[2] Now the public discovered an entirely different truth. "The report of December 11, 1867, reveals *for the first time* to the general public, to the city council, to the entire world that there even exists a third network, that it will be completed by the end of 1868 and that it will have cost 300 million francs."[3]

Ferry's articles in *Le Temps* continued until May. They were a model of political writing: simple, forceful, elegant, and compelling. Ferry compiled the articles into a book, which he presented to the Legislative Assembly in view of the upcoming debate on the finances of the city of Paris. Part of the book's success was its very witty title, *Les Comptes fantastiques d'Haussmann*, phonetically nearly identical to the French title of the compiled tales of German writer E. T. A. Hoffmann: *Les Contes fantastiques d'Hoffmann*.* But instead of being about mad inventors, magical apparitions, and bizarre curses, this was about another fantastical universe, that of the accounts of the administration of the prefecture of the Seine.

The focus of Ferry's argument was the lack of transparency. Disclosure had been limited to periodical triumphal communiqués by the city. There had been no publicity and no competitive tenders for most of the concession contracts. At no point had any independent authority been given the opportunity to exercise informed oversight. For Ferry,

---

* Jacques Offenbach's tremendously successful opéra bouffe of the same name was produced only later, in 1881.

the case of Paris was emblematic of the perverse effects of the Empire's rejection of genuine democracy with its checks and balances.

It is clear to everyone, except to him [Haussmann], that the absence of control has caused the harm. Serious control would have long ago regulated, contained, limited the orgy of expropriations. Serious control would have signaled in time the variance of 230 million francs; the unplanned expenses of 300 million francs would not have suddenly appeared if there had been serious controls. Parliamentary counterweights are often barriers, but they are also often guardrails. Assemblies are naturally scrupulous; they respect legality. Personal government, on the other hand, only endures the brakes of laws with impatience. In the works of the City, the prefect of the Seine covered imprudence with illegality. This time, at least, the case is flagrant.[4]

During the frigid winter of 1867–1868, the economy was not doing well. Many people were unable to find work. Conversation among Parisians centered on these difficulties and on concerns about the size of the national debt, which had now reached 1.4 billion francs. The head of the government, Eugène Rouher, maintained that, even though the deficit had grown, "the government has committed no political fault."[5]

Even those who remained staunchly supportive of the emperor were troubled. Persigny, in a letter to Napoléon III, wrote of the state of "moral anarchy" in the country. "The Empire seems to be collapsing on all sides; the fierce and implacable fight waged by those who have sworn your undoing goes from success to success." "What good," he asked, "is it to make plans for improvement to a house that is on fire?"[6]

The general sentiment was that the regime was exhausting its resources. It appeared that "the trilogy that governed France was worn, the Emperor by illness, the Empress by frivolity, and Rouher by his lies."[7] Important Second Empire figures were dying: Adolphe Billault in 1863,

Charles Auguste de Morny in 1865, Achille Fould in 1867, and Alexandre Walewski in 1868.

A law on civil liberties, promised since January of the previous year, was passed on March 25, 1868. Even though it maintained some repressive practices, it was enough to unleash a flowering of expression and debate. People started criticizing the regime freely; the satirical press flourished; books appeared on taboo subjects, such as Louis-Napoléon's coup d'état of December 1851.

The trial in November 1868 of journalist Charles Delescluze, arrested after starting a subscription for a statue to a representative who had died on the barricades in 1851, was the opportunity for a young lawyer named Léon Gambetta to break onto the scene. Originally from Cahors, in southwest France, he was unknown other than to the patrons of the Café Voltaire, in the place de l'Odéon, where he had honed his rhetoric skills in long political debates.

At the trial, Gambetta gave a fiery, impassioned harangue. Carelessly dressed, with his square jaw and authoritative voice, heedless of the interruptions and protests, he lambasted the regime's refusal to commemorate the day when Louis-Napoléon had dissolved the democratic institutions and taken power by force. Gambetta's visionary and irreverent plea has gone down as a great moment in French public-speaking history:

> For seventeen years now you have been the absolute, discretionary masters of France. We will not seek the use you have made of its treasures, its blood, its honor, its glory; we will not speak of its integrity compromised, nor of what has become of the fruit of its industry, without counting the financial catastrophes that, as we speak, are blowing up like mines under our feet.
>
> What judges you best, because it is the testimony of your own remorse, is that which you have never dared say: we will celebrate December 2nd, we will put it among the solemnities of France as a national anniversary.

Every régime in this country has honored the day of its birth. We have
celebrated July 14th, August 10th, the days of July 1830 and February
24th. There are only two dates, 18 Brumaire and December 2nd, that
were not observed from the beginning, because you know that if you had
wanted it, the universal conscience would have rejected it.

Well! We will claim this date that you don't want, we will take it for
ourselves; we will celebrate it always, incessantly; each year will be the
commemoration of our dead until the day when the nation, once again
master, will impose upon you the great national expiation in the name of
liberty, equality and fraternity.[8]

The footsteps of Francisque Rudel du Miral rang in the corridor of the
Palais Bourbon. A stack of papers under his arm, he walked briskly
through a growing crowd of deputies and assistants converging toward
the plenary assembly hall. On this day, February 22, 1869, there would
be the first discussion of the proposed law on the finance of the city of
Paris, and du Miral, a magistrate from the Puy-de-Dôme who had unfailingly supported imperial policy since his first election in 1852, was to
present the report of the commission. Just weeks before the elections, in
an increasingly electric political climate, it was a keenly awaited session.

The room was full and the crowd restless. The industrialist Eugène
Schneider, president of the Legislative Assembly, opened the session
and called du Miral to the podium to read his report. Du Miral began
by reminding everyone how useful the projects for Paris were, what
great and beneficial changes had been made. He set the ground rules:
The objective was not to critique what had been done, but to examine
the conditions in which the undertaking had been financed and to de-
cide how best to handle the existing liabilities of the city. He explained
in great detail the funding mechanisms, especially the vouchers that
were now mostly in the hands of the Crédit Foncier, as well as the functioning of the Caisse des Travaux de Paris.

The ordinarily dispassionate legislative register recorded that "the administration of the City of Paris was sharply criticized and energetically defended. . . . Partisan spirit and personal animosities played all too large a role in the debate."[9] Deputy after deputy weighed in, many several times, during a debate that lasted eleven sessions. The main voices of the Opposition, Ollivier, Picard, and Favre, approached the sessions as an opportunity to combat the executive's discretionary authority over the city of Paris, as part of the larger struggle for power between the emperor's appointees and the elected representatives of the people. Adolphe Thiers, sensing opportunity, energetically took part.

Since the Legislative Assembly was one place Haussmann did not have a seat, he worked hard to make sure his side of the story was told. He wrote memoranda, detailing the historical failure to modernize Paris and all the improvements that had been implemented in the preceding two decades. He provided all the costs and numbers and developed argumentations for his friends to use. Some of the deputies' interventions follow verbatim the texts Haussmann would later publish in his *Mémoires*.

Deputy Adrien-Charles Calley-Saint-Paul, a banker who had been involved with certain financial dealings of the city of Paris, made a long speech about questionable practices that were embraced or tolerated by the city administration. The response of Rouher, the minister of state, who was responsible for pleading the side of the government in parliamentary proceedings, was awkward, sounding as if he were not prepared to deny the alleged irregularities. When Haussmann heard of Rouher's halfhearted defense, he was furious. Haussmann had been through all the details of his case, articulated again and again until there was no doubt that the strength of his argument was overwhelming. Why, then, was Rouher ceding valuable terrain to the Opposition, who wanted nothing but the downfall of the Empire?

There was a long legalistic debate about whether the payment of contractors over time through tradable vouchers constituted debt or just deferred payments. Haussmann's position was voiced by a number of sympathetic deputies, but both the state council—an institution that had been led by both Baroche and Rouher, and that had consistently opposed Haussmann and his management of the city of Paris—and the court of accounts—populated in large part by friends of the now-deceased Fould—gave opinions qualifying the mechanism used by Haussmann as debt, making it illegal because it had never been ratified by the Legislative Assembly.

There was a debate about the governance of the city of Paris. Thiers pointed out that, with the ability to float its own debt, Paris was a sort of state within a state, without accountability. Assuming it remained out of the question to have elected city councilors or an elected mayor for Paris, some argued that the best form of accountability was oversight by the Legislative Assembly. Deputies close to the government retorted that that would be excessive and would breach the division of power between branches of government.

Haussmann continued to be enraged by Rouher's attitude. Instead of defending the prefect of Paris, as should be the role of a government representative, he sounded sympathetic to the complaints, and even unsure himself of whether the system was legal or if there had been corruption or squandering of the public treasure. If the matter was put to vote, Haussmann was certain the government would win, but Rouher kept granting concessions to the Opposition deputies. When Haussmann finally had the opportunity to express himself directly in a speech in the Senate on April 13, it was too late.

The vote to establish a new law regarding the city's finances was taken five days later. The agreements between the city of Paris and the Crédit Foncier to transform the vouchers into debt to be paid off over an extended term of forty years were approved. But the condition was that the Legislative Assembly would now not just approve Paris's borrowing; it would have complete oversight of the city's finances. The commission had underlined that this was "the natural opportunity to request the effective monitoring and control of an administration whose revenues and expenditures have reached such colossal proportions as to exercise on the situation of the Nation itself a manifest influence."[10] Henceforth, the budget of the city of Paris was to be determined by legislative process.

Just weeks after the passage of the new law, voters went to the polls for the first general election since the new phase of liberalization had been launched in 1867.

Campaigning was vigorous across the country. In Belleville, a committee developed a radical program for their candidate, Léon Gambetta. Its first demand was universal suffrage, "including for the mayors and municipal councils, without distinction of locality"—that is to say, including Paris.

The election led to a new political landscape in France. Many deputies who favored the imperial regime were elected or reelected, but they had a tendency to be supportive of greater liberties and considerably more independent-minded than their predecessors. Republicans nearly swept the big cities and took a quarter of the total number of seats. New figures, such as Jules Ferry and Léon Gambetta, were elected for the first time. At the same time, a series of strikes erupted across France, some of them degenerating into violence. Extremist revolutionary groups gained traction in working-class neighborhoods.

Despite the general upheaval in the country, the spirit of belief in the future continued. In 1869, the Bon Marché began construction on a gigantic new store. Among the elite, the celebrations continued unabated:

In 1868 [Arsène Houssaye, director of the Comédie-Française] gave his first Venetian Masked Ball, and repeated it in 1869. These fêtes were among the most brilliant social events of their seasons, uniting courtesans, actresses and ladies of society and the Imperial Court, all hidden behind their masks, and all of the gentlemen who could wangle an invitation. The secret of success of these balls was that they were unplanned:

witty conversation, plenty of room to dance, an excellent buffet, but no
organized amusement.

Houssaye's greatest entertainment, a "country-fair party," was held in
September 1869, after the success of his book Les grandes dames. *It was*
a fête at his Château la Folie—Riancourt-en-Breuil, not far from Bru-
yères. There were whole oxen, sheep and pigs, partridges, hares and quail
roasted on spits over open fires. The roasting pits stretched for a full quar-
ter of a mile, fountains flowed with wine, one thousand bottles of cham-
pagne were consumed and the tombolas had a thousand prizes. There were
orchestras, clowns, tumblers, games, and a special train to carry the guests
from Paris and back again. It was, almost to the day, a year before the
battle of Sedan.[11]

August 15, 1869, was the last time Saint-Napoléon was grandly celebrated. One year later, the country would be in the midst of a war and
the Second Empire would have only a few more weeks to live. But 1869
was a landmark year: the one hundredth anniversary of the birth of
Napoléon I. The Champs-Elysées was turned into an amusement park,
with orchestras and singers all along its length.

In the days that followed, Napoléon III stopped appearing in public.
All those who had seen him recently remarked on his rapid aging. Officially suffering from rheumatism, he sent his son in his place for the
annual review of the troops in Chalons, an event he had scrupulously
attended since he instituted it in 1857. Rumors circulated that the condition of his health was dire; prices on the stock exchange sharply decreased.

Haussmann had started to dissolve the financing apparatus he had created. Even though he felt these transactions were unwarranted and
would accomplish little more than costing the city money, the contracts
with the Crédit Foncier were replaced by bonds. The city assumed the

debt of the Caisse des Travaux and, effective at the end of the year, the institution would be disbanded. Anyway, the controversial financial mechanisms instituted by Haussmann had already done their work.

In the fall of 1869, Haussmann seemed to have, amazingly, weathered the storm. He was still in place, the financial position of the city had been regularized, and he even had some financial margin for new projects. As long as the Legislative Assembly refused to consider creating a position of elected Mayor of Paris, there was no prospect of him being removed. But things were about to change suddenly.

The wind of freedom sweeping over the nation was threatening to unleash anarchy. The Opposition newspapers became decidedly belligerent. Léon Gambetta made a speech at a banquet, boldly declaring his ambition to "tirelessly pursue the definitive achievement of freedom in its republican form."[12] Strikes broke out at Le Creusot and elsewhere; there were conspiracies to win over the soldiers of the Paris barracks and to assassinate Napoléon III. Now in constant, crippling pain, the emperor vowed to be uncompromising in his repression of the violence.

For some time, Napoléon III had been planning to hand power over to his son when young Louis reached the age of eighteen, in 1874. Napoléon III and Eugénie would retire to Biarritz, the town on the Basque coast they both loved and where they spent each September. But first, he needed to reestablish the footing of the Empire. So Napoléon III decided to take the audacious step of launching a new phase of his reign, with a redrafted Constitution and a revised institutional structure. The Legislative Assembly and Senate would function as a true bicameral parliament, and the ministers would assume political responsibility. It was to be a new incarnation of the Empire to pass on to the future Napoléon IV.

In this political environment, with an emerging generation of pro-worker Republican hard-liners, the old cadre of the regime was only a liability. The emperor decided to do the unthinkable—to work with the moderate Republicans, and even to put them in charge of the government. In October, he began secret negotiations to appoint Emile

Ollivier—one of the Five, the original Republican opposition in the Legislative Assembly—to lead the government.

Ollivier wavered before accepting the position, unsure whether he wanted to compromise himself by working within a regime he had always combatted. When he did accept, one of his conditions was that Georges-Eugène Haussmann resign. The fact that Haussmann was one of the retrograde Bonapartists was only part of the reason. Ollivier had lived in the Var, in the south of France, at the same time that Haussmann was prefect of that *département,* in 1850. Haussmann had, in fact, issued a warrant against Ollivier that could have put him in jail or had him sent to a penal colony had he not escaped to Italy. Twenty years after this episode, it was still out of the question for Ollivier to work hand in hand with Haussmann as a member of the same government.

Haussmann refused to resign. If he were to leave, he insisted, he would need to be dismissed. Although Napoléon III was fundamentally loyal, he knew what he had to do. Ollivier became head of the government on January 2, 1870, and by a decree dated January 5, 1870, Georges-Eugène Haussmann was removed from the position of prefect of the Seine. After sixteen and a half years, his tenure was over.

Although he had many enemies, Haussmann had displayed the political astuteness required to stay in a highly exposed position far longer than any minister of the Second Empire. That political longevity, earned through countless backroom alliances, pleas, escalations, displays of indignation, and arguments, was, without doubt, one of the secrets of the scale of his accomplishment. That remarkable run was now over.

At his last session before the city council, the outgoing prefect made a speech that was not without pathos nor a typically Haussmannian brand of bad faith:

> You know that I have long aspired for the hour of my retirement; but that
> I only wanted to reach it after having put the final hand on our work,

*and fully ensure the complete liquidation of our grand enterprise. It had
to be otherwise.*

*What consoles me, after so many efforts, is to fall with the full confi-
dence of the Emperor; with the esteem and affection of all those present
who have seen me at work. That satisfaction is enough to make me forget
many outrages.*

*Ah! Gentleman, it takes courage and devotion to enter public service
in France; to dedicate efforts and faculties that in private practice would
bring both independence and fortune, and which often bring, in the service of the public interest, only bitterness and disappointment.*[13]

Haussmann stayed in position for a few days as his successor, Henri
Chevreau, finished his business as prefect of the Rhône. On January 10,
1870, Haussmann moved out of his office. The next day, he and his wife
left Paris for Nice.

The *grands travaux* represented a colossal investment. Their total cost,
between 1853 and 1870, was 2.5 billion francs—more than the annual
national budget of France, which averaged between 2.1 and 2.4 billion
francs during the years of the Second Empire[14]—even though it was, of
course, spent over seventeen years and was not actually funded by the
national budget. To give a fairer order of magnitude, the *grands travaux*
represented a little less than 1 percent of the cumulative gross domestic
product of France over those seventeen years—roughly speaking, spending the same proportion of the recent gross domestic product of France
would mean an expenditure of $245 billion, or $14.5 billion a year.*
This did not include projects led by the state, such as the building of the

---

* Calculated from the French GDP 1990–2006; source: World Development Indicators data-
base.

Opéra and Palais de Justice, the restoration of Notre-Dame, or the embankments and bridges along the Seine; nor did it include work funded directly from Napoléon III's "civil list," such as the Palais du Louvre.

The roadworks in Paris accounted for more than half of the expenditure: 1.3 billion francs. Buildings, parks, water and sewage infrastructure, and various other expenses accounted for 800 million francs. Financing fees, including interest payments, accounted for the remaining 400 million francs.

Haussmann estimated the overruns for the roadworks at between 460 and 470 million francs, which means that they came in 55 percent over budget. In Haussmann's view, this was due to the expropriation jury overcompensating private property owners and being susceptible to all sorts of trickery and manipulation. The impact was compounded by the fact that the second network—the most affected by far by the overruns—was spread over ten years, facilitating the rampant gaming. Another factor was the decisions of the appeals court and state council to disallow the expropriation mechanism used by the city to buy entire plots and sell back the remainder at the increased market price, which Haussmann saw as bald attacks on the city administration's ability to implement large-scale roadworks in the existing urban area.

Only a small portion of the 2.5 billion francs—0.3 billion francs—was raised through the sale of land and materials. A meager 0.1 billion francs came from national government subsidies. A large portion—one billion francs—came out of the city budget. The remainder came from new debt, raising the indebtedness of the city to unprecedented levels. When Haussmann arrived in 1853, the total debt of the city of Paris was 100 million francs. When he left in 1870, the number was 1.1 billion francs, including the 482 million francs of ordinary municipal debt and 566 million francs of "covert debt" that had been regularized—466 million francs owed to the Crédit Foncier and 100 million francs inherited from the now liquidated Caisse des Travaux de Paris.

Haussmann was not at all shocked by this. He felt that, out of a total investment for the city of 2.5 billion francs, it was perfectly reasonable to ask future generations, who would benefit from the improvements, to pay less than half of the amount. He was confident the investment would pay for itself, as evidenced by the rapidly increasing tax base of an enlarged and more dynamic city. When he left the city, it was indeed running an annual surplus on ordinary recurrent items, from which the debt could be serviced. Haussmann also pointed out that the national government had hugely benefited from Paris's growth: By 1860, the taxes collected by the national government from Paris had increased by more than 120 million *a year,* compared to the 95 million francs in subsidies the national government had paid the city in total over the entire Second Empire for the *grands travaux.*

For Haussmann, the great flaw of the *grands travaux* was that they had, at the behest of Napoléon III, been carried out without any new taxes. Speaking to the city council on October 30, 1869, he said:

> *We would have saved ourselves a great deal of trouble and of unfair criticism if, instead of conceiving the generous ambition of executing so many useful projects without making taxpayers carry an additional burden, that is, to provide the population with incalculable benefits without requesting any tax burden that could cause the slightest complaint, we had decided to ask for what all the other great cities that followed the example of Paris obtained, the creation of additional resources through a Special Contribution forming the cost of these advantages.*[15]

Haussmann was—and would remain—bitter and defensive. "If Voltaire could see the spectacle of Paris today, he would have difficulty understanding that instead of supporting the administration that had realized them, the Parisian . . . would criticize, combat, obstruct it, like people who do not appreciate what it had done for them."[16]

· · ·

By 1870, the city that Louis-Napoléon Bonaparte had entered by train little more than twenty years earlier had been comprehensively remodeled. The Second Empire journalist Amédée de Cesena wrote, "The day will come when history will say, speaking of the capital of France, transformed as if by magic, in less than a quarter century: *the Paris of Napoléon III*, as it said: *the Rome of Augustus.*"[17]

But the future proved de Cesena wrong. Today, the universal phrase is not "the Paris of Napoléon III," but "the Paris of Haussmann." Extraordinarily, a civil servant who joined the undertaking after its broad direction had been determined has supplanted the emperor of France and the visionary leader behind the project of the new Paris in the eyes of posterity.

In large part, Haussmann's legacy stems from the fact that he had the opportunity to write its story. In the last ten years of his life, living in isolation and relative poverty, Haussmann wrote the three-volume *Memoirs of Baron Haussmann*. Two volumes were published in 1890, the year before his death; the third came out posthumously in 1893. Although Haussmann repeatedly paid homage to the role of Napoléon III, the text was, nakedly, aimed at establishing Haussmann's own paternity of the *grands travaux*. And although irritatingly self-centered and tiresomely loaded down with details and numbers, the book worked remarkably well. Countless authors have used the *Memoirs* as their primary or practically only source, often with little historical discernment.

There is, of course, substance to Haussmann's role. He was the right man at the right time, and he knew it. He did everything necessary to ensure that his opportunity to play a role in history did not slip away.

Haussmann well understood that he offered no particular technical or artistic qualification; the one unique thing he brought was the ability to achieve results at a scale that filled timid spirits with doubt and apprehension, to move beyond debate into action—whatever the forces conspiring to confine the ambition.

> *The idea of a regularized plan of the openings to be made in Paris and of the rectification of existing streets is an old one. . . . Unfortunately, in our country, we have the habit of promptly understanding what is good, but we then quarrel at length on what we should actually do; we establish ingenious plans, but move to action only when stricken by an urgent necessity or under the influence of a genius who carries everything along with him. Although the necessity was present, it is likely that we would have continued to hesitate to put the system of the streets of Paris in accordance with the needs of traffic and of public peace if, since the establishment of the imperial throne, a high impulsion had not made itself felt.*[18]

Haussmann's lasting fame is, at the same time, in no small part due to historical circumstance. In painting Haussmann as the man responsible for the commotion and the ruinous costs, the political opposition of the 1860s actually helped to establish his legacy. The ministers and other imperial personalities who were hoping to see Haussmann fall were also happy to have the program of works for Paris associated with him. As Haussmann wrote, "All the opponents of this idea, in good faith or no, personified it in me . . . ; but it was in order to be able to combat it freely, in all impunity, as the conception of an adventurous favorite to be brought down; it was in order to attack the author through the interpreter."[19]

Haussmann's work of self-promotion was so effective that it reached surprising distances. A 1947 article from the *Milwaukee Journal* gave a racy and telling summary of the accepted narrative:

> *Baron Haussmann, who redesigned Paris almost a century ago, is recognized as the greatest city planner who ever lived. Commissioned by*

Napoleon III in 1852, he slashed away at what to all intents and pur-
poses was a medieval city, as though he were equipped with Paul Bun-
yan's bread knife. He laid his ruler across a map, recognized where
there ought to be a wide boulevard, and he had the energy to make it a
reality. He created broad avenues where there had been foul and mold-
ering relics of the Middle Ages peopled with rats and red-capped citi-
zens who came forth with pikes to build barricades whenever there was
a revolution.[20]

This article's suggestion that Haussmann was "the greatest city planner that ever lived" is amusingly naïve. Yet knowledgeable and sophisticated authors make similar claims, talking about Haussmann as one of
the founders of the discipline of urban planning and as "the first to have
treated the city globally."[21]

In reality, the ideas Haussmann implemented were not original; in
fact, they had been documented by the July Monarchy urbanists, by Napoléon III himself in the colored plan, and by the Siméon commission.
Nor did Haussmann do much actual planning, since the key axes had
been determined for him; for the rest, Haussmann's modus operandi was
more opportunism than foresight. He did little to apply methodological
rigor to social issues, although others were beginning to do so at the
time; his aesthetic conceptions went little beyond systematically ending
avenues with domed structure. Haussmann had many qualities, but he
was a doer, not an urban visionary.

The only sense in which Haussmann was a great urban planner is if
one takes the view that being an urban planner means overcoming and
incorporating all the contingencies of the development of a city to produce a result with extremely strong and recognizable characteristics
that matches the needs of an era. If it is not much about planning at all,
but about action and dealing with what is there, with a keen, even cynical skill for navigating the political and financial obstacles, Haussmann
was as good as they come.

· · ·

In the spring of 1870, the emperor's health grew still worse. He complained of feeling as if he had a ball of needles in his bladder. In June, he
was examined by Dr. Germain See, who became convinced that the
emperor had a bladder stone. The emperor and his doctors decided
against exploratory surgery, as they feared it might be fatal. They hid
their suspicions from the emperor's entourage, understating the gravity
of his condition.

With Napoléon III severely diminished, the Second Empire was
hurtling headlong to its final demise. The seemingly insignificant affair
of the succession of Isabella II of Spain, deposed in 1868, turned out to
be the spark that set off the final conflagration. A proposal to select a
German prince had circulated in European chanceries, outraging France.
The idea was withdrawn, but the French insisted that was not enough:
Wilhelm I should issue a public apology. Of course, the Prussian king
was not prepared to do so. Diplomatic provocations orchestrated by
Otto von Bismarck dovetailed with an increasingly bellicose mood in
France. Adolphe Thiers was an all-too-isolated voice of wisdom and
clairvoyance, fully aware that Prussia held itself ready for war with
France. "Austria was not ready, and that is what caused her ruin," he
warned. "Let us not imitate her."[22]

The frenzy of war escalated. At the Legislative Assembly, deputies
made violent speeches, claiming that France now had no choice but to
take up arms. The French minister of war famously declared that the
army was ready to teach the Prussians a lesson: "not a gaiter button is
missing." On July 19, 1870, France declared war against Prussia.

The army mobilized and Napoléon III went to the front. He was in
such pain that even a carriage ride was excruciating. Still, he tried to
mount a horse. He had to be lifted into place and wear diapers because
of his incontinence, and he could only stay in such a position for a short
time. Naturally, he was of no help to the military command.

The collapse of the Second Empire was as spectacular as its achievements. By September 1, as a result of a series of bumbling miscalculations by the French high command, the Prussian troops had trapped a large part of the French army and the emperor himself in the town of Sedan. The next day, in a final tragic scene, the seriously ill emperor wandered about the battlefield as Prussian shells rained down, no doubt thinking that death in combat was the only hope to ensure the continuation of his dynasty, or at least his honor. In the late afternoon, still alive despite himself, he surrendered.

The news reached Paris on the evening of September 3. Eugénie still did not want to relinquish her role as regent, but with word of the disaster of Sedan spreading a mob had formed at the gates of the Palais des Tuileries and she was finally convinced to flee. She escaped through the Louvre with the help of the ambassadors of Austria and Italy, and jumped into a *voiture de place* in front of the église Saint-Germain-l'Auxerrois. At that moment, Léon Gambetta, Jules Favre, and Jules Ferry were at the Hôtel de Ville, proclaiming the end of the Empire, the creation of a Republic, and the constitution of a government of national defense.

Not knowing where to go, only wanting to get out of the center of town lest she be discovered by a bloodthirsty crowd, Eugénie went to the home of her dentist, an American named Thomas Evans, who lived on avenue de l'Impératrice, away from the turmoil. Evans succeeded in ferrying Eugénie to Deauville and commandeering a small boat to take the now former empress to the safety of England.

Meanwhile, Napoléon III, captive, exhausted, and urinating blood, was taken through Belgium to captivity in Wilhelmshöhe Castle, near Kassel in modern-day Germany.

That winter, the Prussians, wanting to avoid urban combat, set up camps around Paris. As the siege wore on and the weather grew colder, Parisians were pushed to extremes. Many stories have been passed down of people eating rats and cats; of elephants, antelopes, and camels from the zoo being served in restaurants. Equally if not more devastating was the lack of fuel. The coal and natural gas ran out, so people started chopping down trees, including those on the Champs-Elysées. Malnutrition and cold caused many deaths. By the end of January, with the population in a dire state and every attempt to strike out against the Prussian forces resulting in heavy French losses, discussions to prepare for an armistice began. In a ceremony in the Hall of Mirrors at Versailles on January 18, King Wilhelm I declared the creation of the unified German Empire. An armistice was signed on January 26, 1871.

In March 1871, the former emperor of France, of no use to his captors, was released. He settled with his family in Chislehurst, today in the London borough of Bromley. Gravely ill, he had less than two years left to live.

By that same month of March 1871, the mistrust between the national, conservative, antiwar government in Versailles and the anticapitulation Republicans of Paris had reached the boiling point. The city of Paris declared itself a self-administered commune and, before the eyes of the German occupants, a civil war broke out.

The Versailles troops retreated and regrouped. On the afternoon of Sunday, May 21, they returned to Paris and broke through the city's fortifications. They established a position at the Arc de Triomphe and began shelling the federated artillery, set up in the Jardin des Tuileries. Paris became an urban battlefield, with cannonballs flying over the Champs-Elysées and raining down from the heights of Montmartre and with infantry combat on the Grands Boulevards. The more professional regular French army advanced through the city from the west, taking Montmartre and Montrouge. By midweek, the fighting had moved into the center of the city.

On the evening of Tuesday, May 23, the actress Marie Colombier was with friends on the terrace of Saint-Germain-en-Laye, overlooking Paris in the distance. She later described the scene in her *Memoirs*:

We saw a light that slowly began to grow, expanding into sheaves of fire, spreading into blankets of red, filling the horizon. We looked at one another and suddenly understood: "My God! These fanatics have set fire to Paris!"

The flames roared like a continuous bass, interrupted from time to time by dry rifle fire. . . . Little flames, carried by the wind, swirled above our heads: they were the parchments of the Court of Accounts—or rather the history of the Second Empire that was disappearing, page by page. Finished this legendary time of folly and grandeur! Finished Balzac's dream realized in the fanciful adventure of this epoch.[23]

Nineteen

CAPITAL OF A REPUBLIC

As the new week started on Monday, May 29, 1871, the army was still rooting out insurgents in their last redoubts in the north and east of the city. Long columns of prisoners were marched up the Champs-Elysées on their way to Versailles for incarceration, deportation, or execution; terrible stories of atrocities propagated by the Communards whirled around Paris.

The response of the Versailles-based government was of nauseating proportions. During this, the Bloody Week, between 17,000 and 35,000 people were killed, including many women and children. Given the number of dead and all those who had been imprisoned, deported, or exiled, the population of Paris decreased by 100,000 in a few days.[1]

Parisians reemerged after the fighting had stopped to see what state the city was in. The scene was awful. The streets were strewn with debris, the paving ripped open to build the barricades. There was a constant movement of workers trying to dispose of the corpses as quickly as possible. Everywhere one could see remnants of blood, bullets, and cannon fire. Emile Zola recorded his impressions: "Paris in the last six days has been nothing but a vast cemetery, where we lacked arms to bury the bodies. . . . It gave me the impression of a lugubrious necropolis, where fire was unable to purify the odor of death that permeates the sidewalks."[2]

The fire had extracted a heavy toll on the city's structures. The Palais-Royal was severely damaged. At the Louvre, fire had devastated the library and its priceless collection, but it had been stopped before it could spread to the rest of the complex. The Ministry of Finance, located on the corner of the rue de Rivoli and the rue de Castiglione, was a ruin, as was much of the rue Royale, with building after building ripped open. The Palais des Tuileries had been gutted, but most of the structure was still standing.

The magnificent Hôtel de Ville had been completely destroyed, together with the annexes on avenue Victoria, including not only the furniture, artwork, and books they contained but all the city records since the Revolution. The Théâtre-Lyrique, today's Théâtre de la Ville, had been gutted; across the square, the Théâtre du Châtelet, although touched by the fire, had been saved due to the heroism of firemen and employees. The fires had continued in buildings up the boulevard de Sébastopol.

On the Ile de la Cité, the courts complex was heavily damaged, including two medieval towers and parts Joseph-Louis Duc had just finished building, as well as the police headquarters. Surrounded by this landscape of destruction, the Sainte-Chapelle was completely untouched. There had been attempts to set fire to both the old Hôtel Dieu—the new hospital was still under construction across the parvis—and Notre-Dame, but the arsonists had been foiled by vigilant employees.

On the Left Bank, the Palais d'Orsay, which housed the state council and the court of accounts, had been burned down, as had been whole stretches of the rue de Lille and the rue du Bac, including the Caisse des Dépôts et Consignations.

Charred remains of other buildings dotted the city: the Magasins

Réunis on the place du Château d'Eau, the gare de Lyon, the Manufacture des Gobelins, part of the église Saint-Eustache, the warehouses at La Villette, and stores, restaurants, and cafés. The total material damage amounted to at least one billion francs.

Paris was in shock, reeling from the tragic succession of events over the preceding year. It was the capital of a defeated, humiliated, divided country, which was still under occupation. But already some had turned their thoughts toward rebirth. In the sixth arrondissement, the mayor of the district had posted placards that read: "The task now is to repair our tragedies, to dress our wounds. The civil war made many victims, aggravated many misfortunes; we will now courageously put ourselves back to work, guided by duty and the love of our nation; little by little we will lift ourselves up from the ruins."[3]

France, on its third try, was about to establish a durable Republic. Although there was little political consensus, there was unanimous desire to turn the page. Democracy was imposing itself, somewhat by default, as the only workable system.

In the early years of the Third Republic, the judgment of many on the Second Empire transformation of Paris was negative. An article in the Larousse encyclopedia published in 1872 offers a good summary of prevailing opinion:

[Haussmann] put his plan to execution with a singular tenacity, without concern for the obstacles and criticisms, without worrying about legality, carrying out the most reprehensible credit operations without any oversight. . . . If Haussmann had limited himself to cleaning up and embellishing Paris, working with measure and prudence, we would only have praise for him; but by mixing a political intention with his actions, by forcing the working class to a sort of emigration, by provoking an increase in rents disastrous for those with small budgets, by wanting to do

everything at once, by overturning even rich neighborhoods without rea-
son, he brought upon the Parisian population a disturbance of which it
will long feel the deplorable effects.[4]

Others, like Maxime Du Camp, insisted that people recall the benefits brought to the city:

If we were to avoid seeing the capital of France choke on itself and perish
of resorption, it was necessary to accomplish this gigantic work of saniti-
zation and of aeration, unfortunately interrupted today. This produced
for our city an excess of costs that required often painful sacrifices, but
which it would be impossible to repudiate.[5]

In the three years following Haussmann's removal, there were three
prefects of the Seine. Henri Chevreau's short tenure had been occupied
with the politics of the weakening imperial regime. Jules Ferry had been
faced with the extreme difficulties of administering a city under siege.
Léon Say had focused on recovering from the siege and the Commune of
Paris, getting the city's finances in order, and reconstituting the birth,
death, and marriage registers, all of which had been destroyed by fire.
The focus during these difficult times was not on construction projects
or any nonessential expense.

On the evening of October 28, 1873, the building in the rue Le Peletier that had been the temporary home of the Paris Opéra for fifty years
caught fire. By the following evening, the building had been completely
consumed by flames.

For three years, the government had been debating whether finishing a lavish new opera house for Paris was really a priority or the right
symbol, given the state of the nation and its finances. But the building

was so close to completion that it was not clear what else could be done with it. With the company and subscribers of the Opéra suddenly without a home, opening the new Opéra suddenly became urgent. Garnier was instructed to deliver the building as soon as possible.

The previous fourteen years of construction had been filled with trials of all sorts. The first tests had revealed that the site, in addition to having sandy terrain, had an extremely high water table, requiring Garnier to develop innovative pumping and excavation techniques and put in place a novel double concrete shell foundation. There were numerous other difficulties: the design of a ceiling for the main hall that was decorative yet fire-resistant, the puzzling problem of the acoustics of the main hall at a time when the science of acoustics was poorly understood, the design of an orchestra pit of a size and depth that would suit both the audience and the somewhat persnickety musicians, and the obvious challenges of keeping a major construction site going through a siege, a civil war, and three different political regimes.

As the opening approached, there were, of course, a million matters to tend to. But Garnier had one special worry: the ceiling of the grand staircase. The painter Isidore Pils, who specialized in battle scenes, struggled with the mythological subjects requested for this painting: "[H]ow he would have preferred to paint an entire regiment than the torso of just one Venus!" joked Garnier.[6] When Pils produced the four canvases required for the ceiling, Garnier was not dissatisfied with the work, but he was concerned that they would be too dark for the space. With the opening day only two months away, Garnier decided to immediately begin the *marouflage,* the operation of fixing the canvases onto the surface of the ceiling, in order to assess the overall effect.

With the paintings in place, it became clear that Garnier's fears were founded and that the paintings would need to be significantly reworked. Pils gamely climbed the scaffolding and continued his work, painting the canvases in situ, with the help of two of his students. A few

days of the strenuous work of painting overhead and constantly climb-
ing up and down the scaffolding were too much for the sixty-one-year-
old Pils, who fell ill. His students were left to finish the work alone.

The two young men worked with extraordinary energy, singing as
they painted, skipping lunch, smoking excessively, and even bringing
models up to the top of the scaffolding to pose for them, all amid the
hammering and other sounds of the construction site all around. The
day before the opening, they were still working away. Garnier practically had to force the painters to stop. Pils was brought in, on the arm
of his doctor, and the scaffolding was removed. They all lifted their
eyes, holding their breath. Garnier recalled the moment: "A sentiment
of joy invaded us all. There was nothing to regret. The effect was admi-
rable! The painting was soft and shimmering! Pils had succeeded!"[7]

Of course, there was much more to the building than the grand staircase and its ceiling. The entry vestibule, the grand foyer, the lounges, the
dancing studio, the main hall, the balconies, the dressing rooms, the re-
hearsal spaces, the library, the mechanical apparatus, the spaces for the
sets and costumes, the lighting equipment—all were designed and assembled with the greatest care, full of decorations, paintings, and sculptures. The Opéra was not just Garnier's masterpiece; it was a showcase of
the artistic talent of the nation, a total work of art.

The one thing that irritated Garnier was criticism regarding the
expense of the Opéra's artworks:

*This great museum of the Opéra will remain as one of the glories of our
French school of painting and sculpture. . . . It is not to study our politics, I believe, that foreigners will come to our beautiful country; it is not
to study our administration; it is to admire our artistic production, and
as far as I know, despite the pain and sadness that has assailed us, the
works of our artists still are not in a position to fear the supremacy of
other nations. Let us then manifest with fullness, with breadth, these
works that are our life and, if some unfortunates preach savings in this*

area, tell yourself that those savings are as harmful to a nation as savings of quinine are to someone suffering from a violent fever.[8]

The opening of the Opéra, on January 5, 1875, was awaited with trepidation. For weeks, people tried to use their influence to obtain tickets. Every minister and ambassador was planning to attend. The Chamber of Deputies, still holding its sessions in Versailles, even scaled back its schedule for the day to allow the deputies to make it back to Paris in time to prepare themselves for the evening.

By seven o'clock, the square was filled with a large, expectant crowd. For the first time, the audience climbed the front steps into the building, crossed into the low, vaulted vestibule, passed the statues of Rameau, Lully, Gluck, and Handel, and discovered the lounges, staircases, and foyers.

At quarter to eight, the president of France, Patrice de Mac-Mahon, and his wife arrived. Shortly thereafter, the sound of trumpets announced the arrival of the Lord Mayor of London, who appeared in full regalia. The magical space of the staircase was filled with the blazing lights of the gas lamps; the warm hues of the limestone, onyx, copper, and multiple varieties of marble Garnier himself had selected in quarries from Spain to Sweden; the ornamentation and sculpture applied with virtuosity in every corner; and the dizzying architectural motifs on all sides—bays, balconies, and balustrades; columns, capitals, and cornices. High above was the domed ceiling carrying Isidore Pils's renderings of Apollo and Orpheus.

At the intermission, Charles Garnier stepped out onto the landing of the grand staircase. The audience filled the floor below him, the foyer level, and the balconies around and above him on all sides. Applause rose, punctuated by enthusiastic shouts of recognition, as if Garnier himself had just sung the tenor role in *La Juive*. He was radiant, overcome with emotion. Seldom in history has an architect received such a direct and overwhelming expression of the public's appreciation.

. . .

In May 1873, Ferdinand Duval was appointed prefect of the Seine, a position he would keep for six years. Prudent in financial matters, Duval nevertheless resumed the projects for new roads, sewers, and buildings. Gradually, despite the ideological differences between Empire and Republic, the continuation of the program for Paris imposed itself. More than ever, modernization was an imperative. In the new democratic context, the idea of spending to improve the city had lost its political toxicity. And something of the excitement Parisians had tasted in the extraordinary undertaking of making a city that could be a capital for the world remained.

The first undertakings of the Duval administration were the two major projects interrupted by the war: the boulevard Saint-Germain and the avenue de l'Opéra.

The unbuilt middle part of the boulevard Saint-Germain, from the rue Saint-Dominique to the rue de l'Ancienne-Comédie, had the potential to be controversial, as it would destroy historic streets of the Left Bank, most notably the rue Taranne, a good portion of the rue de l'Ecole de Médecine, and some dependencies of the abbey church of Saint-Germain-des-Prés. At the same time as the boulevard was being constructed, a large square would be created in front of the church, replacing the smaller medieval square and the streets leading into it. Despite this, the government was unfazed. The building of the boulevard Saint-Germain was relaunched in 1874. In 1877 the great east-west artery of the Left Bank was complete.

The avenue Napoléon, renamed avenue de l'Opéra in 1873, was only a stub of about one hundred yards facing the facade of the Opéra that remained untouched until 1875. Then, after the opening of the Opéra building, it was felt that the avenue needed to be finished to give the full perspective to Garnier's work—a paradox when one remembers that originally it had been the other way around: The building had been sited so as to give a perspective to the planned road. The decree authorizing the completion of the avenue was published in June 1876. The expropriations were completed by the end of the year and construction began. It was a major undertaking, requiring extensive civil engineering and the destruction of a working-class neighborhood, la Butte des Moulins. The avenue, connecting the Louvre to the Opéra and the gare Saint-Lazare beyond, one of the emblematic realizations of the Second Empire despite the fact that it was actually built during the Third Republic, was opened three years later, close to thirty years after its inception.

Many new streets were conceived and built under Duval and his successors. In fact, the total length of streets created in the twenty years after 1870 is comparable to that built during the Second Empire. Some of these new streets were, in fact, projects that Prefect Haussmann had tried, unsuccessfully, to begin during his tenure: the extension of the avenue de la République to Père Lachaise Cemetery, opened in 1897; the boulevard Raspail, completed in 1906; and the last link of the boulevard Haussmann, not completed until 1927. Others were entirely new ideas.

The government of the Third Republic was, in the final analysis, not against the actual urban projects of the Second Empire as much as it was against their protagonists and their politics. Jules Simon, one of the leading Republican deputies in the Second Empire, a luminary of the Third Republic, and a close ally of Jules Ferry, recalled the days of the 1860s: "[A]nything that was said against our common enemy was good for us. But today it matters little to us if Haussmann's accounts were fantastic. He undertook to make Paris a magnificent city and he completely succeeded. . . . We only wish one thing today: that we complete through liberty what was started by despotism."[9]

There is quite a bit of chronological overlap and many aspects of continuity between the projects of the Second Empire and those of the Third Republic—not least the fact that Adolphe Alphand, who had played a critical role alongside Haussmann, continued as director of Public Works through the various city administrations until the late

1880s. As a result, many people today think of the Third Republic projects as Haussmannian.

Paris held another Universal Exposition in 1878, symbolizing the recovery from the war. The transitional Thiers and Mac-Mahon presidencies came to an end and, in 1879, Jules Grévy, a rigorous parliamentary democrat who played a decisive role in anchoring the nation in its new governance model, became president.

Haussmann himself was still alive, living in a small apartment in the rue Boissy d'Anglas, near the place de la Concorde. However, after a number of unsuccessful business ventures and a brief return to politics, he was thoroughly marginalized. He was now a relic, a man of a bygone era whose key protagonists were mostly dead and whose precepts seemed irrelevant. He died of pneumonia in the bitter cold of January 1891, at the age of eighty-one. Close to three hundred people followed the procession to his final resting place in Père Lachaise Cemetery, but there were no representatives of the national government or of the city council.

The accomplishments of the Third Republic form a separate and important chapter of Paris's urban history. They include numerous streets and buildings, big improvements in the transportation system, including the beginning of the underground Paris Métro system, and a certain three-hundred-meter-tall metal tower. They consolidated the changes of the Second Empire and turned Paris into a modern, industrial city, the capital of a great democracy.

EPILOGUE

Throughout history, kings and presidents of France have built monuments for Paris. The Second Empire made Paris itself into a monument.

The enterprise was governed by an extraordinarily powerful idea: Paris was to be the humanist capital of the world. In Haussmann's words, "[T]his immense city aims to be the head of modern civilization; the primary home of science and arts; the masterpiece of architects and engineers; the model of good administration; the veritable Rome of the present century."[1] The men behind the transformation of Paris were not just improving their city; they were invested with a mission for humanity.

The city that came out of this great enterprise is so coherent that it is tempting to think that it sprang fully formed from the mind of Napoléon III onto the paper of his colored plan. In reality, the process was messy. The projects were constantly being amended and added to, in the midst of changing practical, political, and financial constraints. The undertaking was successful because of the immense pragmatism that governed it, driven by Prefect Haussmann, who was as inflexible about the vision to be achieved as he was shrewd and wily about the means to achieve it. As the historian Christopher Mead wrote, "Second Empire Paris reveals in its history the degree to which any living city remains in a constant and indeterminate state of becoming."[2]

Even if imperfect and in places somewhat improvised, the Second Empire's projects for Paris were amazingly bold. They were so radical compared to what existed before that it is often difficult, on old maps, to place exactly where the squares and avenues we know so well are situated. One can get a sense of how audacious these projects were by looking at streets that were planned but never executed—for example, the stretch of the rue de Rennes from the place Saint-Germain-des-Prés to the Seine, which would have had to go right through the fully built city blocks of a historic Left Bank neighborhood. For years, similar projects were implemented by the prefecture of the Seine almost as a matter of routine.

In New York, the success of Paris generated some envy. "Since the [Civil War], New York's elite had been spellbound by Paris, glittering capital of Napoléon III's Second Empire. Shedding centuries of anglophilia, they had passionately pursued all things French, from boulevards to ball gowns, from the cancan to the Crédit Mobilier."[3] The part that most fascinated New Yorkers was Paris's unabashed top-down approach, precisely at a time when New York was experiencing a real tension between its own elite and its masses. Haussmann's strong, highly centralized power and the successful expansion of Paris's city limits to the whole urban agglomeration were potent examples in the debate about the consolidation and governance of New York City starting in the 1860s. One New Yorker wrote, "Despotic governments are generally bad governments, but when one hears of the marvels Napoléon has accomplished in Paris . . . , it makes us wish that he, or someone like him, could be made Emperor of New York for about ten years."[4]

Ultimately, though, Americans learned the wrong lesson from Second Empire Paris. There was a wave of enthusiasm for civic monuments, overlooking the fact that in Paris it was not just the monuments that were beautiful, but the whole city. Paris's public space was carefully designed and maintained by a city administration full of architects and engineers, who worked to make every park bench and streetlight as elegant as Second Empire society desired. Charles Mulford Robinson, the man behind the City Beautiful movement, understood this reality and was frustrated by Americans' failure to assimilate it. To explain to his compatriots that the focus needed to be on the many little things that make the city, he described the work of the Paris nurseries and gardeners, the rules preventing posting notices on light poles, the regulations imposing harmony among various buildings, and the city's practices for the maintenance of the thoroughfares and promenades. When he brought up the place des Vosges and its "perpetual prohibition to change the shape or design of any structure," he had reached the core of the issue: the willingness to impose restrictions on private rights in the interest of the quality of the shared space.[5] That Second Empire France was decisively prepared to make such societal choices is what, most fundamentally, accounts for the quality of the Parisian urban environment.

There is no glossing over the fact that the principles that governed the transformation of Paris were despotic and socially regressive. The financial and real estate dealings were, when not downright reprehensible, questionable. The moral depravity of many of those involved was appalling. The *grands travaux* destroyed entire neighborhoods of irreplaceable character and history, and overturned the lives of thousands of ordinary people. Once one knows the history, one cannot walk down the boulevard Saint-Germain without thinking of the forgotten rue Taranne, or visit the place de la République without imagining the teeming life of the old boulevard du Temple, or cross the Ile de la Cité without recalling the rich medieval neighborhood that was lost. There is no doubt that, in other hands, the *grands travaux* could have been achieved in a more sensitive way, without such blind sacrifice of the city's historic character to the objective of modernization.

At the same time, Paris was facing the challenges of a new, industrial era, and the leaders of the time deserve our admiration for having risen to it so decisively. It is fortunate that the quality of what was rebuilt was, on the whole, high. Although our feelings remain equivocal and tinged with nostalgia, we must acknowledge that, through the strength of their vision and the quality of their work, the Second Empire architects, engineers, and administrators created something that we can also love.

The Paris of the Second Empire has proved to be durable. Its structure still functions quite well today, without major changes. Every day, millions of people use the streets, train stations, parks, arrondissement town halls, and other urban amenities built during the Second Empire. Tourists continue to flock to the city to marvel not just at the monuments but at the city as a whole. Paris's boulevards still convey an image of elegance, luxury, and beauty recognized around the world.

It is extraordinary that the vision of Louis-Napoléon, the improbable future leader of France who arrived at the gare du Nord on that fateful day in September 1848, became a reality. He, in the end, managed to catalyze a deployment of funds, energy, and human skill that forever changed the face of one of the world's great cities. The city created by Napoléon III's vision, by Haussmann's tenacity, and by the priorities and culture of an entire society became the archetype of a modern, functional, and beautiful city, unlike anything we have ever known or ever will know.

The transformation of Paris is the remarkable story of a grand idea meeting reality, a lesson that a great vision can indeed be transformational. It can only invite us to consider the urban vision of our society and ask ourselves what kind of world we wish to build for our own posterity.

ACKNOWLEDGMENTS

This book would have been impossible without the work of the researchers whose dedication keeps the history of Paris alive. I salute their work and hope that this book will encourage more people to delve further into the many fascinating aspects of Paris's urban history that I have only been able to skim over in this book.

I especially want to thank the professors who, years ago, first instilled in me the passion for this subject, in particular Philippe Gresset, a man with an extraordinarily deep and wide-ranging knowledge of urban history. I also wish to note my gratitude to professors Bernard Huet, Jean-Jacques Dupuy, and Yves Bottineau of the Ecole d'Architecture Paris-Villemin (today ENSA Paris-Malaquais) and the Ecole d'Architecture Paris-Belleville (today ENSA Paris-Belleville), all three men of great knowledge and great pedagogical talent.

I would like to thank my agent, William Clark, for his constant encouragement and for the professionalism of his guidance; Charles Spicer, my editor at St. Martin's' Press, for his belief in the manuscript and his support of its publication; and all those at St. Martin's Press who contributed to the publication process.

Most of all, I would like to thank all those who, through words and gestures of encouragement, have believed in and supported this project through its lengthy gestation.

My heartfelt thanks to Michelina Cairo and my sister, Mirabelle Kirkland, for their thoughtful critique of the manuscript at various stages of development. Thanks to my mother, Catherine Coursaget, for helping with editing and fact-checking, and to my father, Christopher Kirkland, for his support and literary advice.

Thanks to Ryan Fischer-Harbage for his irreplaceable help and advice early in the process, and to David Downie and Ellen Williams for their thoughtful input.

For the research, I am indebted to the staff at the Bibliothèque Historique de la Ville de Paris, the Bibliothèque Nationale de France, the Bibliothèque Forney and other specialist libraries of the Paris municipal library network, the library of the Assemblée Nationale, and the New York Public Library. Thanks to Laure Chabanne of the Musée du Second Empire at the Château de Compiègne, Jean-Marie Bruson at the Musée Carnavalet, and the community of Saint Michael's Abbey, Farnborough.

Thanks, finally, to my spouse and children for their patience and encouragement.

ENDNOTES

*All translations in the text are by the
author unless otherwise noted.*

One: In the Shadow of Versailles

1. Voltaire, "Des Embellissements de Paris," in *Oeuvres complètes de Voltaire,* vol. 38 (Paris: Delangle Frères, 1827), p. 43.

2. Voltaire, "Observations sur MM. Jean Law, Melon, et Dutot; sur le commerce, le luxe, la monnaie et les impôts," in ibid., p. 30.

3. Voltaire, "Des Embellissements de Paris," p. 50.

4. Ibid., pp. 53–54.

5. Michel Ulysse Maynard, *Voltaire, sa vie et ses oeuvres,* vol. 1 (Paris: Ambroise Bray, 1867), p. 494.

6. Louis-Sébastien Mercier, *Tableau de Paris* (Hamburg: Virchaux et Compagnie; Neufchâtel: Samuel Fauché, 1781), pp. 57–60.

Two: A World of Change

1. "Des Machines à vapeur locomotives," *Le Magasin pittoresque* 5 (1837): p. 387.

2. Marie-Louise Biver, *Le Paris de Napoléon* (Paris: Librairie Plon, 1963), p. 36.

3. *Galignani's New Paris Guide* (Paris: Galignani, 1839), p. 148.

4. F. Hervé, *How to Enjoy Paris in 1842* (Paris: Amyot; London: G. Briggs, 1842), pp. 116–117.

5. Frances Trollope, *Paris and the Parisians in 1835* (London: Richard Bentley, 1836), p. 26.

6. Jörg Aufenanger, *Heinrich Heine in Paris* (Munich: Deutscher Taschenbuch Verlag, 2005), p. 40.

7. Marie-Christine Vila, *Paris musique* (Paris: Parigramme, 2007), pp. 134–35.

8. Octave Uzanne, quoted in ibid., p. 135.

9. James Fenimore Cooper, *Recollections of Europe* (Paris: Baudry's European Library, 1837), pp. 227–28.

10. Louis Léger, *Nicolas Gogol* (Paris: Bloud et Cie, 1914), p. 30.

11. Hervé, *How to Enjoy Paris in 1842,* pp. 47, 119.

12. Victor Considerant, *Destinée sociale* (Paris: Libraires du Palais-Royal, 1834), p. 462.

13. Jules Janin, *Un Eté à Paris* (Paris: L. Curmer, 1844), pp. 13–15.

14. *Galignani's New Paris Guide,* pp. 126–27.

Three: A Dreamer in the Industrial Age

1. Eric Anceau, *Napoléon III* (Paris: Tallandier, 2008), p. 43.

2. Louis-Napoléon Bonaparte, *L'Extinction du paupérisme* (Paris: Pagnerre, 1844), p. 11.

3. Anceau, *Napoléon III,* p. 15.

4. Alexis de Tocqueville quoted in ibid., p. 213.

5. Albert Dresden Vandam, *An Englishman in Paris* (London: Chapman & Hall, 1892), p. 154.

6. Joseph d'Arçay, *Notes inédites sur M. Thiers* (Paris: Paul Ollendorff, 1888), p. 166.

Four: The Prince-President and the City

1. Victor de Persigny, *Mémoires* (Paris: Librairie Plon, 1896), p. 2.

2. *Discours, messages et proclamations de S. M. Napoléon III, empereur des Français* (Mirecourt: Humbert, 1860), p. 3.

3. Louis-Napoléon quoted in Pierre Pinon, *Atlas du Paris haussmannien* (Paris: Parigramme, 2002), p. 43.

4. *Discours, messages et proclamation de S. M. Napoléon III, empereur des Français,* p. 57.

Five: A New Empire

1. *Discours, messages et proclamation de S. M. Napoléon III, empereur des Français,* (Mirecourt: Humbert, 1860), p. 58.

2. Eric Anceau, *Napoléon III* (Paris: Tallandier, 2008), p. 207.

3. Ibid., p. 228.

4. Pauline von Metternich, *"Je ne suis pas jolie je suis pire"* (Paris: Tallandier, 2008), p. 36.

5. The duchess of Cobourg quoted in Guy des Cars, *Eugénie, la dernière impératrice* (Paris: Perrin, 2000), p. 245.

6. Albert Dresden Vandam, *An Englishman in Paris* (London: Chapman & Hall, 1892), p. 109.

7. Von Metternich, *"Je ne suis pas jolie je suis pire,"* pp. 75–76.

8. Théophile Gautier, *Spirite* (Paris: Charpentier, 1866), pp. 22–23.

9. Emile Zola, *La Curée* (Paris: G. Charpentier et E. Fasquelle, 1895), pp. 17–18.

10. Christian Merruau, *Souvenirs de l'Hôtel de Ville, 1848–1852* (Paris: E. Plon et Cie, 1875), p. 365.

11. Anceau, *Napoléon III*, p. 294.

12. Merruau, *Souvenirs de l'Hôtel de Ville, 1848–1852*, p. 496.

13. Georges-Eugène Haussmann, *Mémoires du Baron Haussmann,* vol. 2 (Paris: Victor-Havard, 1890), p. 257.

14. Michel Chevalier, *Politique industrielle* (Paris: Religion Saint-Simonienne, 1832), p. 48.

15. Georges-Eugène Haussmann, *Mémoires du Baron Haussmann,* vol. 3 (Paris: Victor-Havard, 1893), p. 43.

16. Anceau, *Napoléon III,* p. 266.

17. Ibid., p. 313.

18. Henry Kepler, *Man About Paris: The Confessions of Arsène Houssaye* (New York: William Morrow, 1970), p. 224.

19. Merruau, *Souvenirs de l'Hôtel de Ville, 1848–1852,* pp. 375–78.

20. Duc de Persigny, *Mémoires du Duc de Persigny* (Paris: H. de Laire d'Espagny, 1896), pp. 238–39.

Six: The Man for the Job

1. Georges-Eugène Haussmann, *Mémoires du Baron Haussmann*, vol. 2 (Paris: Victor-Havard, 1890), p. 9.

2. Duc de Persigny, *Mémoires du Duc de Persigny* (Paris: H. de Laire d'Espagny, 1896), p. 253.

3. Ibid., p. 254.

4. Georges-Eugène Haussmann, *Mémoires du Baron Haussmann,* vol. 1 (Paris: Victor-Havard, 1890), p. 15.

5. Haussmann, *Mémoires du Baron Haussmann,* vol. 2, p. 84.

6. J. M. Gorges, *La Dette publique* (Paris: Guillaumin et Cie et Charavay Frères, 1884), p. 255.

7. Haussmann, *Mémoires du Baron Haussmann,* vol. 2, p. 196.

8. Ibid., p. 87.

Seven: Eviscerating with Glee

1. Haussmann, *Mémoires du Baron Haussmann,* vol. 3, p. 54.

2. Georges-Eugène Haussmann, quoted in Pinon, *Atlas du Paris Haussmanien* (Paris: Parigramme, 2002), p. 55.

3. Haussmann, *Mémoires du Baron Haussmann,* vol. 2 (Paris: Victor-Havard, 1890), p. 191.

4. Ibid., p. 257.

5. Haussmann, *Mémoires du Baron Haussmann,* vol. 3, p. 40.

6. Ibid., p. 479.

7. Emile Zola, *Le Ventre de Paris* (Paris: Charpentier, 1876), p. 218.

Eight: The Empire Builds

1. Pierre Larousse, *Grand Dictionnaire universel du XIXe siècle,* vol. 5 (Paris: Administration du Grand Dictionnaire universel, 1869), p. 471.

2. *Galignani's New Paris Guide for 1867* (Paris: A. and W. Galignani and Co., 1867), p. 210.

3. W. Pembroke Fetridge, *Harper's Handbook for Travelers in Europe and the East* (New York: Harper & Brothers, 1868), p. 92.

4. Adolphe Démy, *Essai historique sue les expositions universelles de Paris* (Paris: Librairie Alphonse Picard, 1907), p. 92.

5. Georges-Eugène Haussmann, *Mémoires du Baron Haussmann,* vol. 3 (Paris: Victor-Havard, 1893), p. 490–91.

6. Ibid., pp. 496–97.

7. Marie-Jeanne Dumont, *Le Logement social à Paris, 1850–1930* (Liège: Mardaga, 1991), p. 11.

8. Catherine Granger, *L'Empereur et les arts: La liste civile de Napoléon III* (Paris: Ecole Nationale des Chartes, 2005), p. 89.

9. Letter from Prosper Mérimée, October 19, 1856, quoted in Louis Girard, *Napoléon III* (Paris: Fayard, 1982), p. 262.

10. Haussmann, *Mémoires du Baron Haussmann,* vol. 3, p. 55.

Nine: Celebrating the New City

1. Georges-Eugène Haussmann, *Mémoires du Baron Haussmann,* vol. 3 (Paris: Victor-Havard, 1893), p. 326.
2. Figures given in Maxime Du Camp, "Les Voitures publiques dans la ville de Paris, les fiacres et les omnibus," *Revue des deux mondes,* May 15, 1867, p. 343.
3. *Rapport sur l'exposition universelle de 1855* (Paris: Imprimerie Impériale, 1857), p. 403.
4. Imbert de Saint-Amand, *Napoléon III et sa cour* (Paris: Librairie Dentu, 1897), p. 405.
5. Albert Dresden Vandam, *An Englishman in Paris* (London: Chapman & Hall, 1892), p. 154.
6. Imbert de Saint-Amand, *Napoléon III et sa cour,* p. 444.
7. "The Peace Conference," *New York Times,* August 23, 1898.

Ten: A Landscape of Ruins

1. Georges-Eugène Haussmann, *Mémoires du Baron Haussmann,* vol. 2 (Paris: Victor-Havard, 1890), p. 523.
2. Théophile Gautier, preface to Edouard Fournier, *Paris démoli* (Paris: Dentu, 1883), pp. 2–3.
3. Jean des Cars and Pierre Pinon, *Paris Haussmann* (Paris: Editions du Pavillon de l'Arsenal, 1991), p. 134.
4. Gautier, preface to Edouard Fournier, *Paris démoli,* p. 1.
5. Figure given in Maxime Du Camp, *Paris, ses organes, ses fonctions et sa vie* (Paris: Librairie Hachette et Cie, 1875), p. 120.
6. Both quotes are from "Le Cygne," in Charles Baudelaire, *Les Fleurs du mal* (Paris: Poulet-Malassis et de Broise, 1861), p. 204.
7. Charles Mangin, "Exposé et analyse du plan et projet présenté à l'Assemblée nationale avec les moyens d'en opérer l'éxécution," Paris, 1791, pp. 10–11.
8. Claude Dufresne, *Morny: L'Homme du Second Empire* (Paris: Librairie Académique Perrin, 1983), p. 191.
9. Pierre Pinon, *Atlas du Paris haussmannien* (Paris: Parigramme, 2002), p. 87.
10. The constraint is quoted in ibid., p. 87.
11. "The Paris Exposition," *New York Times,* May 20, 1867.

12. Eric Hobsbawm, *The Age of Capital* (New York: Random House, 1975), p. 30.

13. Adolphe Démy, *Essai historique sue les expositions universelles de Paris* (Paris: Librairie Alphonse Picard, 1907), p. 81.

14. *Discours, messages et proclamations de S. M. Napoléon III, empereur des Francais* (Mirecourt: Humbert, 1860), pp. 134–35.

Eleven: The 180 Million Franc Treaty

1. Claude Dufresne, *Morny: L'Homme du Second Empire* (Paris: Librairie Académique Perrin, 1983), p. 193.

2. Georges-Eugène Haussmann, "Mémoire présenté au counseil municipal de Paris le 19 Mars 1858," *Journal des débats politiques et littéraires,* April 9, 1858.

3. Charles Simond, *Paris de 1800 à 1900,* vol. 2 (Paris: Librairie Plon, 1900), p. 519.

4. *Discours, messages et proclamations de S. M. Napoléon III, empereur des Français* (Mirecourt: Humbert, 1860), pp. 145–46.

5. Georges-Eugène Haussmann, *Mémoires du Baron Haussmann*, vol. 2 (Paris: Victor-Harvard, 1890), pp. 308–09.

Twelve: The New City Emerges

1. Pierre Lavedan, *Histoire de l'urbanisme à Paris* (Paris: Association pour la publication d'une histoire de Paris, 1975), p. 147.

2. Pierre Lepine, Preface to *Gabriel Davioud, architecte* (Paris: Délégation à l'action artistique de la ville de Paris, 1981), p. 3.

3. Eric Anceau, *La France de 1848 à 1870*, (Paris: Librairie Générale Francaise, 2002), p. 163.

4. Figure given in Jeanne Gaillard, *Paris, la ville* (Paris: L'Harmattan, 1997), p. 136.

5. Charles Barthélemy, *Le Deuxième Empire* (Paris: Librairie Blériot, 1889), p. 129.

6. Robin Middleton and David Watkin, *Neoclassical and Nineteenth Century Architecture* (London: Faber & Faber, 1987), p. 242.

7. Georges-Eugène Haussmann, "Mémoire présenté au conseil municipal de Paris le 19 Mars 1858," *Journal des débats politiques et littéraires,* April 9, 1858.

8. Jean des Cars and Pierre Pinon, *Paris Haussmann* (Paris: Editions du Pavillon de l'Arsenal, 1991), p. 182.

Thirteen: An Expanded Capital and a New Monument

1. Devincik quoted in Pierre Pinon, *Atlas du Paris haussmanien* (Paris: Parigramme, 2002), p. 71.

2. Pierre Casselle, "Napoléon III contre Haussmann?—Commission des "embellissements de Paris: Rapport présenté à l'empereur Napoléon III," Cahiers de la Rotonde, n. 23 (2000).

3. Georges-Eugène Haussmann, *Mémoires du Baron Haussmann,* vol. 2 (Paris: Victor-Havard, 1890), pp. 234–135.

4. Haussmann quoted in Pinon, *Atlas du Paris haussmanien,* p. 71.

5. Bernard Rouleau, *Villages et faubourgs de l'ancien Paris* (Paris: Le Seuil, 1985), p. 236.

6. Letter from Prosper Mérimée, November 27, 1860, quoted in Jacques de Brabant, *Achille Fould et son temps* (Pau: Editions Cairn, 2001), p. 384.

7. The background of the building of the Opéra and the avenue de l'Opéra is given in Christopher Mead, "Urban Contingency and the Problem of Representation in Second Empire Paris," *Journal of the Society of Architectural Historians* 54, no. 2 (June 1995): 138–74.

8. Gérard Fontaine, *Palais Garnier: le fantasme de l'Opéra* (Paris: Noesis, 1999), p. 93.

9. Jean-Michel Leniaud, *Charles Garnier* (Paris: Editions du Patrimoine, 2003), p. 52.

Fourteen: An Embattled Prefect

1. *La Presse,* August 15, 1861.

2. *La Presse,* June 19, 1852.

3. Ibid.

4. *La Presse,* August 15, 1861.

5. Hippolyte Castille, *Les Frères Pereire* (Paris: E. Dentu, 1861), p. 41.

6. Jules Lechevalier Saint-André, *La Polémique et les affaires à l'occasion des grands travaux de Paris* (Paris: E. Dentu, 1861), p. 41.

7. *La Presse,* August 15, 1861.

8. Ibid.

9. Ibid.

10. Ibid.

11. Ibid.

12. Ibid.

13. *La Presse,* August 14, 1861.

14. *Archives diplomatiques,* vol. 3 (Paris: Amyot, 1861), pp. 393–94.

15. *Discours, messages, lettres et proclamations de S. M. Napoléon III, empereur des Français* (Mirecourt: Humbert, 1861), p. 178.

16. Our Paris Correspondence, *New York Times,* December 11, 1861.

17. Ibid.

18. L. Girard, *La Politique des travaux publics du Second Empire* (Paris: Colin, 1952), pp. 338–39.

19. Georges-Eugène Haussmann, *Mémoires du Baron Haussmann,* vol. 2 (Paris: Victor-Havard, 1890), p. 224.

20. Hippolyte Magen, "*Histoire du Second Empire* (Bordeaux: Bureaux des Journaux Illustrés, 1878), p. 332.

21. Georges-Eugène Haussmann, *Mémoires du Baron Haussmann,* vol. 3 (Paris: Victor-Havard, 1893), pp. 129–30.

22. *La Presse,* March 29, 1863.

23. Emile Ollivier, *L'Empire libéral,* vol. 10 (Paris: Garnier, 1905), p. 195.

Fifteen: Razing the Cradle of Paris

1. Jean-Baptiste Antoine Lassus and Alfred Michiels, "Architecture religieuse et civile," in Paul Lacroix, *Histoire et description des mœurs en Europe,* vol. 5 (Paris: 1851), pp. 6–11.

2. "Semaine politique," *Revue nationale et étrangère politique, littéraire et scientifique,* August 24, 1867, p. 95.

3. Herveline Delhumeau, *Le Palais de la cité* (Paris: Cité de l'Architecture et du Patrimoine/MMF/Aristeas/Actes Sud, 2011), p. 115.

4. Georges Poisson in Jean-Marie Pérouse de Montclos, *Le Guide du Patrimoine: Paris* (Paris: Hachette, 1994), p. 72.

5. Georges-Eugène Haussmann, *Mémoires du Baron Haussmann,* vol. 3 (Paris: Victor-Havard, 1893), p. 535.

6. Pierre Larousse, *Grand Dictionnaire Universel du XIXe siècle,* vol. 4 (Paris: Administration du grand dictionnaire universel, 1869), p. 352.

Sixteen: The Beginning of the Fall

1. Guy de Maupassant, "Menuet," in *Oeuvres complètes illustrées de Guy de Maupassant, vol. 2* (Paris: P. Ollendorff, 1901), p. 81.

2. Letter from Georges-Eugène Haussmann to Gabriel Davioud, November 16, 1875, quoted in *Gabriel Davioud, architecte du Paris d'Haussmann* (Paris: Caisse nationale des monuments historiques et des sites, 1982), p. 10.

3. Quoted by Géraldine Texier-Rideau in *République, histoire d'une place,* study commissioned by the Urban Planning Department of the City of Paris, 2009, p. 17.

4. *Le Temps,* July 3, 1865.

5. Jacques de Brabant, *Achille Fould et son temps* (Pau: Editions Cairn, 2001), p. 284.

Seventeen: Glamour and Decay

1. Adolphe Thiers, *Discours parlementaires,* vol. 11 (Paris: Calmon, 1881), p. 91.

2. Napoléon III quoted in Hippolyte Magen, *Histoire du Second Empire* (Bordeaux: Bureaudes Journaux Illustrés, 1878), p. 402.

3. Taxile Delord, *Histoire du Second Empire,* vol. 3 (Paris: G. Baillière, 1874), p. 135.

4. Emile Zola, *L'Argent* (Paris: Flammarion, 2009), p. 288.

5. "The Paris Exposition," *New York Times,* May 14, 1867.

6. Théophile Gautier, "Revue des Théâtres," *Le Moniteur,* September 17, 1867.

7. "The Paris Exposition," *New York Times,* May 10, 1867.

8. "The Paris Exposition," *New York Times,* May 20, 1867.

9. "The Paris Exposition," *New York Times,* May 21, 1867.

10. Victor Hugo in *Paris-Guide* (Paris: A Lacroix, Verboeckhoven et Cie Editeurs, 1867), p. v.

11. "The Paris Exposition," *New York Times,* May 21, 1867.

12. Alfred Delvau, *Les Plaisirs de Paris* (Paris: Achille Faure Libraire-Editeur, 1867), p. 18.

13. Adolphe Alphand, preface to Georges-Eugène Haussmann, *Mémoires du Baron Haussmann,* vol. 3 (Paris: Victor-Havard, 1893), p. viii.

14. A Delvau, *Les Plaisirs de Paris*, p. 14.

15. *Galignani's New Paris Guide 1867* (Paris: Galignani, 1867), pp. 476–77.

16. Guy de Maupassant, "Ce cochon de Morin," in *Oeuvres complètes illustrées de Guy de Maupassant,* vol. 2 (Paris: P. Ollendorff, 1901), p. 12.

17. Emile Zola, *L'Argent*, p. 328.

18. Catherine Granger, *L'Empereur et les arts: La liste civile de Napoléon III* (Paris: Ecole Nationale des Chartes, 2005), p. 89.

19. Marie-Jeanne Dumont, *Le Logement social à Paris, 1850–1930* (Liège: Mardaga, 1991), p. 15.

20. Ibid.

21. Paulus, *Trente ans de Café-Concert* (Paris: Société d'Edition et de Publications, 1908), p. 73.

22. Pierre Larousse, supplement to *Grand Dictionnaire universel du XIXe siècle*; (Paris: Administration du Grand Dictionnaire universel, 1877), p. 977.

23. Ibid.

24. J. B. Duvergier, *Lois, décrets, ordonnances, règlements et avis du Conseil d'Etat* (Paris: Guyot et Scribe, 1867), p. 230.

25. David Van Zanten, *Designing Paris* (Cambridge: MIT Press, 1987), p. 231.

26. Pamphlet entitled "Les Folies Garnier," reproduced in Jean-Michel Leniaud, *Charles Garnier* (Paris: Editions du Patrimoine, 2003), p. 61.

27. Eugène Viollet-le-Duc, *Entretiens sur l'architecture,* vol. 1 (Paris: A. Morel, 1863), p. 1.

28. John Summerson, *Heavenly Mansion and Other Essays on Architecture* (New York: W. W. Norton, 1963, p. 158.

29. Leniaud, *Charles Garnier*, p. 153.

30. François Loyer, "Le Triomphe de Louis XVI sous Napoléon III," in *L'Opéra et son quartier: Naissance de la ville moderne*, ed. François Loyer (Paris: Délégation à l'action artistique de la ville de Paris, 1997), p. 29.

31. Mark Twain, *The Innocents Abroad* (New York: Harper & Brothers, 1869), p. 154.

32. Mosette Broderick, *Triumvirate: McKim, Mead and White* (New York: Alfred A. Knopf, 2010), p.14.

33. Henri Cozic, *La Bourse mise à la portée de tous* (Paris: La Libraire Illustrée, 1885), p. 347.

34. Adolphy Démy, *Essai historique sue les expositions universelles de Paris* (Paris: Librairie Alphonse Picard, 1907), pp. 176–77.

35. "Paris During the Fetes," *New York Times,* June 28, 1867.

36. Letter from Maxime Du Camp to Gustave Flaubert, in Albert Thibaudet, preface to Gustave Flaubert, *L'Education sentimentale* (Paris: Editions Gallimard, 1965), p. 14.

Eighteen: The Last Fight

1. Jules Ferry, "Les Aveux de M. le Préfet de la Seine," *Le Temps,* December 20, 1867.

2. Jules Ferry, *Les Comptes fantastiques d'Haussmann* (Paris: Armand Le Chevalier, 1868), p. 27.

3. Ibid., p. 26.

4. Ibid., p. 34.

5. Taxile Delord, *Histoire du Second Empire,* vol. 3 (Paris: G. Baillière, 1873), p. 325.

6. Hippolyte Magen, *Histoire du Second Empire* (Bordeaux: Bureaux des Journaux Illustrés, 1878), p. 490.

7. Taxile Delord, *Histoire du Second Empire*, vol. 5 (Paris: G. Baillière, 1875), p. 263.

8. Léon Gambetta, *Discours et plaidoyers politiques,* vol. 1 (Paris, Charpentier, 1881), p. 18.

9. J. B. Duvergier, *Lois, décrets, ordonnances, règlements et avis du Conseil d'Etat* (Paris: Guyot et scribe, 1869), p. 55.

10. Ibid., p. 58.

11. Henry Knepler, *Man About Paris* (New York: William Morrow, 1970), p. 294.

12. Quoted in Charles Barthélemy, *Le Deuxième Empire* (Paris: Librairie Blériot, 1889), p. 269.

13. Georges-Eugène Haussmann, *Mémoires du Baron Haussmann,* vol. 2 (Paris: Victor-Havard, 1890), p. 186.

14. L. Bouchard, "Les budgets du Second Empire et le régime financier en France," *Revue des deux mondes* 91 (1871): 212.

15. Haussmann, *Mémoires du Baron Haussmann*, vol. 2, p. 262.

16. Ibid., p. 533.

17. Amédée de Cesena, *Le Nouveau Paris* (Paris: Garnier Frères, 1863), p. 1.

18. Georges-Eugène Haussmann, "Mémoire présenté au conseil municipal de Paris le 19 Mars 1858," *Journal des débats politiques et littéraires,* April 9, 1858.

19. Haussmann, *Mémoires du Baron Haussmann*, vol. 2, p. 59.

20. Frances Stover, "The Man Who Remade Paris," *Milwaukee Journal,* July 15, 1947.

21. Françoise Choay, introduction to Georges-Eugène Haussmann, *Mémoires* (Paris: Editions du Seuil, 2000), pp. 34, 12.

22. Emile Ollivier, *Thiers à l'académie et dans l'histoire* (Paris: Garnier Frères, 1879), p. 11.

23. Marie Colombier, *Mémoires* (Paris: Flammarion, 1893), p. 318.

Nineteen: Capital of a Republic

1. Marc Ferro, *Histoire de France* (Paris: Editions Odile Jacob, 2001), p. 299.
2. Zola quoted in Jacques Marseille, *Nouvelle Histoire de la France* (Paris: Librairie Académique Perrin, 1991), p. 814.
3. *Le Temps,* June 1, 1871.
4. Pierre Larousse, *Grand Dictionnaire universel du XIXe siècle*, vol. 9 (Paris: Administration du Grand Dictionnaire universel, 1873), p. 108.
5. Maxime Du Camp, *Paris, ses organes, ses fonctions et sa vie* (Paris: Librairie Hachette et Cie, 1875), pp. 2–3.
6. Charles Garnier, *Le Nouvel Opéra de Paris*, vol. 1 (Paris: Ducher et Cie, 1878), p. 352.
7. Ibid., p. 355.
8. Ibid., p. 357.
9. Haussmann, *Mémoires du Baron Haussmann,* vol. 2, p. ix.

Epilogue

1. Georges-Eugène Haussmann, *Mémoires du Baron Haussmann,* vol. 3 (Paris: Victor-Havard, 1893), p. 274.
2. Christopher Mead, "Urban Contingency and the Problem of Representation in Second Empire Paris," *Journal of the Society of Architectural Historians* 54, no. 2 (June 1995): 156.
3. Edwin G. Burrows and Mike Wallace, *Gotham: A History of New York City to 1898* (New York: Oxford University Press, 1999), p. 1002.
4. From the *Real Estate Record and Builders' Guide,* 1868, quoted in ibid., p. 923.
5. Charles Mulford Robinson, "Municipal Art in Paris," *Current Literature* 31 July–December 1901): 271.

Index

PARIS EN 1871.

Les Opérations de Voirie exécutées de 1854 à 1871
sont indiquées par des teintes jaunes et rouges.
(Le millésime indique la date d'achèvement.)

LES BATIGNOLLES

CLICHY

NEUILLY

17

8

BOULOGNE

1856

PASSY

LA MUETTE

16

ESPLANADE
DES
INVALIDES

CHAMP DE MARS

2

AUTEUIL

GRENELLE

Partie

15

ISSY

VAUGIRARD

VANVES

MONT

EXTENSION DES LIMITES DE PARIS EN 1860
(Loi du 16 Juin 1859)

COMMUNES ENTIÈREMENT ANNEXÉES	COMMUNES QUI ONT CÉDÉ DES PORTIONS DE TERRITOIRE
Auteuil	Neuilly
Passy	Clichy
Les Batignolles	St Ouen
Montmartre	Aubervilliers
La Chapelle	Les Prés St Gervais
La Villette	Pantin
Belleville	Bagnolet
Charonne	St Mandé
Bercy	Ivry
Vaugirard	Gentilly
Grenelle	Montrouge
	Vanves
	Issy

Surface de Paris avant l'Annexion   3 402ʰ 56ᵃ 07ᶜ
d°   après   d°   7 949ʰ 43ᵃ 85ᶜ

Echelle de 0,125 pour 2,000 Mètres (1/16000)

Gravé chez L. Wuhrer, R. de l'Abbé de l'Epée 4.